Trans Am & Firebird Restoration 1970½–1981

Melvin Benzaquen

CarTech®

CarTech®

CarTech®, Inc.
838 Lake Street South
Forest Lake, MN 55025
Phone: 651-277-1200 or 800-551-4754
Fax: 651-277-1203
www.cartechbooks.com

© 2015 by Melvin Benzaquen

All rights reserved. No part of this publication may be reproduced or utilized in any form or by any means, electronic or mechanical, including photocopying, recording, or by any information storage and retrieval system, without prior permission from the Publisher. All text, photographs, and artwork are the property of the Author unless otherwise noted or credited.

The information in this work is true and complete to the best of our knowledge. However, all information is presented without any guarantee on the part of the Author or Publisher, who also disclaim any liability incurred in connection with the use of the information and any implied warranties of merchantability or fitness for a particular purpose. Readers are responsible for taking suitable and appropriate safety measures when performing any of the operations or activities described in this work.

All trademarks, trade names, model names and numbers, and other product designations referred to herein are the property of their respective owners and are used solely for identification purposes. This work is a publication of CarTech, Inc., and has not been licensed, approved, sponsored, or endorsed by any other person or entity. The Publisher is not associated with any product, service, or vendor mentioned in this book, and does not endorse the products or services of any vendor mentioned in this book.

Edit by Paul Johnson
Layout by Monica Seiberlich

ISBN 978-1-61325-732-6
Item No. SA316P

Library of Congress Cataloging-in-Publication Data

Benzaquen, Melvin, author.
 Trans Am & Firebird restoration 1970-1/2 to 1981 / author, Melvin Benzaquen.
    pages cm
  ISBN 978-1-61325-172-0
1. Firebird automobile–Conservation and restoration. I. Title.
TL215.F57B46 2015
629.28'722–dc23
                                        2015006501

Written, edited, and designed in the U.S.A.
Printed in the U.S.A.

Title Page: *If you plan on restoring your Trans Am or Firebird body, you most likely need to weld in body patch panels. When welding thin sheet metal, proper heat management is imperative, and this is the case when stitch welding in a patch panel. You need to effectively quench the welds with air once you have welded it in.*

Back Cover Photos

Top:
This 1978 Formula W72 was a limited performance model with a 400-ci engine, which produced 220 hp at 4,000 rpm and 320 ft-lbs of torque at 2,000 rpm.

Middle:
Once the car has been completely disassembled and only the body shell remains, you can mount it to a rotisserie for bodywork and painting. The rotisserie allows easy access to all surfaces of the body so you can strip, repair, and paint the body before you assemble the car. The rear axle and leaf springs need to be removed. Another option is to purchase a wheeled body dolly.

Bottom Left:
The second-generation F-Body car is 34 years old or older, and many have some form of rust that needs to be repaired. Often, the best course of action is to cut out the area that has rusted and weld in a patch panel. In this step, you need to properly fit the patch panel in place and use body clamps to firmly hold it. Drill holes into the adjoining panel for spot welds. Tack weld the panel starting at the corners.

Bottom Right:
The second-generation Firebirds used the "corporate" 10- and 12-bolts axle assemblies. This 10-bolt is being reinstalled in a Firebird.

CONTENTS

About the Author 4
Acknowledgments 4
Introduction 5

Chapter 1: Models and Numbers 6
Model Search 7
VIN Tag Decoding 11
Firebird and Trans Am Values 15

Chapter 2: Getting Started 21
Type of Restoration 22
At-Home or Professional Shop Restoration 22
Restoration Process in a Nutshell 24
Evaluating the Car 24
Buying Parts 25
Organize Your Parts 27
Tools and Equipment 29
Basic Disassembly 30

Chapter 3: Bodywork Part I: Body Panels 39
Safety 40
Preparation 40
Tools for Bodywork 40
Quarter Panel Patch 40
Trunk Extension 42
Rear Body Panel Sectioning 48
Patch Panel Fabrication 51
Fenders 55
1970–1973 Front End Removal 63
Engine Accessories and Related Component Removal 64
Basic Techniques 68
    Sheet-Metal Stripping and Fiberglass Application .. 68
    Fiberglass Resin Application 69
    Shaping and Sanding 71

Chapter 4: Bodywork Part II: Doors, Spoilers, Bumpers and Wheel Flares 73
Door Panel 73
Door Glass 75
Interior Door Panel Installation 79
Endura Bumper 80
Rear Spoiler 86
Wheel Flares 87
Panel Alignment 92

Chapter 5: Painting 95
Environmental Laws and Safety Considerations .. 96
Paint Job Types 97
Painting at Home 99
Selecting the Right Shop 100
Panel Sanding and Cleaning 102
Masking 102
Paint Type and System 103
Prime Time 104
Color Coat Process 105
Clear Coat Process 107
Wet Sanding 107
Polishing and Hand Glazing 108

Chapter 6: Engine Rebuilding 109
Through the Years 109
Engine Identification 110
Rebuilding Considerations 111
When to Rebuild 114
Original Appearance Is Key 117
Procedure Overview 117

Chapter 7: Transmission Rebuilding 121
Manual Transmissions 121
Automatic Transmissions 124

Chapter 8: Drivetrain 126
Differential 126
Clutch 126
Driveshaft 131
Rear Axles 131

Chapter 9: Brakes 135
Front Disc Brakes 135
Rear Disc Brakes (1979–1981) 140

Chapter 10: Suspension 144
Inspection 144
Frame-Off Preparation 145
Front Suspension 145
Rear Suspension 151

Chapter 11: Electrical System 154
Electrical Harness 154

Chapter 12: Interior 158
Documentation and Damage Assessment 159
Interior Carpet 159
Dash 164

Chapter 13: Other Systems and Components 170
Cooling System 170
Fuel System 171
Wheels and Tires 172

Source Guide 176

DEDICATION

To my wife, Renita, my shining sun each and every day, and whose love is boundless. And to my family, especially my son, Jake, for everything they do and providing so much meaning in my life.

ABOUT THE AUTHOR

Melvin Benzaquen is a nationally recognized authority on restoring classic and muscle cars. Melvin has been involved with cars since early childhood. After starting Classic Restorations in 1995, he specialized in Pontiac Firebird restorations. During the next 18 years, he grew Classic into the largest restoration facility in the United States.

Melvin also was a contributing editor answering technical Q&As for *High Performance Pontiac* magazine and has written dozens of articles for various publications. Melvin has been featured in various publications, including *Hemmings Muscle Machines*, *Hemmings Motor News*, *Classic Truck*, *Super Chevy*, *Corvette*, *Auto Trader*, *GM High Tech & Performance*, *Muscle Mustangs*, *Hot Rod*, *Car Craft*, and many others.

He also is credited with inventing in-car computing. He installed a Mac Mini into a vehicle that drew worldwide attention. He and the concept were featured in *The New York Times*, *The Austin American Statesman*, *Mac Mini Hacks & Mods for Dummies*, and thousands of websites all over the world in 2005.

Melvin has hosted a radio talk show called *Resto Talk* (available on iTunes) for two years, discussing restoration and other related subjects. He has also been an expert contributor to Motor Trend Radio and Auto World Radio hosted by Bob Long.

ACKNOWLEDGMENTS

I want to thank the people who assisted me in writing this book. Their help was given without hesitation and is appreciated. My sincere thanks to Tom DeMauro and Terry McGean of *Hemmings Muscle Machines*; Rocky Rotella; Don Keefe; Jeffrey Kleinberg; John Angiolillo; Arthur Poltorak; Greg Schwark and the staff of Premier Restorations; Gil Monge of Gillin Custom Design; and Frank Chicherchia of Frank's Auto Body.

INTRODUCTION

When CarTech contacted me about the idea of writing a second-generation Firebird restoration book, I was excited about the project. After speaking on multiple occasions with Paul Johnson, my editor, I came to understand that the proposed book was to be about restoring your Firebird in a practical manner. This is not a book for someone who is looking for a guide to get into a national points judging competition. This book focuses more on techniques on how to restore your Firebird so you can get out and enjoy it. These processes yield results that will make you stand out at almost any car show. If you follow the techniques described, your Firebird will turn out to be absolutely stunning.

I do provide some information on identifying the correct components and identifying what you have. It is important to note that you should always buy the very best Firebird you can afford. Numbers matching is important from a value standpoint. The better off the starting point is and the more complete the Firebird is, the more you will be rewarded down the road in restoration costs. It costs the same to restore a matching numbers car as a non-matching one.

Although Pontiac Historical Services (PHS) offers factory-to-dealer documentation, that only verifies how the Firebird was originally built. Having your Pontiac inspected by a professional to verify its authenticity is invaluable. So is confirming that the numbers are indeed matching.

This book does not get much into the rebuilding of engines, transmissions, and differentials. CarTech already has books on these subjects. Rocky Rotella's *How to Rebuild Pontiac V-8s* covers these great engines in detail. Furthermore, these operations require specialized tools that exceed the costs of having the job done. Using a professional rebuilder also gets you a warranty, which is invaluable should there be a problem. There are only so many pages available.

This book is geared to the do-it-yourself home restorer. Even if you are not restoring your Firebird yourself, this book will give you good insight on what is involved in the various processes so that you can be knowledgeable in dealing with a restoration shop. It is always helpful if you can understand and talk with a professional restorer about what is needed and going on with the restoration.

CHAPTER 1

MODELS AND NUMBERS

Although the first-generation Firebird and Trans Am put the Pontiac F-Body on the performance map, the spectacular performance and styling of the second-generation models established the Pontiac Firebird and Trans Am as some of the most potent muscle cars ever made. The Firebird Formula 400, Trans Am Ram Air IV, 455HO, SD 455, and many other models became legendary muscle cars.

The performance of these new muscle cars was not their only attribute. The styling featured clean, flowing lines; a fastback roof design; and a European influence. But more important, the body profile was much more aerodynamically efficient than the first-generation Firebird's. The Firebird and derivative Trans Am became instant hits, still recognizable today. After the gas crisis of the early 1970s and the rise of insurance rates, the muscle car era's swan song was sounding loud and clear, but Pontiac seemed to not hear the music. Not only did the company continue to offer the Firebird and all of its performance models, but also it upped the ante by introducing engines that rivaled all others. The sister Camaro lost its Z28 model after 1974 and only offered a somewhat anemic 350 V-8. Pontiac introduced the 455 Super Duty in 1973 and continued with it in 1974.

When everyone thought large displacement engines were finished after 1974, Pontiac came right back with the venerable 455 still on the option list until the 1977 model year. In fact, Pontiac continued to offer the 400-ci engine until 1979. The hit movie *Smokey and the Bandit* in 1977, which used Special Edition Trans Ams, sparked a sales bonanza for Pontiac. In 1979, the company had

The revered 1974 Trans Am SD 455 is one rare bird as only 943 were made in 1974. This one is adorned in Buccaneer Red. Not only is this rare among Firebird models, it's rare among all muscle cars because, by 1974, it was the only remaining muscle car.

Pontiac didn't cut corners when it built the Super Duty. It was fitted with a cast nodular iron crankshaft, four-bolt main bearing caps, Magnafluxed 5140 forged steel connecting rods with 7/16-inch bolts, and TRW forged aluminum pistons. Although the compression ratio was 8.4:1, the high-flow heads helped to make up the deficit. It delivered 390 ft-lbs of torque at 3,200 rpm and 290 net hp at 4,000 rpm.

MODELS AND NUMBERS

All 1970–1981 Firebirds have their VIN plate located on the driver-side dash visible from the outside. All Firebirds had hidden rivets on VIN plates until 1980. In model year 1981, the VIN was revised to a federally mandated 17 digits and the rivets were visible.

This 210-mile 1977 Black Special Edition Trans Am is a prime collector car and was used as a reference source for this book.

Search Resources

Finding your Firebird is not difficult today because you have so many venues in which to look for a car. Major city collector car auctions, car show auctions, eBay, Craigslist, and other online listings can help you find the car that fits your needs and budget. Unfortunately most of the printed materials have disappeared, but a few, such as *Hemmings Motor News*, *DuPont Registry*, and *Want Ad Press*, are left.

its highest sales year for the entire Firebird lineup, including the Trans Am. The black Special Edition Trans Am is still the most sought-after late-model second-generation Firebird; sales prices continue to reflect that. Want proof? Burt Reynolds' personal 1977 Special Edition Trans Am sold at Julien's Auctions in December 2014 for $450,000. This was not an actual movie car!

The second-generation Firebird offered a variety of models that stayed fairly consistent throughout its 11-year model run. The models offered were base Firebird, Esprit, Formula and Trans Am. Each model has its own VIN (Vehicle Identification Number) designation, which makes identifying the individual model easy.

Model Search

The second-generation Firebirds certainly evolved and changed during their 11-year-model run. The 1970–1973 models are the most sought after and also among the fewest produced, especially the 1972 model year. The SD 455 Trans Am and Formula Firebird garner the highest collector values.

The 1974 and 1975 models are not as plentiful as other model years, and the collector value and fan following aren't as strong as the other model years.

The 1976 model is pretty much a standalone year as far as the exterior styling. The 1977 and 1978 model years brought in the "cat's-eyes" styling, which was a big hit, especially with the popularity of the *Smokey and the Bandit* movies.

The 1979, 1980, and 1981 models years share similar exterior styling, but the 1979 stands alone in value and popularity because this

TRANS AM & FIREBIRD RESTORATION 7

CHAPTER 1

VIN Numbers

When you are contemplating a purchase or simply want to verify the part numbers of a Firebird, here are some of the basic vehicle identification numbers (VIN) to consider:

1970 and 1971 Model Years

This is an example of a VIN for a 1970 Formula digits.

1971 was the first year of the 455 in the Trans Am.

1st Digit = GM division
2 Pontiac

2nd and 3rd Digits = Car line series
23 Base Firebird
24 Esprit
26 Formula
28 Trans Am

4th and 5th Digits = Body Type
87 2-door sport coupe

6th Digit = Model Year
0 1970
1 1971

7th Digit = Assembly Plant
N Norwood, Ohio
L Van Nuys, California

Last 6 Digits = Production sequence number
100001 up   8-cylinder engines
600001 up   6-cylinder engines

1972 Model Year

In 1972, the VIN format changed to include the engine option. The 13-character format remained, but the model designation was changed to a single letter in the second position.

Example of 1972 Trans Am VIN: 2V87X2N500001

1st Digit = GM Division
2 Pontiac

2nd Digit = Model Designation
S Base Firebird
T Esprit
U Formula
V Trans Am

3rd and 4th Digits = Body Type
87 2-door Sport Coupe

5th Digit = Engine Code
D 250 1-barrel inline 6-cylinder
M 350 2-barrel V-8 single exhaust
N 350 2-barrel V-8 dual exhaust
P 400 2-barrel V-8 dual exhaust
R 400 2-barrel V-8 single exhaust
T 400 4-barrel V-8 dual exhaust
X 455 4-barrel V-8 HO round-port heads

6th Digit = Model Year
2 1972

7th Digit = Assembly Plant
N Norwood, Ohio
L Van Nuys, California

Last 6 Digits = Production Sequence number
500001 and up

MODELS AND NUMBERS

1973 Model Year

The 1973 model year VIN changed slightly to reflect the addition of the Super Duty option. The infamous X code was used specifically for the SD 455 performance engine and was only available on Formula (U) and Trans Am (V) models. This 1973 example is for a Formula Firebird.

The 1973 model year VIN changed slightly to reflect the addition of the famed Super Duty engine option. The infamous X code was used specifically for the SD 455 performance engine and was only available on the Formula (U) and Trans Am (V) models.

A new identifier was added: a Y code to designate the D port 455 4-barrel carburetor engine. This was also the first year that two separate 455 engines were offered. The sixth digit shows a 3 for the 1973 model year. The last six sequential production number again begin with 100001.

Example of a 1973 VIN for a Formula: 2U87T3N100001.

1974 Model Year

The 1974 model-year VIN changed slightly, with the sixth digit now a 4. The infamous X code was used again for 1974 specifically for the SD 455 performance engine and was only available on the Formula (U) and Trans Am (V) models.

The 1974 model year VIN only changed the 6th digit to a 4.

1975 Model Year

In 1975, the VIN was revised again with changes to the model designation and engine options.

Example of a 1975 VIN for an Esprit: 2T87S5L100001.

1st Digit = GM Division
2   Pontiac

2nd Digit = Model Designation
S   Base
T   Esprit
U   Formula
W   Trans Am

3rd and 4th Digit = Body Type
87 Sport Coupe

5th Digit = Engine Code
D   250 1-barrel inline 6-cylinder
E   350 4-barrel V-8
M   350 2-barrel V-8
S   400 4-barrel V-8
W   455 4-barrel V-8

6th Digit = Model Year
5   1975

7th Digit = Assembly Plant
N   Norwood, Ohio
L   Van Nuys, California

Last 6 Digits = Production Sequence Number
100001 and up

1976 Model Year

In 1976 the VIN was slightly changed to reflect engine code changes, and the 6th digit shows a 6 to reflect the 1976 model year. This was the last year the 455 was available.

5th Digit = Engine Code
D   250 1-barrel inline 6-cylinder
M   350 2-barrel V-8
P   350 4-barrel V-8
W   455 4-barrel V-8
Z   400 4-barrel V-8

1977 Model Year

In 1977 the VIN was slightly revised to reflect the changes in engine availability. The 6th digit now shows a 7 to designate the 1977 model year.

This also was the beginning of GM installing engines from different divisions.

VIN Numbers CONTINUED

5th Digit = Engine Code
- C 231 2-barrel V-6 (Buick)
- K 403 4-barrel V-8 (Oldsmobile)
- L 350 4-barrel V-8 (Chevrolet)
- R 350 4-barrel V-8 (Oldsmobile)
- Y 301 4-barrel V-8 (Pontiac)
- Z 400 4-barrel V-8 (Pontiac)

1978 Model Year

In 1978 the VIN was revised slightly for changes in engine availability.

The 6th digit is an 8 for the 1978 model year.

5th Digit = Engine Code
- A 231 2-barrel V-6 (Buick)
- K 403 4-barrel V-8 (Oldsmobile)
- L 350 4-barrel V-8 (Chevrolet)
- U 305 2-barrel V-8 (Chevrolet)
- Z 400 4-barrel V-8 (Pontiac)

1979 Model Year

In the 1979 model year, the VIN again had engine code changes, but for the first time, a special model designation with the X code was used for the 10th Anniversary Trans Am. The W code in the second position reflects all of the Trans Am models with the exception of the 10th Anniversary Trans Am, which uses the X code in the second position. This VIN is for a 1979 Trans Am.

The 1979 model year VIN again had engine code changes but also, for the first time, a special model designation with the X code for the 10th Anniversary Trans Am. The W code as the 2nd digit represents all Trans Am models with the exception of the 10th Anniversary Trans Am, which uses the X code as the 2nd digit. The 6th digit of the VIN changes to a 9 to reflect the 1979 model year.

This was the last year that the Pontiac 400 was available. The 400 was only available with the 4-speed manual transmission.

5th Digit = Engine Codes
- A 231 2-barrel V-6 (Buick)
- G 305 2-barrel V-8 (Chevrolet)
- K 403 4-barrel V-8 (Oldsmobile)
- L 350 4-barrel V-8 (Chevrolet)
- R 350 4-barrel V-8 (Oldsmobile)
- W 301 4-barrel V-8 (Pontiac)
- Y 301 4-barrel V-8 (Pontiac)
- Z 400 4-barrel V-8 (Pontiac)

1980 Model Year

The 1980 model year VIN changed slightly because of new engine availability. The X as the 2nd digit was again used to reflect a special model. This year the Indianapolis Turbo Trans Am Pace Car received the X code in the VIN.

5th Digit = Engine Codes
- A 231 2-barrel V-6 (Buick)
- H 305 4-barrel V-8 (Chevrolet)
- S 265 2-barrel V-8 (Pontiac)
- T 301 4-barrel V-8 Turbocharged (Pontiac)
- W 301 4-barrel V-8 (Pontiac)
- Y 301 4-barrel V-8 (Pontiac)

1981 Model Year

The 1981 VIN was revamped due to the National Highway Traffic Safety Administration (NHTSA) mandating a standardized format. All over-the-road vehicles were required to use the 17-character format. The letters O and Q could not be used. The special X code was now relocated to the fifth position to designate the Pace Car.

MODELS AND NUMBERS

The 1981 VIN was revamped due to the National Highway Traffic Safety Administration (NHTSA) mandating a standardized VIN format. All over-the-road vehicles were required to use the 17-character format. The letters O and Q could not be used. The special X code was now relocated to the 5th digit to designate the Pace Car.

Example of a 1981 Trans Am VIN: 1G2AW87W_BN100001

1st Digit = Country of Origin
1   USA

2nd Digit = Manufacturer
G   General Motors

3rd Digit = GM division
2   Pontiac

4th Digit = Restraint System Type
A   Nonpassive-type restraints (seat belts)

5th Digit = Models
S   Base Firebird
T   Esprit
U   Formula
W   Trans Am
X   Indianapolis Turbo Trans Am Recaro Pace Car

6th and 7th Digits = Body Type
87 Sport Coupe

8th Digit = Engine Codes
A   231 2-barrel V-6 (Buick)
H   305 4-barrel V-8 (Chevrolet)
S   265 2-barrel V-8 (Pontiac)
T   301 4-barrel V-8 Turbocharged (Pontiac)
W   301 4-barrel V-8

9th Digit = Check Digit
The number used verifies that the VIN is correct.

10th Digit = Model Year
B   1981

11th Digit = Assembly Plant
N   Norwood, Ohio
L   Van Nuys, California

12th through 17th Digits = Production Sequence Number
100001 and up

was the last year of the Pontiac 400 engine. The 1980 and 1981 models had a light-cast 301 engine, in naturally aspirated and Turbo versions.

Although the 1979 model year saw the highest numbers of Firebirds ever produced, 1980 and 1981 were some of the lowest as people moved away in droves from the low-powered Firebirds.

Once you find that particular Firebird, verify the VIN as being the true Firebird, Formula, or Trans Am you are searching for. Given the ease of interchanging body parts, it is really easy to make a base Firebird appear to be a Trans Am. The VIN for all years defines the equipment package for a particular Firebird.

VIN Tag Decoding

Using these VINs helps you identify the model of Firebird, and as of the 1972 model year, they verify what engine the car originally had. In some instances, the VIN confirms the vehicle as being an original Super Duty 455–equipped Firebird (1973–1974) or a 10th Anniversary Trans Am (1979) or an Indianapolis Turbo Trans Am Pace Car (1980–1981). Using a VIN chart is the first step in identifying the Firebird model you are interested in and ensuring you are making an informed decision.

Given the extensive production run of Firebirds, each year has its own valuation, earlier models due to special performance engine options and later years with the offerings of the Limited Edition (1976), gold Special Edition (1978), and black Special Edition (1977–1981). The 1976–1981 Limited and Special Edition Trans Ams have dramatically increased in value over other comparable Firebird models. Unfortunately, these models are not verifiable by VIN, and the cowl tags are not to be relied upon. Therefore, original paperwork, such as the build sheet or original window sticker, is very important for documenting the authenticity of a particular car. Many excellent forgeries of original paperwork are out there; they may look original but should not be solely relied upon.

CHAPTER 1

1972 Engine Identification

All Series

HP	Disp	Trans	Block	Model	C.R.	Cam	Headcast	Carb & Number	
175	350	A	VV	X	8.0	335	7H1	1-2	7842062
175	350	M	WR	A, F	8.0	555	7H1	1-2	WGD 488062 (6311S)
475	350	A	YR	A, F	8.0	555	7H1	1-2	7042062
200	400	A	YX, YZ	A, B, F	8.2	555	7J2	1-2	7042060
200	400	A	ZX	A, B, F	8.2	066	7J2	1-2	7042062
250	400	M (3SP)	WS	A	8.2	067	7K3	1-4	7042263
250	400	M (4SP)	WK	A, F	8.2	067	7K3	1-4	7042263
250	400	A	YS	A, B, F, G	8.2	067	7K3	1-4	7042264
250	400	A	YT	A, B, F, G	8.2	067	7K3	1-4	7042272 (Alt.)
200	455	A	YH	B	8.2	066	7L4	1-2	7042064
250	455	A	YC	A, B, G	8.2	067	7M5	1-4	7042262, 72
250	455	A	YA	B, G	8.2	067	7M5	1-4	7042262, 72
250	455	A	ZH	B	8.2	067	7M5	1-4	7042262
300	455*	M (4SP)	WM	A, F	8.4	068	7F6	1-4	7042273 RA
300	455*	A	YB	A, F	8.4	068	7F6	1-4	7042270 RA
300	455*	M (4SP)	WD	F	8.4	068	7F6	1-4	7042273 RA
300	455*	A	YE	F	8.4	068	7F6	1-4	7042270 RA

* Denotes 4-bolt main caps, 455 H.O. engine. Standard on Trans Am.

1972 GTO option (W62) with LS-5 (455 H.O.)
Style: 23527: with M22 = 3, with M40 = 7
Style: 23537: with M22 = 310, with M40 = 325

1972 GT option (WU2) with LS-5 (455 H.O.)
Style: 23527: with M22 = 10, with M40 = 4, with L75 (455) = 24
Style: 23867: with M22 = 2, with M40 = 5, with L75 (455) = 2

From an engine identification chart, you are able to identify your engine and get a lot of information about your engine package. This example is for 1972. The head casting number and carb number are particularly useful.

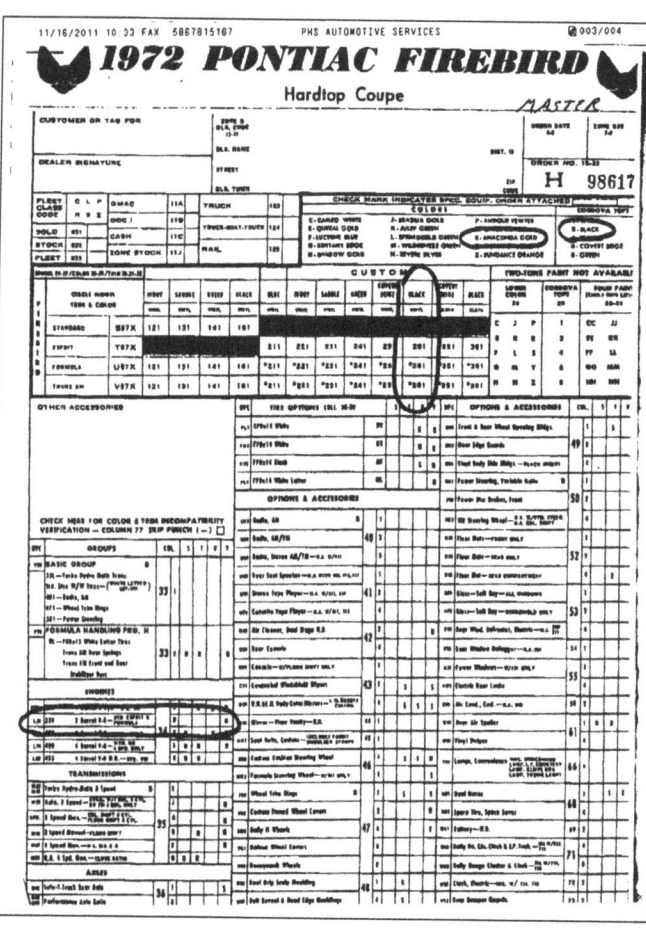

Contacting Pontiac Historical Services (PHS) to obtain the dealer order paperwork is the next step to make sure the Firebird model in front of you matches the way it originally left the factory. Given the vast numbers of Firebirds built in its 11-year model run, many options could have been added to offset the value. This is a photocopy of an original vintage document.

Pontiac Historical Services (PHS) documentation is irrefutable and always should be obtained directly from PHS for the best assurance, even when the seller presents it. I have had personal conversations with Jim Mattison of PHS, who related that he has seen doctored paperwork that even fooled him until he checked his records. Pontiac also made special models, and these designations are for the 1973, 1974, 1979, 1980, and 1981 model years to identify limited production models using an X in the VIN.

For 1979, the X reappeared as the second digit of the 13-digit VIN to identify the 10th Anniversary Trans Am. The X was not used to identify the engine for the 1979, 1980, and 1981 model years but rather a special model. In 1980, the X was again used in the same format as on the 1979, but this time it designated the Indianapolis Turbo Trans Am Pace Car. In 1981, the X made a curtain call in the fifth position of the newly mandated 17-digit VIN to identify the Indianapolis Turbo Trans Am Recaro Pace Car. No other model year received any special VIN coding, not even the Special Edition models whether they were the 1976–1981 black SE or the 1978 gold SE versions.

For 1973 and 1974, the X was placed in the fifth position of the 13-character VIN to identify the Super Duty engine (SD 455) when ordered in the Formula and Trans Am models.

MODELS AND NUMBERS

Obtaining the original paperwork from Pontiac Historical Services is the only way to absolutely verify the originality of a Firebird. Pontiac supplied this paperwork to the selling dealer. This has been a valuable resource for preventing rampant fraud for the Pontiac community. With the paperwork, collectors can verify that a prospective car for purchase really is optioned correctly. This service not only gives peace of mind, but also helps sustain value as it eliminates the question as to whether the Firebird was equipped that way from the factory. One can only imagine what would happen if Chevrolet offered this service.

The VIN also identifies a particular model as being an authentic Formula or Trans Am, so you don't waste time looking at a clone. It is extremely easy to make a base Firebird appear to be a Trans Am because all the parts interchange within every model. Not only do the parts interchange within models within the same year, but it is also not difficult to bolt on a 1970 front bumper onto a 1979 or vice versa.

The engine code is on the passenger's side just below the head on the engine block. This indicates the engine type and displacement.

Check the engine pad on the passenger's side of the lower pulley for the last eight characters of the VIN.

The cowl tag contains information pertaining to when and where the Firebird was built, its interior and exterior colors, and some option codes. The cowl tag is located on the top portion of the cowl at the base of the windshield by the hood hinge on the driver's side and is visible when the hood is opened. The identification of other special models that did not have a special VIN require more research beyond what the cowl tag may show.

The cowl tag, however, was not consistent in showing all the option codes. As an example, it is entirely possible that a 1979 black Special Edition may not show a Y84 code on the cowl tag. The cowl tag should be viewed as an accessory piece of information but not as an absolute.

The last two digits of the year of the engine are cast by the distributor opening. The date code for the engine also appears near the distributor opening.

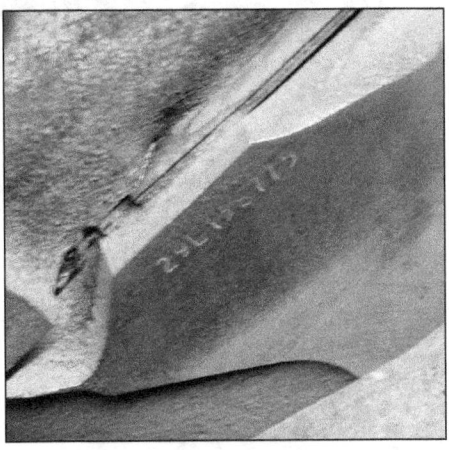

Font style and size differ depending on the year and plant. Placement of the VIN stamp on the engine can vary also. I have seen them stamped below the head on the passenger's side of the block and several other locations near the lower pulley on the block face.

The block casting number is on the passenger-side rear portion of the block where the transmission bellhousing is attached.

TRANS AM & FIREBIRD RESTORATION

CHAPTER 1

Macho Trans Am

The Macho Trans Am is an example of a "tuner" Firebird that was offered from 1977 to 1981 by Dennis and Kyle Mecham of Mecham Pontiac of Glendale, Arizona.

A tuner or dealer special Trans Am was built in the late 1970s and early 1980s. Starting in 1977 and through 1981, Mecham Pontiac, a dealer in Glendale, Arizona, began offering tuner Macho Trans Ams. DKM Design and Performance built the Macho Trans Am. The DKM designation represented Dennis and Kyle Mecham, who were brothers working in Evan's (their father) dealership. In 1977, the Mecham brothers wanted to improve the lackluster performance of Trans Ams.

Given the declining performance since the early 1970s, the Firebird was really the only car with anything over 200 hp other than the Corvette. The Firebird 400 engine with the W72 option was rated 10 hp more (220) than the Corvette optioned with the L82 engine. Things looked dismal on the performance horizon.

So, in the spirit of the Royal Pontiac, Baldwin Motion, Mr. Norm's Grand Spaulding Dodge, and Yenko dealerships, Dennis and Kyle Mecham started modifying the Firebirds while still walking the fine line of emissions compliance. Earlier dealers did not have such constraints, as there were minimal emission laws in place in the early 1970s. Dennis Mecham relayed the following story to me during an interview regarding the emission laws.

Mecham Pontiac removed the Trans Am's monolithic factory catalytic converter and replaced it with true dual exhaust with dual high-flow catalytic converters (one on each side) behind Hooker headers. However, the Mecham Firebirds did not pass the visual part of emissions test in many states because the factory emissions were no longer in place.

In one particular instance, Dennis was having one Macho Trans Am emissions tested in California. And it not only passed the tailpipe test, it actually tested much cleaner. However, the California smog station technician told Dennis that the car would fail the visual test as the factory equipment had been modified or replaced. In the midst of the conversation Dennis had with the technician, the technician remarked that if someone already owned the car and was relocating it to California, then it would pass.

A lightbulb went off in Dennis' head. He went back to Arizona and came up with a creative solution. Although other Pontiac dealerships in the network could order the car, it would be drop shipped to Mecham Pontiac. The selling dealership would then "sell" the car to Mecham Pontiac, and it would "resell" the car back to the selling dealership. The end result was that the dealership that delivered the car to the customer sold it as a used car. That made passing the visual inspection easier as the cars were technically used cars, even though the person who ordered the car owned it.

My personal 4-speed 1979 Macho Trans Am was ordered in Virginia at Rosenthal Hayman Pontiac; built in the Van Nuys, California, assembly plant; and shipped to Mecham Pontiac in Glendale, Arizona. After it received the Mecham Pontiac modifications, it was shipped to Rosenthal Hayman in Virginia. I have all of the documentation and the checks that were exchanged between Rosenthal Hayman and Mecham to show that this is truly what happened.

Production History

The Macho Trans Ams were certainly limited in number, and now these cars are highly coveted on the collector market. From 1977 to 1981, each car was individually numbered. In the first year, DKM Design and Performance sold 26 Macho Trans Ams; in 1978 it sold 203, and in 1979 it sold 96. These numbers are not an absolute. Some Macho Trans Am conversions were done after their sale. Rumor has it that DKM wanted to leave room for the anticipated sales so it started the numbers above 200. In 1980, Pontiac discontinued the venerable 400, and instead DKM used the Turbocharged 301. Sales dramatically fell for the 1980 and 1981 model years.

The Macho Trans Ams were not a simple appearance package. Instead, these were genuine high-performance cars in the dark ages of muscle cars. The standard list of upgrades and modifications included ignition timing, distributor advance curve modification, carburetor jetting changes, Hooker headers, dual-catalytic converters, and true dual exhaust. In addition, the shaker scoop was opened up at the back for improved airflow, Koni shocks were installed, and front coil springs were tempered for a lower stance and to introduce some rake. Also added were sway bar bushings and specific numbered decals.

Interior upgrades included a console numbered plaque, steering wheel center emblem, and unique paint schemes, depending on the color of the Firebird and whether it came with the hood bird.

Few Macho Trans Ams were assembled with T-tops because DKM felt the T-top roof compromised the structural integrity of the car.

A vast array of options was available, such as turbocharging (on the Pontiac 400), an oil pressure restorer from H-O Racing Specialties (used for hard cornering to keep the oil in the oil pump), and Scheel seats. A Doug Nash 5-speed manual transmission was also available. On automatic-equipped Machos the shift points were reprogrammed. Lift-off tilt fiberglass hoods, custom paint, and stereos were also on the option list. These Macho Trans Ams are extremely rare to find, and collectors have not yet set their sights on them. ■

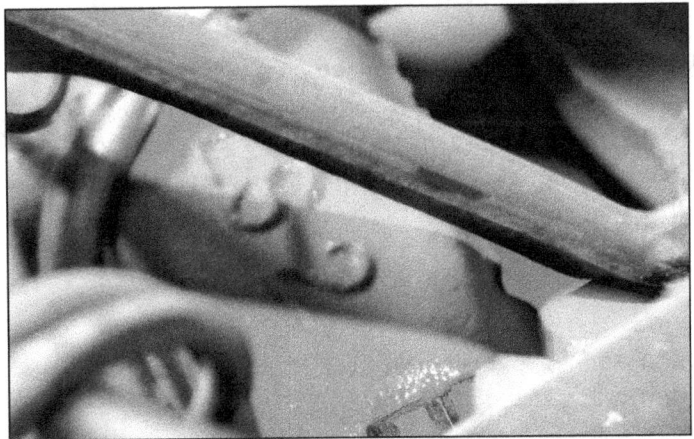

Intake manifold numbers are located near the thermostat housing on some engines and closer to the carburetor on others. The LS2 designation on this intake is for 1973–1974 Super Duty 455 engines.

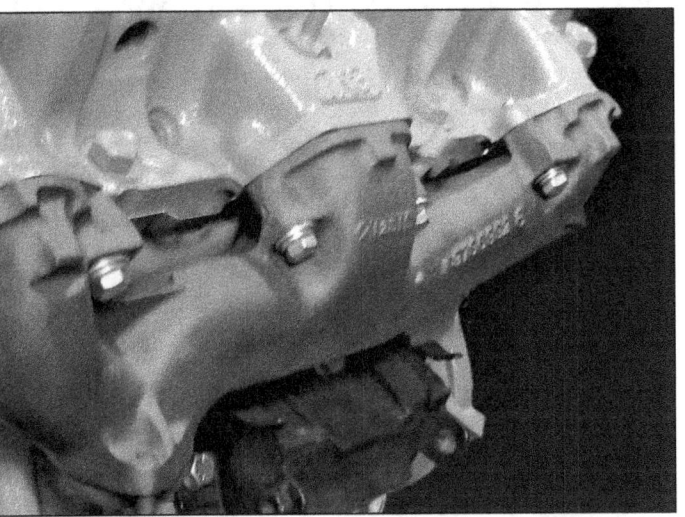

Exhaust manifold numbers are cast into the face of the manifold, easy to find and read.

Firebird and Trans Am Values

The value of a Firebird is not always tied to top models and engine offerings, but also to how much it is desired. A rare model or engine offering does not necessarily translate to value. The old adage about what was popular then being popular now holds true in the car collector market. However, sometimes a particular engine offering was so prohibitively expensive that few were produced, and now they are highly sought after. As an example, a 1973 Trans Am base price was $4,186 and the SD 455 engine option was $521. That represents 12.5 percent of the base price, which was largely out of reach for most people. When you consider that most options usually only added 1 to 2 percent of the base price, you understand why so few Super Dutys were ordered.

A 1970 Trans Am equipped with the Ram Air IV engine option is another example. The base price of a 1970 Trans Am was $4,305. The Ram Air IV engine option was $390, almost 10 percent of the base price. That's pretty hefty. Only 88 Ram Air IV Trans Ams were produced that year.

In addition, 213 1979 Trans Am black Special Editions with the 301-V-8 and 4-speed manual transmission were produced. However, the same black Special Edition with the 400 V-8 and 4-speed manual transmission garners almost double the value,

Cylinder Head ID Codes

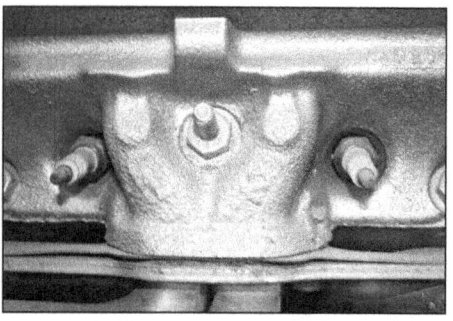

Heads generally have the casting numbers on the center ports. Head codes vary from year to year. All Pontiac heads interchange among years and displacements. The only exception is the 301 heads. They do not fit onto any other Pontiac block. The 326-, 350-, 389-, 400-, 428-, and 455-ci engines all have different valve sizing and different exhaust port configurations. These heads can physically bolt onto any of the aforementioned blocks. Some external differences affect the intake manifold and accessory bracket placements but that is generally on pre-1968 engines.

The 1969 and later heads physically interchange without any issues. Casting numbers for the heads are located between the center exhaust ports with the exception of the Ram Air IV heads. The Ram Air IV head casting numbers are a three-digit code located above the number-1 and number-8 exhaust ports.

Model	Code
1970	
Base 400, 265 hp	11
400, 330 hp, manual transmission	12
400, 330 hp, automatic	13
Ram Air III, 345 hp, manual transmission	12
Ram Air III, 345 hp, automatic	12 or 13
Ram Air IV, 370 hp	614
1971	
Standard 400, 265 hp	99
Standard 400, 300 hp	96
455, 325 hp, D port	66
455 HO, 335 hp, round port	197
1972	
400, 200 hp	7J2 (2-barrel)
400, 250 hp	7K3
455 HO, 300 hp, round port	7F6
1973	
400, 170 hp	4C
400, 185/230 hp	4X
455, 250 hp	4X
SD 455, 290 hp, round port	16

Model	Code
1974	
400, 190 hp	4C or 4X
400, 200/225 hp	4X
455, 250 hp	4X
SD 455, 290 hp, round port	16
1975	
400, 185 hp	5C
455, 200 hp	6H, 6X, 6S (AIR)
1976	
400, 185 hp	6X, 6S
455, 200 hp	6H
1977	
400, 180/200 hp	6X
1978	
400, 180/220 hp	6X
1979	
301, 135/150 hp	01
400, 220 hp	6X

Transmission ID Codes

Automatic transmissions have the last nine characters of the VIN stamped on the passenger's side of the case just above the pan. The transmission code is on an aluminum plate attached just above the pan on the passenger's side of the case. Usually the plates have their printing worn off and only the difficult-to-read stamp remains.

The side case of the transmission has the casting number and build date. This particular transmission date is November 15, 1978.

All are M40/Turbo 400s until 1975 model year.

Model	Code
1970	
400, standard hp	PX
400, Ram Air III and IV	PQ
1971	
400, with 3.08 ratio	PX
400, with 3.42 ratio	PY
455, with 3.08 ratio	PW
455, with 3.42 ratio	PR
455 HO	PQ
1972	
400, standard hp	PG
455 HO	PQ
1973	
400, standard hp	PG
455/SD 455	PQ
1974	
400, standard hp, California	PW
400, standard hp	PG
455	PZ
SD 455	PQ
1975	
All are M38/Turbo 350s.	
400, standard hp	MF, MG

Model	Code
1976	
400	MG
1977	
400	MG, MK, MT
403 Olds	MZ
1978	
400, standard hp	MG, MT, MC
400 W72	MK
403 Olds	MZ
403 Olds, California, High Altitude	LP
1979	
400 Pontiac engines were only available with manual transmissions for 1979.	
301	ME, MJ
403 Oldsmobile	LM
403 Oldsmobile, California, High Altitude	LP
1980	
301	ME, MJ
301, Turbocharged	MT
1981	
The service manual does not break down the Turbo 350 transmission codes by model. There are too many transmission codes used for 1981 (57!) to list here.	

CHAPTER 1

Rear Axle Assembly ID Codes

Gear Ratio	Code	Gear Ratio	Code
1970		*1975*	
3.08	COF	2.73	PUG
3.31	COV	3.08	PWG
3.55	COX	*1976*	
3.73	COZ	2.73	PUG
1971		3.08	PWG
3.08	GYG	3.23	LDG
3.42	CJG	*1977*	
3.73	CGG	2.56	PTG
4.10	CBG	3.08	PWG
1972		3.23	PXG
3.08	GYG	*1978*	
3.42	CJG	2.41	2PS
3.73	CGG	2.56	2PT
1973		3.08	2PW
3.08	GYG	3.23	2PX
3.42	CMG	3.42	2PY
1974		*1979*	
3.08	GYG	2.41	2PS
3.42	CMG	2.56	2PT
		2.73	4PR
		3.08	2PW
		3.23	2PX, 2PP

The rear axle code is stamped into the passenger-side tube closest to the center on the forward side. This particular axle stamp PP designates this as a 1979 Safe-T-Track 3.42 ratio. The G is the manufacturer's code. The ratio is also stamped on the tube.

Gear Ratio	Code
1980	
2.41	2PS, 5PV
2.56	2PT
3.08	2PW
1981	
2.41	2PS
2.56	2PT
2.73	2PU
3.08	5PQ, 2PW

The production Trans Am is the most commonly sought-after model. Some special high-performance Firebird models are also highly sought after. The 1973 and 1974 Formula equipped with the X code SD 455 engine is one such example. The SD 455 Formula models are extremely rare and the market reflects their desirability.

even though 1,107 were made. The 301 simply was not a desirable option and fewer Trans Am Special Edition models with the 301 were made. That does not mean it has more value simply because it is more rare.

In your quest to buy a Firebird, a car that has a numbers-matching

Carburetor ID Codes

Model	Code
1970	
400, 330 hp, manual	7040263, 7040563 California
400, 330 hp, automatic	7040264, 7040564 California
400, Ram Air III and IV, manual	7040273, 7040573 California
400, Ram Air III and IV, automatic	7040270, 7040570 California
1971	
400, 300 hp, manual	7041263
400, 300 hp, automatic	7041264, 7041271 High Altitude
455, 325 hp, automatic	7041262, 7041271 High Altitude
455 HO, manual	7041273, 7041267
455 HO, automatic	7041270, 7041268
1972	
400, 250 hp, manual	7042263
400, 250 hp, automatic	7042264, 7042272 High Altitude
455 HO, manual	7042273
455 HO, automatic	7042270
1973	
400, 230 hp, manual	7043263
400, 230 hp, automatic	7043264, 7043274 High Altitude
455, 250 hp, automatic	7043262, 7043272 High Altitude
455, 250 hp, manual	7043265
SD 455, manual	7043273
SD 455, automatic	7043270
1974	
400, 225 hp, manual	7043263
400, 200 hp, automatic	7044266, 7044274 High Altitude
455, 250 hp, automatic	7044262, 7044374, 7044272 High Altitude
SD 455, manual	7044273
SD 455, automatic	7044270
1975	
400, 185 hp, manual	7045263
400, 185 hp, automatic	7045274, 7045564 California
455, 200 hp, manual	7045263
1976	
400, 185 hp, manual	17056263
400, 185 hp, automatic	17056264, 17056564 California
455, 200 hp, manual	17056261
1977	
400, 180 hp, automatic	17057274
400, 200 hp, manual	17057263
400, 200 hp, automatic	17057266
403 Olds, 185 hp, automatic	17057550, 17057553 A/C
403 Olds, 185 hp, automatic	17057258 High Altitude
1978	
400, 180 hp, automatic	17058276, 17058278
400, 220 hp, manual	17058263
400, 220 hp, automatic	17058266
403 Olds, 185 hp, automatic	17058553 California
403 Olds, 185 hp, automatic	17058258 High Altitude
1979	
301, 150 hp, manual	17059271
301, 150 hp, automatic	17059272
400, 220 hp, manual	17058263, 17059263
403 Olds, 185 hp, automatic	17059250, 17059253
403 Olds, 185 hp, automatic	17059553 California
1980	
301, 155 hp	17080270
301 Turbo, 210 hp	17080274
1981	
301, 150 hp	17081270
301 Turbo, 200 hp	17081274
305 Chev, 145 hp (49 State)	17081203, 17081207 A/C
305 Chev, 145 hp (California)	17081202, 17081204 A/C

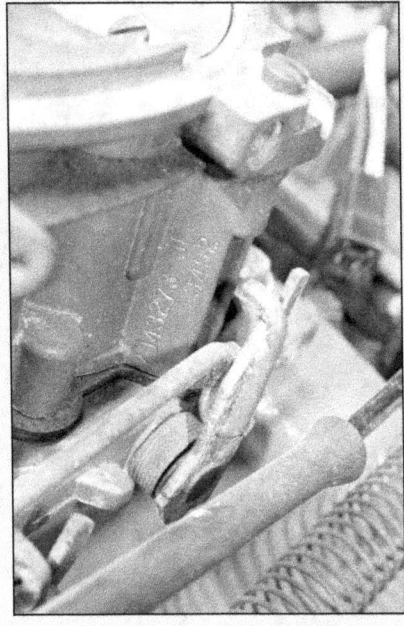

The carburetor code is stamped on the driver's side just behind the throttle lever.

> ## Most Valuable Firebirds
>
> Here is my list of the most valuable Firebird models with engine and transmission options in chronological order:
>
> | Year | Model |
> |---|---|
> | 1970 | Trans Am 400 Ram Air IV, auto or manual |
> | 1973–1974 | Formula and Trans Am SD 455, auto or manual |
> | 1975 | Trans Am 455, manual |
> | 1976 | Limited Edition Trans Am 455, manual |
> | 1977–1978 | Special Edition Trans Am 400, manual, black |
> | 1977 | Macho Trans Am 400, manual |
> | 1978 | Special Edition Trans Am 400, manual, gold |
> | 1978 | Macho Trans Am 400, manual |
> | 1979 | Special Edition Trans Am 400, manual, black |
> | 1979 | 10th Anniversary Trans Am 400, manual |
> | 1979 | Macho Trans Am 400, manual |
> | 1980 | Turbo black Special Edition Trans Am 301-T Auto |
> | 1980 | Special Edition Trans Am 305, manual, black |
> | 1980 | Indianapolis Turbo Trans Am Pace Car |
> | 1980–1981 | Turbo Macho Trans Am |
> | 1981 | Turbo black Special Edition Trans Am |
> | 1981 | Indianapolis Turbo Trans Am Recaro Pace Car |
> | 1981 | Special Edition Trans Am 305, manual, black |

installed engine is the most collectible and commands the highest value. A Firebird with a matching-numbers engine has a gold standard of value when it includes the previously mentioned documentation and an appraisal and verification from a known expert. Collectors want everything to be as correct and original as possible, and this documentation and appraisal establishes the car's value. When considering a Firebird for restoration, bear in mind that the cost of performing a restoration does not change whether the engine is the original numbers-matching one or not.

If you are purely interested in a Firebird for aggressive street driving, I recommend buying the very best condition and completeness you can afford so you limit your restoration costs. Remember, there is still value in a Firebird that does not have its original engine or if it is not a Trans Am. However, when you are spending a substantial amount of money on a restoration and want to maximize the return on your investment, it is best to invest in the best possible candidate you can afford from both option and condition standpoints.

Before buying a Firebird, you need to carefully inspect the body. Rust is not your friend. It is the single most expensive part of a restoration because rust repair involves an enormous amount of labor. Labor is the highest percentage of cost in a restoration. Sometimes you may not have a choice. If you found one of the 88 1970 Ram Air IV Trans Ams that needed a lot of rust repair but was numbers matching and complete, it would obviously be difficult to walk away from it. Restorations are expensive. You have to be aware of that, especially when significant rust is involved. The cost will be substantial and quite probably exceed the value of the Firebird. However, passing on a car such as that may mean you never find another such example.

Anyone can authenticate a vehicle by verifying the VIN, cowl numbers, and identification numbers. However, it is important to have an expert look at the drivetrain numbers, especially the engine, because this component holds the most value for a car. This is most important regarding a high-performance, low-production, high-option-equipped Firebird. With these models, engine re-stamps are not uncommon because unscrupulous sellers are trying to increase the value of the original engine.

Although every effort has been made to be correct and factual in this book, there can be differences of opinion and conflicting information. One thing I have certainly learned in my past experiences is that you can never say never when it comes to how a vehicle was originally built. The vast majority of vehicles were nothing more than a product meant to be mass-produced and to be as profitable as possible. The assembly line was not stopped because of a part that did not match.

The people who purchased the vehicles are the ones who made them special through their passion and experiences.

CHAPTER 2

Getting Started

Restorations are performed on many different levels. Before you start your project, you need to have a clearly defined restoration plan. I have always said that you have two types of potential candidates when shopping for a restoration project. One is the car that demands the restoration. The other is a restoration that satisfies the owner's personal desire for how the car should look.

A Firebird that demands a restoration has rust in various body parts, damage, has been sitting for a very long time, or is just plain worn out. It would be difficult to get away with not performing a restoration given the forlorn condition of the car. The car's appearance has simply declined to an unacceptable point, and you cannot safely or reliably drive the car.

In the case of performing a restoration for personal preference, the Firebird has been maintained throughout its lifetime and maybe has been the subject of an earlier restoration. Often, many areas of the body or interior need attention; they need to be repaired or replaced. Maybe the drivetrain is starting to wear out also, so it needs some mechanical repair. Although the Firebird may be fine, it just does not inspire the confidence you used to have in it to get you from Point A to Point B. It may constantly have minor issues or failures that necessitate repair. A full restoration also may not be needed. If you cannot afford a full restoration all at once or you restore sections as time and money allows. In this event, you may be planning to do the restoration in stages and paying for it as you go.

If you are disassembling the Firebird yourself, make sure you have ample room to work. You generally need at least a full two-car garage or workshop just to be able to have the proper amount of room to work around the car. You need an additional one-car space just for parts storage so they are accessible and safe. Throwing all of the parts on the

This 1970 Formula has been disassembled down to the bare unibody shell, subframe, and core support.

CHAPTER 2

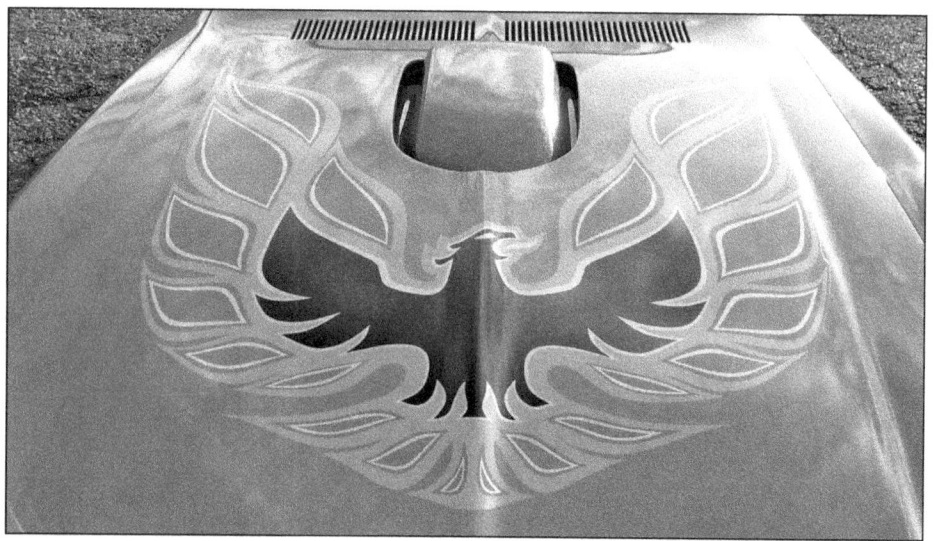

The iconic Firebird decal graces the hood of this 1973 Trans Am; it is available from various parts suppliers for your restoration project.

floor or in boxes without any type of organization is going to be extremely frustrating and problematic later on. Take the time to develop an organized space, and mark bags and tag all parts with information about where they were placed on the vehicle.

Type of Restoration

Planning is a key step of restoration, maybe the most important step. You're not going to achieve the intended results if you don't take the time to target the final results and plan the steps to get those results. Planning not only involves choosing what parts you want to use, how much power you want your engine to produce, and what colors you want to use inside and out, but also what you want for a finished product. How do you plan to use the Firebird?

This book is not about restoring a Firebird to win at a national points judging event. Instead, this book shows you how to restore a vehicle to be a reliable, well-performing weekend driver that has an original appearance.

Concours-Level Restoration

If you have your Firebird judged at a national level, it requires parts that match or precede the date the Firebird was built. Some of these parts include the starter, alternator, carburetor, master cylinder, engine, transmission, and rear axle.

However, it doesn't stop there. This also includes correct appearing bolts that are plated in the original finishes, the trunk, and hood latches with unique plating characteristics. The number of different finishes used throughout your Firebird can boggle the mind. Replicating all of these finishes and locating the correct components can add tremendously to the complexity and cost of the restoration, not to mention greatly extending the time it takes to restore the Firebird.

High-End Restoration

This type of restoration means you're not so concerned with the configuration of bolts or their plating. Although you use proper accessories, such as the alternator and starter, they are an appropriate GM part. The same applies to using a Rochester Quadrajet carburetor. The Firebird needs to look correct for its particular year, but it does not need all matching dates and numbers. The Firebird can still be completely dismantled and all components and parts stripped and renewed to appear as new, but it might not necessarily hold up under the intense scrutiny that a national points judging competition entails. This particular type of restoration is a hit at the local car show where it's judged on how fresh and beautiful it looks.

Driver-Quality Restoration

This type of restoration generally addresses the functional and cosmetic parts of the Firebird. The exterior may look pristine, but looking under the car reveals an original or unrestored undercarriage. The interior also appears to be in good condition. All or most of the mechanical and electrical functions of the Firebird are operable. The suspension may also be restored and is serviceable. The engine and transmission may not necessarily be original or numbers matching.

Basically, a driver-quality restoration is a fully functional and operable vehicle that, from all practical aspects, looks like a restored car. It does not hold up under the scrutiny of a national points judging competition. A collector who wants to purchase the car to make it into a national points judging car would view it as being in need of a restoration.

At-Home or Professional Shop Restoration

Once you've determined the level of restoration for your Firebird or Trans Am project, you need to determine your personal involvement

GETTING STARTED

Mecham Pontiac in Arizona offered Macho Trans Ams from 1977 to 1980 that were more potent than production Trans Ams. Mecham sold 200 or fewer Macho Trans Ams each year, so now these are very highly sought after collector cars.

in the restoration project. In doing this, you need to honestly and accurately assess your own mechanical, body restoration, electrical, and other restoration skills.

Typically car owners have some mechanical acumen so performing some engine, rear axle, suspension, and other aspects of restoration is feasible. On the other hand, bodywork is a skill and art that many have not undertaken, and many do not have the skill or the equipment. Suffice it to say that most car owners do not possess all of the necessary skills to restore the entire car. A person needs to restore the engine, transmission, and axle assembly; repair and/or install new body panels; replace electrical system components; reupholster seats; and work on many other systems. These different components require a specialized skill set. Therefore, most owners choose the components they can competently restore themselves and leave other component restoration to the professionals.

Another option is to leave the entire restoration to a professional shop. This decision is also dictated by your budget for the project. The average pricing per hour at a professional restoration shop could range from $35 per hour in the South to well in excess $100 per hour in the Northeast. Be wary of shops that say they do everything in house. They should be upfront with what exactly work they perform in house and what they sublet. Ask them if they guarantee the work of the shops that they sublet to. It is common for one-stop shops to farm out machine shop–related work, automatic transmission overhauls, gauge restorations, and interior-related work, but that should be about it.

You could also assume the position of a general contractor. You can have your car spread all throughout the city, state, or country and deal with all the different entities and manage their production. It all depends on what you can and are willing to do. But remember: It is very easy to think the project will take far less time than it actually does.

A typical high-end restoration for a Firebird in fairly solid condition can range between $40,000 to more than $100,000. A concours restoration can run well north of that figure, especially if there is a lot of rust and critical parts are missing. Obviously, the dollar range varies drastically depending on the starting condition of your Firebird, the completeness or lack of it, and what your ultimate goal is for the finished product.

Restoring a car presents certain challenges and complexities. Typical restorations involve many component groups, so the planning, timing, and execution of each restoration process are important. A restoration shop that can handle everything in house is the most preferable way to go about getting the best restoration. When you have many different subcontractors performing many different tasks on your car and something goes wrong, they always point the finger elsewhere, leaving you with little to no recourse.

If you subcontract work on your restoration project, you have to be an involved and astute project manager. You need to accurately inspect and evaluate the work being performed so problems can be recognized and resolved if and when they crop up.

When selecting a restoration shop, you should visit it multiple times if possible. See what cars are being worked on and talk to the employees. You don't need to go into details but just have some general automotive conversation.

Of course, you want to make sure the shop is knowledgeable about Pontiacs, especially Firebirds. As with all other makes and models, Firebirds have their eccentricities, and a knowledgeable shop is familiar with their quirks. The last thing you want is to pay for those at the shop to learn on your car. Don't take their word for being familiar with Firebird restorations. Take a tour of the shop and see if Firebirds are in the process of being restored. If not, ask for references, especially Firebird owners. Ask if any of the shop's customers' Firebirds have been featured in a magazine or on a website. See if the employees are friendly and knowledgeable and if they appear to be enthusiastic about their jobs.

You want to know if the shop has the proper equipment to restore your car too. Does it have MIG welders, rotisseries, a paint booth, lifts, air compressors, and sandblasting cabinets? Is it in the backyard of someone's home or in a proper building? Does the owner or shop manager answer your questions with knowledgeable and direct answers? Are completed vehicles at the shop so that you can judge their quality? Ask about the shop's hourly rate and how billing works. Most professional shops work on an hourly rate.

Whether you have decided to perform the restoration on your own or to subcontract out the work, the same principle applies to whomever you are looking to do business with. You want to feel confident that whoever is going to be working on your car or parts is responsive to you and will get the job done.

Restoration Process in a Nutshell

Another aspect of planning is determining the sequence of how to proceed. If you are going into a full restoration, you need to take steps to avoid performing redundant labor. You also have to plan the necessary sequence of events to keep the project rolling smoothly.

Organization is key when restoring a car: not only to save time, but also to save money. You should disassemble your Firebird from the outside going in. Exterior trim should be the first component removed. A variety of reveal molding tools are available for efficiently removing the trim.

The first stage of actual restoration starts with the subframe, suspension, rear axle, and underside of the body. You should restore these components first so you have a rolling vehicle because it's much easier to work on than one that is not mobile.

In addition, the Firebird should have all four wheels and sit on the suspension because this is the foundation for restoration. This means that when you are correcting gaps or replacing welded-on panels, they are placed and gapped as the vehicle sits. There will be no further need to correct gap issues later on if you follow this approach.

The next sequence is to work on the body shell, then install and align the front fenders, bumper, and hood. Then do the same for the doors and trunk lid. Once all of the gaps have been corrected and aligned in this test fit, they need to be removed, but the hard work is done.

Then it's time to block sand and primer the body and bolt-on parts. Engine, transmission, wiring, accessories, and all other operational systems are the next stage in the restoration process. The edging of the bolt-on body parts and the body shell need to be refinished in the correct paint and clear coat. You can now reassemble your previously aligned parts.

Once that is all done, the car is ready to go into the booth for a complete refinishing. Next is wet sanding and polishing the body. Exterior trim reassembly is next. The interior should be the last operation you do for completion.

Also, in my experience, machine shops that rebuild engines always take longer than they say they will. One of the first things you should do is get your engine ready for transport to a machine shop. I have had engines come back in several weeks and I have had engines come back after 16 months. Obviously that kind of time can seriously impact completion of your restoration.

Evaluating the Car

Evaluating a car for restoration is also important. I provide some guidance below for inspecting and evaluating a car. But it is wise to use a qualified professional to inspect the particular car. This person can recognize telltale signs of big and costly problems that can easily go undetected by someone who is unfamiliar with the cars. Bear in mind that these second-generation Firebirds are more than 34 years old. The Firebirds all have typical areas for rust and common wear areas and issues. Most have already had some work done to them as described earlier.

If you are looking at a Firebird for potential purchase, you want to ensure that it is properly evaluated for its current completeness and functionality. The better the condition of the car, the easier the restoration. This is especially true if you are contemplating a driver-quality restoration as you will not be replacing or

---

> ### Organizing Parts
>
> It is a good idea to have boxes ready if you are going to send items out to subcontractors. For example, the stainless-steel trim could be removed and placed into a single box and labeled for shipment once all the pieces are in there. It is easier to do it now when you are removing the parts than later. You can waste a lot of time trying to remember if you have everything or where it is placed. Worse yet, it could become damaged or lost if not in a box.

GETTING STARTED

The shop is prepping this 1979 Macho T/A for paint. The body technicians completed final body touch-ups to ensure that the body is straight and wave free.

restoring every single component as you would in a high-end or concours restoration. Completeness is still paramount when considering the higher end or concours restorations as any critical parts that are missing drive the costs up even further. This is especially important when correct numbered parts are not present. Also, it is important to have an experienced appraiser who is familiar with Pontiacs because these cars have some unique characteristics.

Take your time when inspecting and look everywhere for evidence of past and present leaks. Pay particular attention if an area is cleaner than the surrounding area as that may indicate recent repairs or an attempt to cover up a problem.

Buying Parts

Parts acquisition is an important piece of your restoration. You must determine which parts need to be replaced, the available budget for them, and order the parts at the correct time during the restoration. You don't need parts sitting around for long periods of time.

Although the Firebird is a popular vehicle to restore, all OEM parts are not available as reproduction parts. Hence, do not make the assumption that everything you need is available. And if an OEM part is beyond repair or restoration, you need to source a used part that can be restored.

Typical parts that are not reproduced are the one-year-only 1971 Firebird fender, the front bumper for 1970–1972, the front bumper for 1973, the 1974–1976 front and rear bumpers, the 1976 front bumper cover reinforcements and header panels, the 1977 and 1978 rear reinforcements, and the 1979–1981 rear bumper reinforcement to name a few. Taillights for the 1979–1981 Firebirds and Trans Am models are also not reproduced. The padded dash and instrument cluster bezels with gold, silver, and wood grains are not reproduced either.

Do not throw anything away until you not only have located the new part, but actually have it in your hand and have test fitted it to ensure it functions the same as the part it is replacing. The last thing you want to do is to throw out a part only to find it is not commonly available. Finding a used OEM part can slow the progress of your restoration.

It is also important not to purchase "perishable" parts too early on. For example, purchasing a new battery at the beginning is not a good idea because it can go dead from sitting. The warranty period also starts as soon as you purchase it, not when you install it. This is especially important if you are using a reproduction restoration battery because they are very expensive.

Tires are another example. I wait until the car is painted and the drivetrain is installed before purchasing tires. This way they are not becoming flat spotted from sitting or possibly having overspray on them from the painting process.

NOS Parts

NOS (new old stock) parts were originally manufactured either by the factory or the original parts vendor. Their intent was to be used either on the assembly line or in the dealer network as a warranty replacement or for retail sale.

Obviously, these parts have not been made for quite some time. Usually a collector hoards these parts, and when they do come up for sale, they are generally very expensive. I am not saying that you should not consider an original (NOS) part for your restoration, but you need to recognize that you will pay a premium for it.

CHAPTER 2

Creating and Analyzing a Parts List

Although you can simply look over online listings, I recommend ordering catalogs from several distributors that carry Firebird parts. It is still most helpful to have an actual book in your hand when standing near your Firebird and deciding what needs to be replaced. Searching online parts listings can be done after you have compiled your list and is a much more efficient way of ensuring your order is complete. Ames Performance Engineering, Classic Industries, Original Parts Group, The Parts Place, and Year One all offer catalogs and online ordering.

Depending on the condition of your Firebird, you need almost all the parts that degrade over time, such as weather-stripping and interior components. Mechanical components can be obtained from local auto parts stores and online resources such as Kanter and RockAuto.

Taking the time to go over every inch of your car greatly enhances your ability to order the majority of the parts at one time. Whatever appears to be worn, broken, or missing should be researched in the catalog. Make the determination whether you will purchase the part (if it is available) or repair it (if you have the skills and tools). Use original factory parts manuals so you can determine any missing parts and their original part numbers.

It also helps to figure out the original name of the part. Every manufacturer can give the same part a different name, so it is important to know what Pontiac originally called it. For example, you may look at a plastic disc that goes between the window crank handle and the door panel and call it a washer or a spacer, but Pontiac may have called it an escutcheon. The Pontiac arrowhead-shaped emblem is called an ornament. Knowing the original part name will help greatly because having most of your parts will keep the project going.

Used parts can be found online through eBay, Craigslist, Frank's Pontiac Parts, Desert Valley Auto Parts, GM Sports Salvage, and many others. Searching online can reveal many other dismantlers. ∎

For example, an NOS door skin simply clamps on and requires minimal fitment to sit correctly on your car. An aftermarket door skin requires much more additional work to fit correctly on the door shell. That labor difference could quickly close the gap (no pun intended) to the cost of the NOS skin. In addition, the aftermarket door skin uses thinner-gauge sheet metal and is therefore more susceptible to dings.

Reproduction Parts

Most, if not all, reproduction parts start out as a copy of an original or used part. Factories generally do not release (if they still have them) original blueprints of the individual parts, and the stamping dies are usually worn beyond any further use. When an overseas manufacturer sets up dies, molds, and other tooling, they are using an existing part, so it's a copy of a copy. As a consequence, these parts often are not precision manufactured and do not fit properly.

As you well know, the vast majority of the reproduction parts are manufactured overseas. Whenever you build a product to a price point instead of a quality point, there are bound to be issues. Check carefully if a particular part is supposedly made in the United States. A part can be made overseas and assembled here and the company can legally claim it as "Made in USA."

This is not to say that *all* reproduction parts are inferior. It is in your best interest to ask knowledgeable restoration shops what parts they use; they know what installs easily and what takes an inordinate amount of time to fit correctly. This problem is not unique to classic automobiles. The collision industry has had a long-standing feud with the insurance companies that require shops to use aftermarket parts and do not allow them the proper amount of time to fit the parts correctly.

Bear in mind that the businesses that commonly sell these parts are simply distributors, not manufacturers. When it comes to sheet metal, only so many manufacturers of the reproduction parts exist. Stamping dies are expensive to make, so manufacturers make sure the particular panel they are stamping will sell in high numbers.

Some distributors that sell aftermarket or reproduction parts also may make their own parts. It is a good idea to call them and ask them who makes their parts and where they were made. Where can you purchase reproduction parts? A lot of places, but you may have to hunt around a little.

Ames Performance Engineering, The Parts Place, Original Parts Group (OPG), Classic Industries, Year One, Goodmark Industries, and Dynacorn are all good sources for finding reproduction parts for your Firebird. Many reproduction part sellers also can be found on eBay. Do your research.

If you buy an inferior part, don't assume that this is the only way it comes. There might be a different manufacturer that offers the same part, which may or may not be better quality. To avoid disappointment, just assume that any reproduction part you purchase will require some degree of additional work to fit properly.

Organize Your Parts

As you disassemble your Firebird, you need to have tags, markers, plastic zip-type bags, and other containers on hand. The bags with the white writing areas on them are the best. It is important to use individual bags for each panel or component you remove. One reason is that it keeps the guesswork to a minimum as to where those bolts and associated hardware came from. Another reason, and probably the most important, is that if a bag is lost, you have not lost an entire section of your car. I also like to include a separate identifying tag inside the bag in case the outer writing is somehow blurred or wiped off.

Document the Details

Be sure to document the disassembly of your Firebird so you correctly reassemble it and avoid time-consuming hassles. You don't want to waste time figuring out how it came apart and how it needs to go back together. Although shop manuals and this book detail disassembly and assembly procedures, they cannot cover specific aspects.

You should have a notebook in the shop and write down specific items that are needed for proper reassembly.

Photographs taken before and during disassembly are also very important. Take an enormous number of photos and download them daily into your computer. Separate them according to each part of the car and make sub-folders so they are easily found when you need to look at them. That way you are not looking through a bunch of photos when you need to find something.

Parts Storage

It is important to designate an indoor area to hold the parts. The storage space should also be sealed from rodents. The last thing you want is to have your wiring and seats damaged. It also is important to make sure soft items do not come in contact with heavy items so designate separate areas for these. Another area should be designated for parts that are being sent out for other people to work on: the carburetor, distributor, stainless trim, interior items, and whatever other items are being subcontracted out. It should also be an area that is close by and you are able to roll heavy items in or out easily.

Never make the assumption that something, such as a molding on a door panel, can be easily replaced. If that door panel is damaged because something heavy was placed on it, you may be surprised just how difficult it could be to find a replacement or try to get it repaired so it doesn't look as if it were damaged previously.

Also, *do not* throw anything out until you are sure that you will not need it. One never knows what the replacement wiring harness may be missing. It could be missing a correct connector or a sub-harness that is not reproduced. The reproduction door panels may not come with a particular piece of trim. Maybe the reproduced part is so awful that you would rather reuse the original part. Another possibility is that the reproduction part may be missing a small but nearly impossible part to attach it to wherever it goes or for it to function properly. You can, however, throw away the rubber coolant hoses, weatherstrip, and rubber components because they can be replaced. Old carpet and seat covers, along with the padding, can also be tossed as they are usually just nasty and smell awful. Air-conditioning hoses and lines should be kept as you may need them to have a pattern should those lines or hoses not be reproduced. A typical car has more than 20,000 parts. On a total restoration, you remove every part and purchase a substantial percentage of those parts as replacements. That should give you an idea of just how much space you really need and how important being organized is.

Cleaning Supplies

Greasy, rusty parts require cleaning for any restoration project. Properly cleaning pieces takes time and it's a dirty job. You should clean as many parts as possible during disassembly with good old mineral spirits. All the oil and grease must be completely removed for best results. When bead blasting, grease and oil contaminate the blasting agent, plus it forces the contamination into the parts. Older mineral spirits–based wash tanks with recycling capabilities can be used.

You need a number of cleaning brushes to ease the removal of all the grime. Stainless steel bristle brushes work great on aluminum surfaces to remove corrosion and baked-on grease.

Carbon-steel brushes work well on iron castings and all internal iron engine pieces (engine blocks, cylinder heads, connecting rods, etc.).

CHAPTER 2

Expect the Unexpected

Expect the unexpected. It's that simple. You need to recognize this and accommodate it during the planning process. When you start disassembling a Firebird, you often find that trapped moisture in various body panels and areas of the car has led to much more extensive rust than was initially visible. The secrets a car holds and many details of its past life are revealed during disassembly.

The varied stories about the long and hard lives of many Firebirds and Trans Ams could fill a book. These cars were driven aggressively and in some cases severely abused. These high-performance cars were the only American muscle cars that had an amount of respectable horsepower during certain years. They were daily drivers, hot-rodded, drag raced, and exposed to the weather in all different types of climates. No one had a clue that many years later these cars would become cherished possessions and valuable collector cars.

This 1974 Super Duty Trans Am in Buccaneer Red has no-additional-cost optional honeycomb wheels.

Many have been wrecked, rusted out, and put back together. And as you would guess, many amateurs have made poor, incorrect, or what could otherwise be termed Band-Aid repairs throughout the years to keep them on the road.

An infinite number of things could have happened to a Firebird over the decades. Haphazard, poor, or flat-out wrong repair jobs are not uncommon, and these need to be effectively remedied. It's good to have a positive attitude, but be prepared for unexpected problems to pop up. They almost always do.

Even if your car has not experienced any of the horrors that can occur to cars, wear and tear is a major factor. Wear and tear happens whether the car has been driven a lot or is a low-mileage example.

Sitting is the worst thing for an automobile. Seals dry up, mechanical parts stick together, tires dry rot, brakes seize, rats eat interiors and wiring, and the list goes on. A well-maintained high-mileage car is probably a better candidate for a restoration than a lower mileage vehicle that has been sitting outside or a barn-find car that has not had any attention to it whatsoever for the past 20, 30, or 40 years.

This is not meant to scare you off but just to point out the realities of the restoration industry.

Another concern is buying an already restored vehicle. A car being represented as restored does not necessarily mean it has been properly restored. I have seen some of the best-looking cars that turned out to be the worst nightmares because of the repairs or restoration that you cannot see when the car is assembled. The term *restoration* has been loosely defined and used over the years. Many talented sculptors can make body filler look like metal and make body contours look solid and proper.

Hire a professional to inspect and evaluate your potential purchase whether it is already restored or not. A qualified professional uses tried-and-true inspection methods and knows what a correct original car looks like.

If you're considering a disassembled or basket case project car, it could be missing many parts and oftentimes all the good parts. These missing parts can drive up the cost of a restoration dramatically. For example, a correct distributor for a Ram Air IV or SD 455 costs $1,800, a correct Rochester Quadrajet is $2,000, and correct SD 455 emission components are $1,500, just to name a few. A replacement correct engine block could run well over $10,000 and proper heads could cost more than $3,500. Yes, you need to expect the unexpected, but if you are well prepared, you can minimize them. ∎

GETTING STARTED

Brass brushes work best on bronze or brass fittings.

Brass brushes transfer brass from the bristles to aluminum and iron when scrubbing pieces.

Nylon bristle brushes work well to loosen the grease and dirt buildup on parts.

Then the correct metal bristle brush is used to do the final corrosion removal and cleaning.

Tools and Equipment

The tools required for restoration depend on the work planned for your Firebird and your skill level. Some of the more expensive tools and larger tools such as an engine hoist are usually available for rental from a tool rental facility.

A small fortune in tools may be needed to perform the restoration. Depending on your preference and wallet, you may want to use air- and battery-powered tools rather than manual tools. If you plan to do more than one restoration, you might want to invest in tools made by a high-quality (and high price point) tool company, such as Snap-on or Blue Point. Sears probably offers the best bang for the buck and its tools are good quality.

These companies offer lifetime warranties, which come in handy when a tool fails. All tools fail, so don't be surprised when they do. Other tool companies are out there, but check their warranties. Cheap tools make the job harder and can actually damage the fasteners, which, in turn, make the restoration that much more difficult.

The same goes for materials. Using off-brand sandpapers and body supplies will come back and haunt you in a big way. I have tried all sorts of

Required Tools

Before you begin a restoration on any vehicle one of your best strategies is to have the needed tools handy. Different projects require different tools, but it's a good idea to gather them near your work area. You are basically setting up a job-specific shop each time. Although the following list is not comprehensive, it is a good one to start you on the right track.

- Digital camera
- SAE and metric 1/4-inch-drive socket set
- SAE and metric 3/8-inch-drive socket set
- SAE and metric 1/2-inch-drive socket set
- 1/4- and 3/8-inch for 2-, 4-, and 6-inch socket extensions
- 1/2-inch-drive 2- and 4-inch extensions
- SAE and metric open- and closed-end wrenches (I prefer ratcheting wrenches)
- Line wrenches (for power steering hoses, brake lines)
- Oil filter wrench
- Lug wrench
- Torx sockets
- Distributor hold-down tool
- Carburetor adjusting tool
- Drain pans: one for coolant, one for oil, and one for transmission fluid
- MIG welder (preferable 240V, but 110V will do)
- Acetylene torch setup
- Air compressor capable of maintaining 40 psi for 5 minutes when in use
- Air compressor hose, 25 to 50 feet
- Air compressor connectors for tools to hose
- Air impact tools
- Air chisel
- HVLP spray gun
- Primer spray gun
- 3-ton jackstands
- 3-ton floor jack
- Engine hoist
- Engine stand
- Screw jack, 5-foot
- Transmission jack
- Body dolly
- Phillips and flat-blade assorted screwdrivers
- Allen wrenches
- 3- or 4-inch cutoff tool
- 6-inch grinder
- 6-inch DA sander
- Snap-ring pliers
- Channel-lock pliers
- Assortment pliers
- Test light
- Multimeter
- Pry bar assortment
- Tool chest
- Long-board sander
- Sanding block
- Flexible sanding block set
- LED or fluorescent work light (regular bulbs can cause fires)
- Heavy-duty extension cord
- Heat gun
- Windshield glass removal tool kit
- Reveal molding removal tool
- Rivet gun
- Electric drill with drill bit set
- Body hammer
- Claw hammer
- Rubber mallet
- Hog-ring pliers (if you are installing your own seat covers)
- Sandblast cabinet
- Rotisserie
- Coil-spring compressor
- Vise
- Hydraulic press
- Bench grinder
- Polisher
- Reciprocating saw ∎

brands and I recommend using 3M or Norton for the majority of your materials. Yes, they cost more, but they last longer. Rage Gold for body filler is another recommendation. Cheap body fillers do not provide professional results so don't cut corners when it comes to selecting them. If your body filler shrinks or cracks, you have wasted a lot of time and money.

And the same goes for paint. Name brands, such as PPG, Sikkens, Dupont, and Glasurit, provide exceptional-quality products. Bear in mind that it is important to stay within the same manufacturer family for all of the chemicals that mix with the paint.

Basic Disassembly

The disassembly of a second-generation Firebird requires organization, paying attention, and, most important, patience. These vehicles were assembled many years ago; even in the best of environments, they do not come apart easily. Clips break, bolts seize and eventually snap, moldings bend, and something almost always gets damaged or lost. Add in prior work that may or may not have put parts or hardware back on and you can have a real headache on your hands.

The actual procedures may be somewhat unique to a particular model, but the process is the same as for many vintage cars from this era. Taking on a restoration project at your home or having a restoration shop tackle the job is not for the faint of heart.

Exterior Trim

Start by removing the exterior trim. Make a plan to start at one end of the car and work your way toward the other end. Which end you start at is not important. Just be methodical in your approach. Make notes as you go, especially if some part had hidden fasteners or was particularly difficult to remove and reference it in a snapshot.

Reveal moldings close the gap between the body and the glass on the windshield and the rear window. Spring clips that slide over a welded stud attached to the body hold the moldings.

You can also use a small flat-blade screwdriver to pop the molding out of its retaining clip. The technique is to insert either the flat-blade screwdriver or the reveal molding tool in between the bottom side of the molding and the glass where the clip is located. Then you slightly twist the tool or screwdriver, which, in turn, applies pressure to the molding and makes the molding pop out of the clip.

Take care so you don't crack or scratch the glass, or bend the molding. The quality of the aftermarket moldings is not nearly as good as that of the original equipment moldings. The aftermarket versions bend easily and are then generally unusable. The original moldings can stand repairs, but they should be sent to someone who specializes in aluminum and stainless-steel molding repair. (*Hemmings Motor News,* for example, includes businesses that specialize in molding repair and polishing in its Services Offered section.)

Almost all of the other exterior trim on your Firebird is held in by screws or just pops off with some pressure (similar to the technique for the front and rear glass moldings). The trim that is similar to the front and rear glass moldings is the vinyl top (if equipped) trim, or the upper door trim if your Firebird has the exterior decor trim.

The easiest way to tell if your Firebird was equipped with the exterior trim is to look at the trim on the back side of the hood and the top of the fender ears in addition to

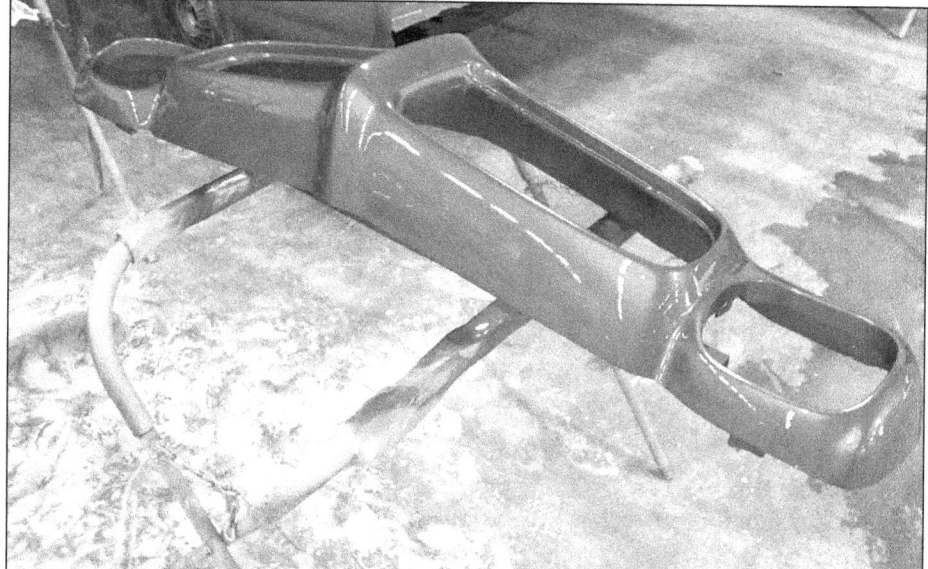

If you are disassembling a 1970–1973 Firebird, you must be careful when removing the front bumper. Do not place it on its side or front as the weight of it deforms the material edges and creates additional labor to repair. It should be placed with the beak facing upward on a clean, flat surface. This requires removal of the brackets attached to the bumper.

GETTING STARTED

the doors. If your Firebird does not have that trim, refer to PHS paperwork to see if it is listed on the manufacturer-to-dealer invoice.

Wheel flares and spoilers are often considered trim items. Make sure they are removed. Most of the attaching hardware is specialized for that individual component and is difficult to replace. Properly label the hardware and bag it. Reinstall the nuts and bolts onto the removed parts so they're not lost or you're not confused when reassembly time comes.

Once the trim has been removed, bagged and tagged, relocate it to a safe and organized place for storage.

Windows

You need to remove the 1/2-inch bolts securing the tracks and mechanisms in order to remove the components. The glass, inner and outer window weatherstrip, regulator hardware, door lock and handle along with the door latch mechanism are all in the door. If your Firebird has power windows and door locks, the wiring harness connectors need to be disconnected at the window motor, door lock switch (if a later-year model), and power lock actuator.

Removal starts at the glass mounts at the base of the glass. Once the glass is loose, simply grab the glass on each end and lift it out. As you lift, it may be necessary to lift the rear of the glass up to a 45-degree angle to allow the roller to escape the track.

Next is to disconnect the plug from the power window motor and power lock actuator (if equipped). Then, remove the bolts to the window regulator; they are attached to the inside of the door shell. On cars with power windows, the regulator may be riveted in. These rivets can be drilled out. Once the regulator is loose, it can be lifted out through the top of the door.

The harness can be threaded through the harness boot that goes between the door and hinge pillar. The harness boot needs to be gently removed with a flat-blade screwdriver to pop the boot out. Reproductions of these boots are not accurate and fit poorly.

Various Panels

Remove the doors next. Use a 9/16-inch socket and ratchet to

Disassemble the doors while they are still on the car. The doors weigh more than 100 pounds each and any weight that can be removed from them is helpful in preventing injury and minimizing the potential for damaging the door.

Remove the door glass and window regulator from the door using a 1/4-inch drive socket and ratchet set. The door glass lifts out from the top. The glass may need to be tilted at a 45-degree angle from the back so the rollers clear the track.

The window regulator is bolted or riveted to the door shell. Most of the time the factory riveted in the power window regulators but bolted in the manual window regulators. If your door has rivets, simply drill the center of the rivet all the way through to release them.

Make sure the glass has already been removed. The outer glass weatherstrip located at the top of the door; Phillips-head screws hold it in.

Once you have removed these items, the door is still heavy but weighs less. Place a floor jack covered with a thick blanket or pad under the center of the door to help support it while you remove the hinge-to-hinge pillar 9/16-inch bolts. It is very helpful to have a friend hold the door as you do this. If no one is available, loosen the hinge bolts but do not fully remove them until you have the door well situated so it does not fall off when you remove the last bolt.

remove the four bolts that connect the hinge to the doorjamb.

The trunk lid is held on with two 1/2-inch bolts on each side.

How to remove the fenders, bumpers, radiator support, and hood is covered in Chapter 3.

Be sure to inspect parts as you remove them along with the attaching hardware. If you see a problem that creates rust or another systemic problem, you need to correct it before you assemble the car.

For example, cowl side panels commonly rust at the lower triangulated portion, so use a medium-size flat-blade screwdriver to poke the side panel to see if it's rusted. You should poke all around using a good amount of force. Leaves, twigs, and other organic material fall on top of the cowl and into the sides. Over the years, the debris builds up, clogs the drains, and moisture accumulates. Add in car washing, rain, snow, and other wet environments and over time you have the perfect recipe for rust.

Transmission

Once the inner and outer fenders have been removed, you have easier access to the engine and transmission, which makes removal easier. It is a good idea to drain the engine oil and transmission fluid at this point. Do not use the same drain pan for both fluids because waste recyclers do not accept mixed fluids.

The engine and transmission are easier to remove from the car with the front sheet metal removed. This also prevents any body panels from potential damage during engine removal.

My experience is that it is a much cleaner job and takes less time to remove the engine and leave the transmission in place. The transmission can be easily removed later in the restoration process and with much less mess. However, if you have already removed the engine or you want to remove the transmission at an early stage in the process for rebuilding, you can use the following process.

To remove the transmission, you need to first remove the exhaust manifolds, head pipes, and starter. Move to the motor mounts that have 5/8-inch bolts to hold the engine to the 3/4-inch nut. It may be possible to still have access with the exhaust manifolds present, but it depends on the individual setup. In this area, oil leaks play into your favor and you can often avoid removing rusted fasteners. The engine and/or transmission gaskets and seals have deteriorated. Years of seeping oil have coated these bolts, so they are rarely rusted and come out quite easily. A couple of 1/2-inch-drive ratchets with extensions are usually sufficient to remove the nut and bolt. Once you remove the nut, you can lift the engine just slightly to take the weight off of the mount so the bolt slides through the mount ears.

The transmission mount is held in by a single 15-mm nut attached to the transmission crossmember. On earlier models, the bolt is most likely an SAE size. The transmission crossmember is held in with four nuts and bolts on each end at the subframe. It takes several steps to separate the transmission from the car.

First, loosen and remove the bolts that attach the transmission bellhousing to the engine. Next, remove the exhaust head pipe where it attaches to the exhaust manifold with sockets. Disconnect all electrical harness connectors by pressing the connector tabs or pulling them off (depending which connector is used). Use a flat-blade screwdriver to depress the tab on the fuel-line clip and pull the fuel feed and return line from the fuel pump.

Use a line wrench to disconnect the power steering pressure hose, and disconnect the return line with a flat-blade screwdriver. If equipped with A/C, remove the A/C compressor at its mounting bracket and lay to the side. Remove any vacuum lines that connect to the body. The vacuum lines are pressure fitted on which can be removed by simply pulling on the hose. Some of the larger lines may have spring clamps that can easily be removed with a pair of pliers.

Remove any engine ground straps at the engine block. Disconnect the positive battery cable at the battery end. Remove the engine.

If you have a manual transmission a few more parts need to be disconnected. Clevis pins hold in the clutch pedal linkage rods. The "Z" bar requires removal because the pedal linkage attaches to it. It just slips off once the engine is removed. Remove the nut that holds the lockout rod. The shifter handle bolts can be removed from the interior side with a socket by pushing down on the shifter boot.

I do not recommend removing the engine and transmission as a unit because there really is not enough room in the engine compartment to slide the engine forward enough to allow the transmission to clear the firewall. The front of the car would have to be lifted very high to allow the transmission enough clearance to swing. The angle that would be required to allow the transmission to clear would result in the transmission leaking substantially even if it had been drained.

Transmission Removal

Removing the motor-mount bolts is pretty easy and straightforward once the exhaust manifolds, head pipes, and starter have been removed. Use a socket and ratchet to remove one 5/8-inch bolt that holds the engine to the 3/4-inch nut. It may be possible to still have access with the exhaust manifolds present but it totally depends on the individual setup.

Given that there are usually oil leaks, the bolts are rarely rusted and come out quite easily. A couple of 1/2-inch-drive ratchets with extensions are usually sufficient to remove the nut and bolt. Once the nut is removed lift the engine slightly to take the weight off the mount; the bolt slides through the mount ears.

A single 15-mm nut attached to the transmission crossmember secures transmission mount. On earlier models the bolt is most likely an SAE size. The transmission cross member is held in with four nuts and bolts on each end at the subframe.

Sheet-Metal Cage

Four bolts and cage nuts secure the body mount bushings to the body of a second-generation Firebird. Generally, these bolts are rarely removed, and corrosion sets in from exposure to the elements over time. As such, these bolts and nuts are often very difficult to remove. The nuts are simply thick, solid-steel square nuts through which the bolt threads. The nut is held in place by a sheet-metal cage that is tack welded at four corners to prevent the nut from spinning when loosening or tightening the bolt.

You may try to remove the bolt, and the corrosion is so solid that the weakest link lets go. When the front two cages break loose, they are easily accessible and can be tack welded. The rear two-cage nuts become more of an issue when the cages fail because they are located below the floor and are not accessible from underneath. The mount and frame rail are in the way.

If the bolts spin while you are removing them, you need to gain access to the cage nuts. Use a rotary tool with a cutting wheel to cut through the floor, peel back the sheet metal, and access the cage nut.

If the cage has simply broken loose, use a wire brush to clean the threads. Use a MIG welder to tack weld the cage back together.

If the cage is rotted, tack weld the nut itself, so you can remove the bolt. In my case, the cage was in good condition. I recommend spraying a rust penetrant onto the bolt from the cage side and allowing it to soak for a few hours. Use a socket and ratchet to remove the bolt rather than an air ratchet or impact wrench because you don't want to strip or snap the bolt.

Once you have removed the bolt, push the floor flap back and tack weld it in place to hold it closed. Using the techniques described in Chapter 3, weld the flap fully and perform bodywork to finish the repair properly so no evidence of it having been done can be found.

Cage Removal

Remove Subframe

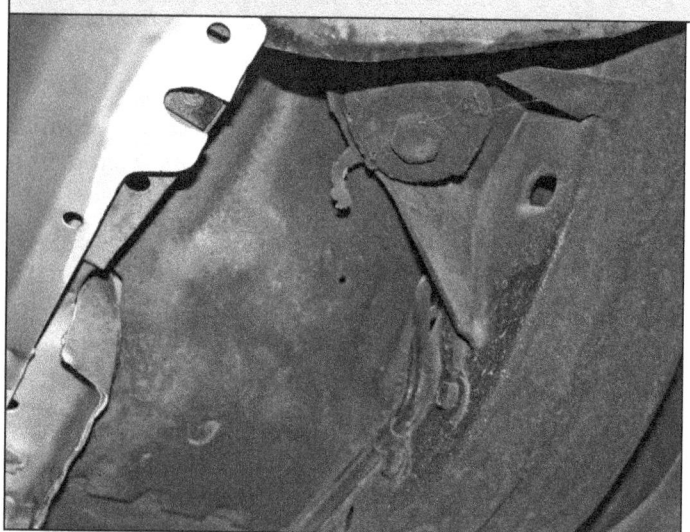
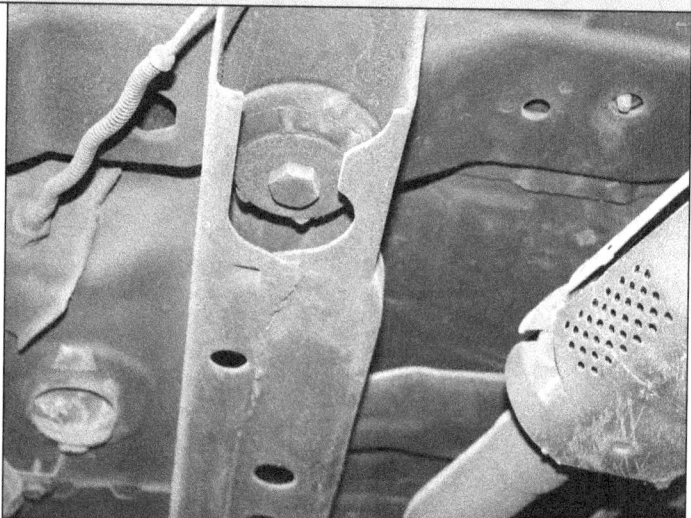

1 The forward bolt is located at the base of the firewall next to the rear of the front fenders. The bolt can be removed with a 1/2-inch-drive socket and ratchet. If you experience difficulty in loosening the bolt you may need to replace the ratchet with a breaker bar to gain leverage. These bolts hold in the forward portion of the subframe. It also may be necessary to lubricate the threads of the bolt, which are accessible from the other side just below the firewall in the engine compartment.

2 The rear frame bolt is located underneath the front seats on the underside of the body at the rear portion of the frame. Removing the rear frame bolts requires the same technique as the forward bolts. Unfortunately, you cannot access the other side of the bolts to lubricate the threads. I do not recommend the use of an air impact tool because the extreme amount of torque may break the cage nut in the floor, or even worse, break the bolt.

Remove Subframe (CONTINUED)

3 The entire subframe can be removed with the front suspension still attached by removing two bolts on each side. (The front sheet metal should have been already removed.) The subframe bolts should be fully removed only after making sure the body shell is properly supported on the rocker panel ridge and the front of the subframe is supported with small jackstands under the lower control arms.

Two floor jacks under the control arms makes it easier to roll the subframe out from the underside of the body when you have finished disconnecting everything. I do not recommend using a single floor jack placed under the suspension crossmember because the subframe would be unbalanced and rock from side to side. Additionally, the underside of the suspension crossmember is thin steel and dents easily.

Strip Paint

4 The body requires additional jackstands placed under the forward portion of the rocker panels to allow the subframe to be removed as the front suspension is supporting the front with jackstands placed there previously.

As far as stripping the paint off the body, you have some choices. I usually determine the method based on how many paint layers are on the car.

If the car has the original paint or one repaint, it is more productive to hand and power sand along with chemically strip the paint. If there have been multiple paint jobs and a large presence of body filler, it makes sense to have the body media blasted. I prefer the 80/20 plastic media as it does not generate excessive heat and the material can be re-used.

If the car is between those two examples, I use soda blasting. Bear in mind that if any of the high-pressure blasting material gets into cracks and crevices you may not even know it. It is imperative that a high-pressure blow out be performed on the car several times during the bodywork stage and before the paint process begins.

I do not like to use chemical-dip processes as they are extremely caustic and get into areas that you will never be able to treat. These exposed areas could possibly start rusting from the inside out.

Take Measurements

5 First, measure the distance from the head of the bolt on the underside to the inner rocker pinch weld. (The pinch weld is where the outer and inner rocker panels are joined together and the lip runs from front to rear between the front and rear tires.) Then, measure in the top of the floor and you have the location for your cage. With a magic marker, indicate where you will cut (on three sides). The size of the panel only needs to be as wide as the frame rail underneath.

Cut Floorpan

6 There is no easy or convenient way to access the cage nut when the cage has failed. You have to cut through the floorpan using a metal cutting tool. A pneumatic or electric rotary tool with a small 3-inch cutoff wheel works well for this job. Bodywork or home improvement stores sell cutting discs such as the one shown. A 100-grit wheel is just fine. Use a Sharpie or scratch awl to mark the cut lines. Wear eye protection. Simply press the trigger and cut along the previously marked lines on three sides. Use the cut-off wheel on three sides. Peel back the metal flap you have created with a flat-blade screwdriver or pry bar.

Remove Nut

7 After you have pried the flap up, the cage is revealed. Obviously in this case the measurement was correct. The intent is not to have to make many cuts so that closing the hole is easily done and does not turn into a repair patch. Once the cage nut has been revealed, you can see where the cage welds have failed. If you have a broken bolt, you peel back the cage and remove the nut. Often the cage nuts are rusted so it is a good idea to apply lubricant.

Remove Steering Box

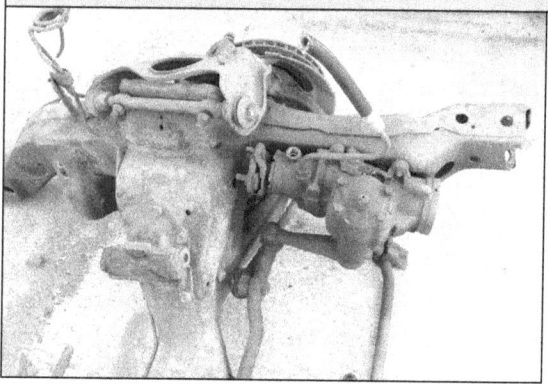

8 Once the subframe has been removed, you can remove the three steering box bolts with a socket. In many cases, an impact wrench or air ratchet comes in handy when removing large fasteners. But you need to take a look at the condition of the fastener before you start. If the nuts or bolts are damaged or rounded off, you may need to use a breaker bar or large ratchet with a handle extension and apply consistent and moderate force until the fastener starts to turn.

In addition, you should treat most bolts with a thread lubricant, such as WD-40 or PB Blaster. Impact wrenches apply an enormous amount of torque and can easily strip bolts and nuts.

Use a ratchet or impact wrench to remove the nuts on the steering linkage. Once you have removed the nuts, turn them upside down and re-install them with a few turns. With a hammer, tap the nuts to break the end loose. Once the linkage pops down remove the nut and drop the link at that point.

The front suspension can be removed at this time also; the procedures are covered in Chapter 9.

Crack and Fastener Inspection

Once you have separated the subframe from the body, you need to thoroughly inspect it. A lot of chassis and suspension forces are driven through the subframe and they crack, bend, and often sustain damage over time. Visually inspect for cracks or bends from prior accident damage. If the frame is bent or cracked, I recommend replacing it rather than repairing it. Finding a good used subframe is usually not difficult or very expensive.

Body mounts typically rust and openings often become irregular or egg shaped. The subframe can be effectively repaired and the repair process is not that difficult. The procedure for repairing the mounts begins with cutting out the rust area. Obtain a large thick washer with an opening of sufficient size to allow the body mount bolt to slide through. Weld the washer into place using welding techniques as described in Chapter 3.

Glass Removal

A multi-piece reveal molding covers the edge of the front and rear glass. This molding covers the gap between the body and the glass and is held in by clips that slide onto studs welded to the body and allow the molding edge to pressure fit onto the clip. Use a reveal molding tool, which is available from most auto supply stores, because it makes the removal much easier and helps avoid damage.

You need to take all measures to prevent bending these expensive moldings. The technique is to slide the tool between the glass and the molding until you encounter some resistance. Once you are at that point, slowly and steadily twist the tool, and the clip should release the molding. The molding pieces interlock into each other; gently remove them. Place the moldings in a secure place. A good idea is to tape them to a board such as plywood or MDF so they cannot get bent.

Now you are ready to remove the glass. Adhesive holds the front and rear glass in and is very difficult to remove. The front windshield is a large piece of heavy glass that's not easy to hold and move. Like other parts on the car, it deteriorates and weakens over time. It's very easy to crack it during removal.

All Firebird windshields, and those on other similar-year cars, are laminated and they deteriorate over

GETTING STARTED

Mounting the body on a rotisserie allows you to easily access all surfaces of the body so you strip, repair, and paint the body before you re-assemble the car. The rear axle and leaf springs must be removed (see Chapter 9).

If you are not using a rotisserie, place another set of jackstands under the rear portion of the body. Or you can purchase a wheeled body dolly. Auto Twirler and Eastwood sell these tools. You can also check Craigslist, eBay, and other sources for used equipment.

time. This laminate is a clear plastic layer sandwiched with glass on either side. It is designed to hold the glass in shape during an impact, which minimizes potential injury to passengers from large shards of glass that would come from an unlaminated windshield.

Most windshields have been replaced from normal exposure and usage. Even if windshields do not crack, they are typically pitted from road debris, chipped, and not nearly as clear as when new. A new and correct windshield is available in tinted or clear applications. The windshield can even be ordered with the correct markings and date code if so desired. That makes the decision for keeping the original windshield not so difficult.

At the rear the glass is tempered, and it's designed to shatter into small round pieces and not sharp shards. The tempered glass can take a fair amount of abuse before breaking. It is pretty difficult to cause the rear window to shatter when removing it.

A simple and cost-effective method is available when performing the replacement job yourself. Buy a windshield removal tool kit for about $18. The kit consists of two pull handles, windshield wire, and a tool to pierce through the glass sealant so the wire can be threaded through the sealant.

Once the wire has been threaded through the opening in the sealant, you need a helper. Attach the windshield wire to the pull handles on each end. Then, you and your helper move the wire in and out as in a sawing motion while exerting upward pressure to cut through the sealant. Do not become too eager and decide to start pushing the windshield out when you reach the last couple of inches; the glass will definitely crack.

The same technique is also used for the rear glass. If your Firebird has the optional heated rear glass, it is necessary to disconnect the connectors on each side prior to starting the removal process.

Miscellaneous

Screws hold all of the other trim panels in place and are easily removed. A Torx-head bolt holds the seat belts to the floor. The roof-mounted shoulder belts on the 1970–1973 models have a single Torx-head bolt on each side. The 1974 and later Firebirds have shoulder belt retractors mounted in the roof, which are held in by three bolts. The seat belts require a ratchet to remove the bolts.

The center console removal is covered in Chapter 12. After removing the screws in the sill plates, remove the carpet by lifting it out.

Windshield Replacement

I highly recommend having a mobile glass company remove the old and install the new front and rear glass. These companies guarantee their work. An experienced technician, who replaces glass every day, performs a professional-quality job. The likelihood of having a leak is greatly minimized when a professional installs the glass. The Firebird glass can even be purchased from them, making the process painless.

GETTING STARTED

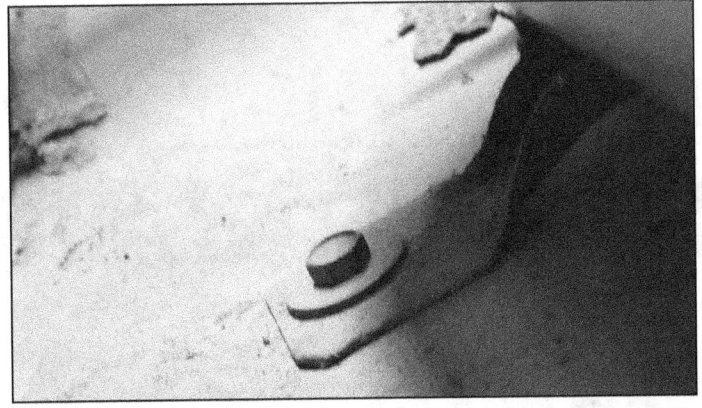

Two bolts hold the front seats in the front tracks and two bolts hold the rear portion of the tracks. The seats should be moved fully rearward to gain easy access to the front bolts. Then the seats should be moved to the full forward position to fully access the rear mounting bolts. A short socket should clear the seat, but if you encounter difficulty use a wrench.

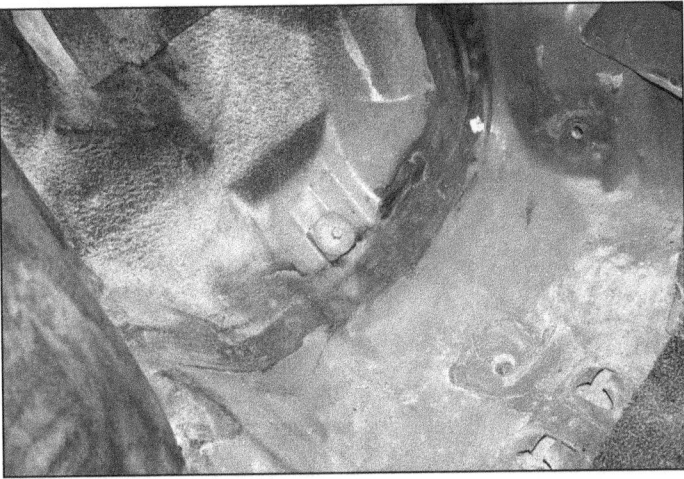

Push in on the front leading edge of the seat while lifting to pop it out and remove the rear lower seats. Use a deep-well socket to remove the two bolts, which are at the bottom to hold the rear upper seat. One bolt is positioned at each side around the seat frame. Lift up the rear upper seat from the bottom and push up to disengage the upper portion of the seat from the three hooks that the seat frame rests on.

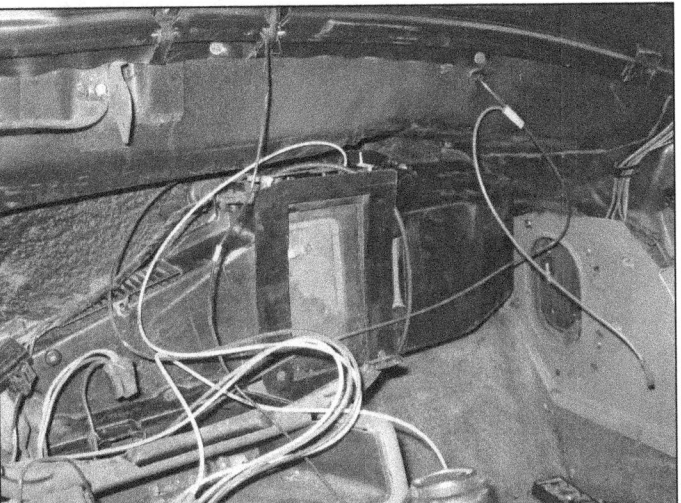

Once you have removed the dash, the heater or A/C box is accessible. To extract the firewall pad from the car, use a door panel removal tool to take out the push plugs. The opposite side of the heater or A/C box is located on the engine compartment side of the firewall. All of the bolts can be removed using a ratchet. (Dash removal is detailed in Chapter 11.)

Removal of the bolt-on components on the firewall on the engine compartment side is straightforward. The power brake booster is attached to the firewall with nuts accessed by wrenches. All other ancillary components attached to the firewall require removal by using a socket and ratchet. Some wiring harness clips may need to be popped open by inserting a flat-blade screwdriver into the lock flap and twisting. Make sure you take a lot of pictures before you remove any of these components. Take close up shots and overall shots, so you can orient yourself when the time comes back to re-install everything. You would be surprised at how different everything looks after the firewall has been cleaned and is bare.

CHAPTER 3

BODYWORK PART I: BODY PANELS

Bodywork on your Firebird is the most important part of your restoration. For many enthusiast restorers, it's the most challenging part of restoration and the results are critical to the quality of the overall restoration process. Think of the body as the foundation of your house. If the foundation is not solid, everything else attached to it is compromised.

The Firebird, or second-generation, F-Body car is a unibody vehicle, and therefore the body is constructed as one unit. The floors, rear frame rails, inner and outer wheelhouses, quarter panels, trunk floor extension panels, rocker panels, rear body panel, roof, and cowl are all welded together to form this one unit. Any of these parts that become compromised due to accident or rust require proper repair procedures to maintain the structural integrity of the body.

These cars have had at least 35 years of ownership and road history. Most of them have lived an interesting life . . . if they could only talk. As most people suspect, and as many experienced owners know, these cars often possess and hide many problems. Many things have happened over the course of these years, and this includes overaggressive use, accidents, and excessive rust. In some cases, routine maintenance has been almost or completely ignored, and this has significant consequences. It means you have more to repair and restore. In addition, some cars may have been improperly stored, and this leads to more rust and mechanical problems.

Taking all of this into consideration, you need to be well aware that many cars have been repaired, restored, and in some cases messed up over the years. In my experience, the vast majority of repairs are substandard. You need to correct that substandard work while you are at it so the

The importance of bodywork cannot be stressed enough. The overall quality of the restoration is largely determined by bodywork underneath the paint. The quality of the bodywork is evident in this 1970 Formula. The paint has been applied and wet sanded; the results are beautiful. The fender is installed and will be aligned.

vehicle has a consistent overall look when your restoration is complete.

The doors, trunk lid, and front sheet metal need the unit body to be in proper shape for them to correctly work. Four 15/16-inch bolts hold the front subframe to the underside of the forward portion of the floors and directly under the firewall, which requires the body to be square or it throws off the alignment of the front suspension and sheet metal as well as the engine and transmission.

Safety

Safety cannot be compromised. The whole point is for this process to be enjoyable for you and for you to enjoy the car when it is finished. Missing a finger, a limb, becoming visually impaired, partially paralyzed, or dead will not help you enjoy your car. Using the proper safety equipment such as welding gloves, a good-quality auto-darkening welding helmet, safety glasses, and the proper tools to do the particular task are important. Using a dust mask, paint respirator, and well-ventilated areas are also critical to maintaining a safe environment. Make sure you are not welding near open combustibles, as the fumes are what explode, not the liquid. Always use common sense and read the warning labels.

Make sure you clean up properly and allow time to do so before stopping for the day. Never keep working when you're tired because it is too easy to make a bad call or have an accident when you are tired. Never work under a car without using jackstands underneath. The coil springs are under immense pressure and can pop out of the control arm and cause major physical harm and death if one loosens. Do not assume that if a mechanic makes a particular procedure look easy that it really is easy.

Don't wear open-toed shoes; wear steel-reinforced work boots. Wear non-flammable clothing and long-sleeved shirts. Keep your hair out of the way. Make sure you wear gloves, especially when handling fluids and chemicals. A majority of the chemicals with which you'll come in contact will absorb through your skin on contact and can make you very sick very quickly. Make sure you have at least two sufficiently sized Class B fire extinguishers in each end of the workspace.

Preparation

This chapter discusses the most common rust issues Firebirds have and the proper procedures to deal with rusted areas as well as superficial dents. I do not believe in replacing entire panels unless absolutely necessary. Think of replacing panels as overly invasive surgery. Why cut more than you need? The original sheet metal is unquestionably the best to have, so why remove more metal than you need to?

The bodywork procedures I discuss will make for a proper and long-lasting repair. I cannot emphasize the importance of these steps to ensure a good-quality repair as well as stunning results once your Firebird is painted. Prep is paramount when working on the body and the paint reflects that hard work.

After all, the paint job is only a reflection of the level of bodywork and prep performed.

Tools for Bodywork

Performing bodywork is an acquired skill. Although a beginner can learn this skill, body panel replacement techniques and welding are not skills that are learned in a day. That's why you need to assess and accept what you can reasonably accomplish on your own.

To perform body repair and restoration procedures yourself, you need to rent, borrow, or buy a fair number of specialized tools. You should have a full selection of crimpers, formers, notching tools, an anvil, a bench vise, and metalworking hammers. A basic kit that includes dollies, shot bags, bossing mallets, and hand-held shears costs $200 to $500. Remember, with tools, you get what you pay for; high quality does not come cheap. You can purchase these tools from Snap-on, Sears, Eastwood, Jegs, and a number of automotive supply stores.

Beyond the specialty metalworking hand tools, you need a compressor to run the air flange and punch tool. In addition, you need a MIG welder and a high-quality welder from Lincoln, Hobart, Miller, or another brand; it can cost $900 or more. And of course, when welding, a weldor's mask and gloves are always essential apparel.

If you're restoring one car, my recommendation is rent or borrow the tools needed to complete the restoration job. If you plan to restore several cars over the coming years, investing in all the tools necessary to complete more serious restoration jobs is most likely worth it.

Quarter Panel Patch

Firebirds are known to commonly rust behind the rear wheels, especially where the lower portion of the quarter is joined to the trunk extension panel. It is important to evaluate the rusted area and to find

BODYWORK PART I: BODY PANELS

In almost all cases, the three- and four-decade-old 1970–1981 Firebirds need some body panel replacement because after such a long period of time, rust almost inevitably sets in. Bodywork requires metalworking and welding skill; you cannot become proficient overnight. But certainly, these skills can be learned with discipline and practice. In this case, the amount of rust warranted a quarter panel replacement.

where the weakened metal ends and the good metal begins. It is a good idea to cut at least 1½ inches into the solid metal when making a patch. When welding, you need to be sure there is no burn-through because of compromised metal integrity.

Look inside the trunk at the back side of the quarter panels to find any evidence of prior work, such as a line of newer metal indicating where a prior patch may have been made. Also look on the underside of the top of the quarters because larger patch panels generally end at the transition from the side to the top.

Most body shops do not take the time to hide the inside line that is left when doing patch panels, but if you do not see one, that does not mean it has not been patched. It just means that the seam may be hidden or just out of view due to other panels blocking it.

To start preparing for work on the panel, it is important to disassemble surrounding items. All these items, such as bumpers, moldings, lights, and spoilers, can be in the way and exposed to damage if not removed. They have to be removed anyway to prepare for paint so you might as well do it as you work in that area.

1974–1981 Component Removal

Open the trunk lid and remove the two 3/8-inch nuts for the side-marker lights using a socket. Remove the lightbulb socket with a slight twist and pull. The lamp comes out from inside and the lamp bezel comes out from the outside.

Two 7/16-inch nuts hold the spoiler ends. They are located at the top of the quarter panel; remove them from inside the trunk.

Remove the license plate lamp lens. Remove the two Phillips-head screws with a Phillips screwdriver, and twist the bulb retainer, then remove it.

Remove the three taillight bulbs and one reverse lamp bulb by twisting the sockets from inside the trunk. Remove the taillight assembly 7/16-inch nuts (eight total) from inside the trunk. The lamp lens and outer trim are now loose and require some wiggle and twist to remove from the rear body panel. It may be necessary to rotate the top out slightly to allow the lamp to clear the bumper cover.

Next, remove the two 7/16-inch nuts holding each end of the bumper cover to the quarter panel. They are accessible from the underside of the trunk at the quarter panel ends.

Remove the two 11/16-inch bumper bracket nuts, which are accessible from inside the trunk.

1970–1973 Component Removal

The 1970–1973 Firebirds were equipped with a chrome rear bumper, smaller taillights, and a fiberglass finish panel, so these components need to be removed. The spoiler and side-marker removal procedures are the same, but taillight and rear bumper steps are slightly different.

Place the jack under the center portion of the rear axle and use it to raise the rear of the car; raise it high enough so the rear tires clear the ground by 4 to 5 inches. Place jackstands under each end of the rear

Here, the rear bumper, spoiler, and taillight have been removed in preparation for bodywork. Firebirds often develop rust around the rear spoiler, particularly if they have not been sealed correctly. In addition, it's not unusual for Firebirds to rust on the rear body panel or in the trunk.

CHAPTER 3

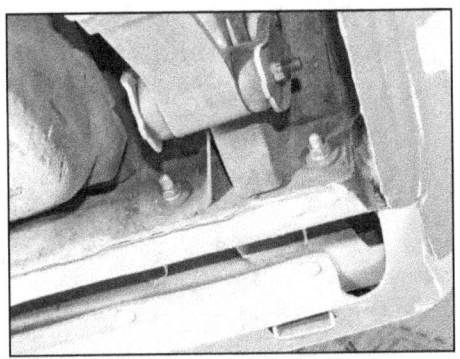

Two additional 11/16-inch nuts for each side sit below and behind the bumper on the rear body panel. Slide the bumper straight back and place the bracket facing down so the cover does not get damaged.

Brackets hold the rear bumper to the vehicle. They are easily accessible from the trunk.

To remove the quarter panel, taillight assembly, finish panel, and related parts, use a 7/16- and 9/16-inch socket and ratchet. Two 9/16-inch bolts hold the outer brackets on the quarter panel side while two 9/16-inch bolts hold the back side outers. A single 9/16-inch bolt holds an inner rear bracket on each side. The taillights are held in with six 7/16-inch nuts on each side: three on the top and three on the bottom. The finish panel also has four 7/16-inch nuts. The license bracket is held in with two 7/16-inch bolts accessible from the outside lower edges. The bracket also holds the finish panel in place. The taillight sockets are held in below the lamp housing. They twist to remove, as do the side-marker lamp sockets. The rear bumper has six brackets attached to it.

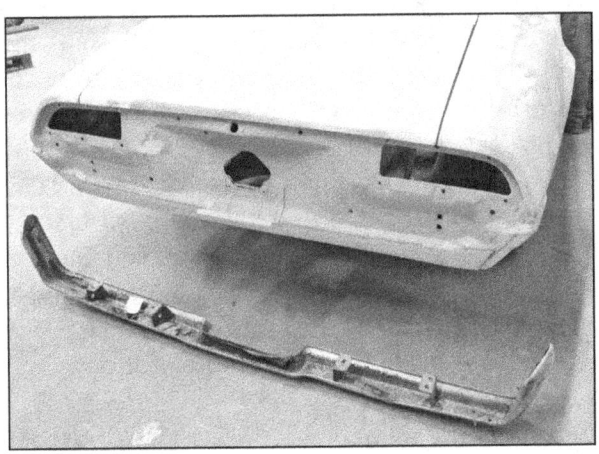

You need to reach inside the trunk to remove the bolts that secure the bumper to the car. Like many bolts, these can be very rusty and may require application of a lubricant such as PB Blaster. This rear view of the bare body panel also includes the back side of the rear bumper and its brackets.

axle and then lower the floor jack. It is important to have the weight of the car on the suspension and not on the body when replacing panels.

Rear Quarter Panel Rust

Remove the wheel-opening molding (if equipped) and eight Phillips-head screws. Cover the exhaust tip extension with a couple of masking tape wraps so it is not damaged while you work in the vicinity.

With a 24-grit wheel, start grinding where you identified the prior patch (as in this case) along the seam. If you could not identify a prior seam, start grinding around the rusted area and work your way out until you see solid metal. You may be grinding through a white powdery substance, which is body filler. Keep grinding through that until you hit metal. Think of this procedure as exploratory surgery.

Check the inside of the trunk and the drop-off areas for any rags or flammable objects before cutting the body to minimize the possibility of a fire. Also make sure the vehicle does not have any fuel leaks. Have a suitably sized Class B fire extinguisher nearby.

Now you can see how thick the body filler is and also where the metal is sound on the remaining panel so you can trim the replacement quarter panel patch to fit once this area is properly prepared. As you can see here, substandard prior repairs have compromised the panel behind the quarter panel. This panel is called a trunk extension or a trunk drop-off. Trunk extensions are extremely rust-prone and may require replacement.

Trunk Extension

The trunk extension panel is part of the trunk floor. One side attaches to

BODYWORK PART I: BODY PANELS

General Welding Tips

Use a high-quality MIG welder that allows you to do quality work. I use a Miller Matic 175 with .023 wire. When working on thin sheet-metal body panels, you need to use a suitable low-amp setting because you don't want to apply too much heat and deform the body panels.

Welder settings vary depending on the panel upon which you are working. One of the best ways to tell if you have the correct settings is that the welder should not throw off spatter. And most certainly, you should not burn through the sheet metal quickly. This process is commonly referred to as *plug welding*.

It is important to know that when welding, you want to weld all the corners first so the panel is set in the proper position. Next, start at the farthest end and then your next weld is the opposite farthest end, and you repeat that process until all of the punched holes are filled with weld. This welding creates extreme heat and causes the metal to warp if it gets too hot. By welding at the farthest points and working your way inward, you prevent the panel from warping or distorting from heat.

Spray Paint Trunk Extension

Spray paint the trunk extension panel and the back side of the quarter panel patch prior to welding the panel so corrosion protection is increased. The coating applied by the manufacturer (known as E-coat) is not very durable and really is only meant to prevent corrosion during storage and shipping of the part.

---

a flange at the floor; the other side ties into the bottom of the quarter panel and also has a flange. The forward portion attaches to the rear of the outer wheelhouse. The rear portion attaches to the rear body panel. This is an important part of the structure of the body. This panel usually rusts behind the quarter panel and is not visible from the inside of the trunk. Therefore, it is commonly overlooked.

Patch Panel

A trunk extension replacement quarter panel patch is not of great quality and often needs some minor reworking to make it fit and function as original. Having access to a shrinker and stretcher is helpful. This is a difficult skill to master. If you do not have access to a shrinker and stretcher, you can use a hammer and dolly to get the shape you need once the panel is installed.

Most sheet metal for patch panels is 16-gauge, but the thickness can vary depending on the manufacturer. These patches are generally available for about $50. Using the stretcher part of the tool is a matter of inserting the panel and working the metal with the handle to stretch the metal.

The same goes for the shrinker to make the curve that you need. It takes multiple times to place the panel on the body panel to compare your progress. Small steps are necessary because you really do not want to go too far too fast with this procedure.

The procedure works by trial and error. Starting out with just some scrap sheet metal gives you the feel and technique necessary to figure out how the tools work. Practice will make you much more proficient.

Place the patch panel in the proper position. Use body clamps to clamp it down, and make sure all mating surfaces are flush. Body clamps are available in small, medium, and large sizes and you should purchase an assortment. Almost any tool supplier (Eastwood, Sears) carries them. Make sure you have at least 10 clamps because every panel will use a different number of clamps to hold it.

Whenever you are mating a replacement panel to an existing panel, you must have enough clamps to hold the panel in place correctly to allow for proper welding. Once you have welded in the patch, be sure to look at the panel from all angles and adjust your clamps as necessary until you are satisfied that you have the panel sitting in the right place. You can obtain the anti-heat compound from many sources, including Eastwood.

Trunk Extension Patch Panel Installation

Evaluate Patch Panel

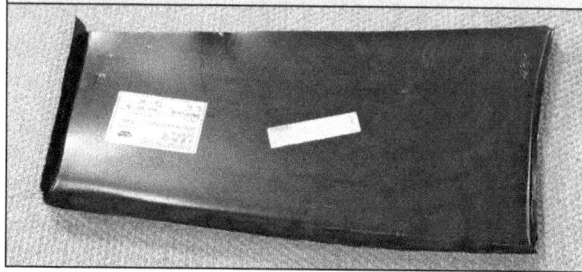

1 *Measure and trim the patch panel. It is important to make sure you do not cut off too much metal. Use a marker to draw a line to follow with the cut-off wheel.*

TRANS AM & FIREBIRD RESTORATION

CHAPTER 3

Cut Quarter Panel

2 Many second-generation F-Body cars no longer have solid sheet metal below the paint on the rear quarter panels, and rust may be poking through. This 1978 Firebird had a lot of body filler; I had to cut through it to find solid metal all the way around. I had previously tested the area with a magnet and knew I had a lot of filler to deal with.

Simply rapping your knuckles on the panel tells you if it has a lot of filler. When you rap the panel and hear a thud sound instead of a tinny metal sound it is a pretty good bet that there is body filler hiding behind the paint. Before you start cutting make sure you wear safety glasses and thick gloves to protect yourself from flying metal shards. Also make sure that no flammable fluids or rags are in the general vicinity.

Once you start the tool, slowly lower it into the metal and smoothly push the tool along the line. Use a cut-off wheel on a pneumatic rotary tool to make the first cut. It should be about 2 inches below where you designate the final cut across the top of the sheet metal. Remember, if you remove too much sheet metal you may need to replace the entire panel.

Mark Your Second Cut Line

3 Once again, measure several times and make sure your lines are accurate. It is better to cut smaller sizes later than to cut too much now. You can mark this cut line with a magic marker or you can simply drag a flat-blade screwdriver across the metal so you can see a line in the e-coat. A good solid line is important to use as a guide when you cut the metal with your cutoff tool. Make sure the metal is clear underneath so you do not accidentally cut something you did not intend to. Another tip is to place a strip of masking tape along the line you have drawn to give you a better visual as you cut.

Cut Other Sides of Panel

4 Cut the other two sides of the panel and peel back the panel. The technique is the same to cut the sides of the panel. You just want to be sure not to cut the metal underneath it.

Scrape Off Seam Sealer

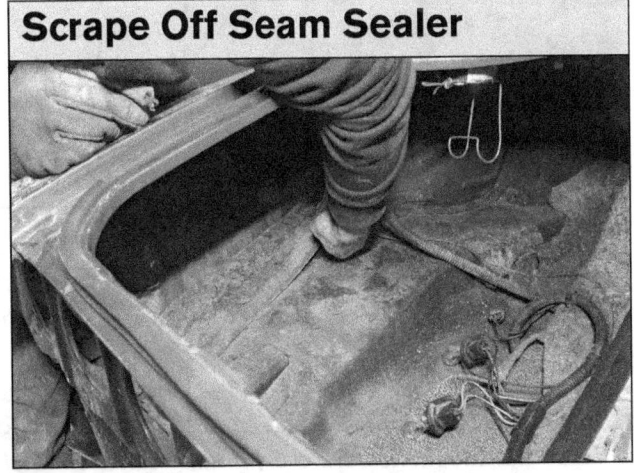

5 Use a scraper or utility knife to remove the thick seam sealer that hides the seam between the trunk floorpan and the extension. Once you get under the sealer, you can peel it off.

BODYWORK PART I: BODY PANELS

Cut Quarter Panel Seam

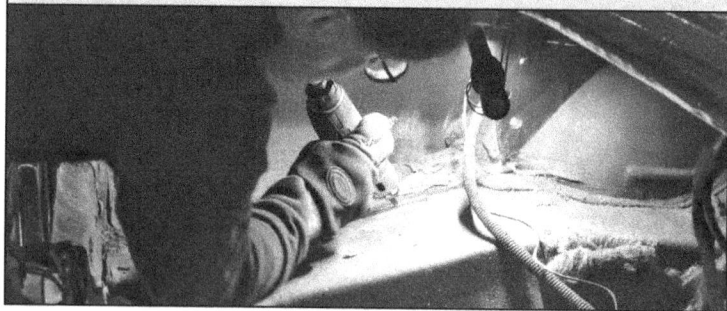

6 Use the cutoff wheel and make a small cut at the metal seam where the extension and floor meet. Use an air saw to cut along that seam. The air saw cut only needs to be about 2 inches long to allow the cutoff tool wheel to smoothly engage the line. If you did not make an initial cut with an air saw, your cutting tool could move back and forth before actually making a cut. That may result in the cut being in the wrong place.

Remove Quarter Panel

7 Cut off the rest of the panel where it meets the rear body panel and wheelhouse. Remove the quarter panel and extension. This panel had serious issues and the seam line of the prior patch is now visible.

Trim Metal in Quarter Panel Area

8 With the cutoff wheel trim the rest of the remaining metal edges to reveal the flanges. Remove the spot weld fragments to provide a smooth surface to attach the new trunk extension panel. It may also be necessary to use tin snips, hammer, and chisel to remove the remnants.

Remove Excess Sheet Metal

9 Now that all spot welds and excess metal have been removed, you have a flush surface for attaching the new trunk extension panel. It can be fitted against the edge to verify that the two flanges are flush. Simply using a hammer and dolly on the metal edge to straighten the flange makes the two panels mate together. The rusted panel below the taillights is also being replaced.

Check Fitment of Panel Patch

10 Check the fitment of the new extension against the floor, wheelhouse, and rear body panel. You must straighten the flanges as necessary to ensure a flush fitment. It is not uncommon for the metal to have distorted somewhat during the remnant removal process. The edges of the new panel need to be checked, because it is common for the edges to distort during manufacturing or shipping.

You want to make sure every mating surface matches up squarely for a proper fit. This is accomplished by constantly checking and re-checking every edge of the existing panel and the new panel to make sure the flanges are going to fit flush. When you correct one side, double-check the other side; modifying one side can slightly change the other. This has to be done over and over again until the part fits perfectly. Leaving gaps can, at a minimum, cause leaks or debris to get in or worse, cause an adjacent panel to not fit correctly.

CHAPTER 3

Clamp Panel in Place

11 Test fit the panel and use body clamps to hold it in place. It should fit flush against all flanges. Be sure that all the mating surfaces fit flush against the existing panel as you clamp them into place. This is how the panel will sit after you have welded it. This is not a step to take lightly and should be checked multiple times until you are satisfied with the fitment.

Punch Spot Weld Holes

12 Once you have verified that the panel fitment is good as described previously, remove the panel. Use an air flange/punch tool (available for less than $75) to punch holes in the new panel flanges about 1 inch apart. These holes provide an opening for the spot welds to join to the panel. Take your time and punch the holes in the middle of the flange so the work is clean and professional. This trunk extension is part of the body structure so it should have many spot welds to hold it in place and provide strength.

Strip Paint off Panels

 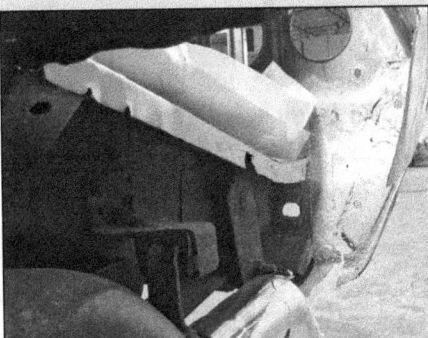

13 Use a wire wheel to clean up the edges of both panels (new and original joining) until they are shiny bright metal. This ensures a clean surface. Use a good-quality weld-through primer, such as 3M Weld-Thru Primer (PN 0511 31-05917). This reduces spatter and distortion caused by excessive heat that occurs during the welding process and replaces certain properties in the metal that are burned off. Spray some weld-through primer on all surfaces that will be welded. A few light coats are sufficient. Let the panel sit 5 minutes between coats and approximately 10 minutes after the final coat.

Install Trunk Extension Panel

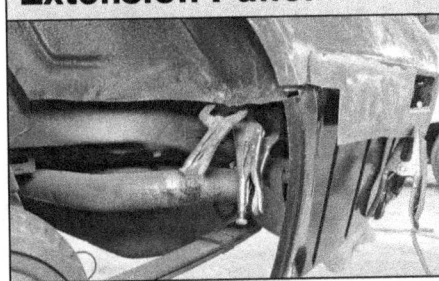

14 Clamp the panel into place. Use as many clamps as needed to properly hold the panel in place but still allow enough space to properly weld it. It is critical to fit this panel precisely. The quarter panel attaches to it and any mistake could make the quarter panel look distorted.

Tack Weld Trunk Extension

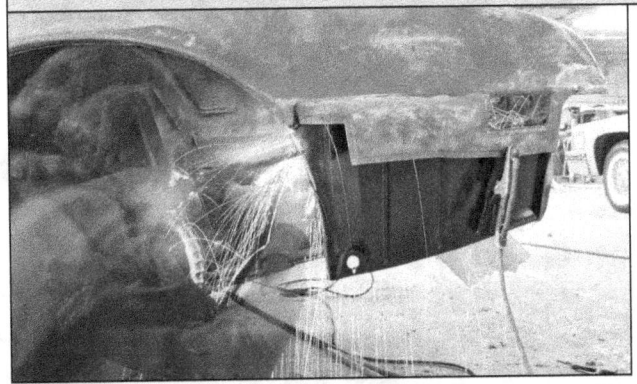

15 Using a good-quality MIG welder perform some test welds on scrap sheet metal to determine the settings to achieve a good weld. Burning a hole in the metal means that the setting is too hot. Lots of spattering can mean that the setting is too cold or that contaminants are on the panel. Every welder requires a different setting depending on its level of power and what material you are welding. Starting the welding at the farthest points and working inward prevents the panel from warping or distorting from heat. This is the same procedure to be used when welding on other panels where you are not plug welding but rather stitch, butt, or tack welding.

BODYWORK PART I: BODY PANELS

Inspect Tack Welds

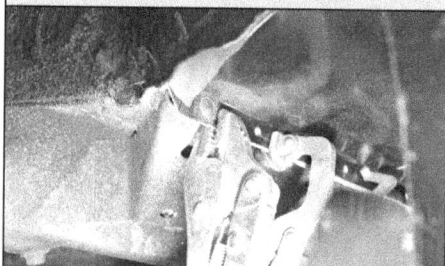

16 Take a good look at your tack welds before you continue because you want to be sure the welder settings are correct and you're not transferring too much heat to the weld area. An excellent plug weld should look like this on both sides.

Adjust Patch Panel Radius

17 A shrinker/stretcher tool lets you easily fabricate gentle radius bends and contours. These tools generally sell for less than $200 at most restoration supply stores. The technique for shrinking and stretching metal takes time and practice. Perform some tests on scrap metal to practice making the metal bend the way you need it to bend. Wear leather gloves at all times.

Secure the tool to a workbench. The better the tool is secured, the easier it is to use. Pre-drill and tap two holes into the base; it accepts 3/8-inch bolts. Bend the metal to be formed 90 degrees on a corner or a brake, if you have one. Create a flange that is no longer than 2 inches. Make a template out of cardboard. Trace the outline of the section you want to form. Work the leading edge first. This reduces the resistance and allows for easy and accurate working of the metal.

For best results, place the metal halfway into the jaws. Any metal that rises can be hammered out. Control the amount of pressure you exert on the handle and the number of strokes used while forming the metal. Move the metal back and forth until the desired radius is obtained. The jaws of the tool are serrated to bite into the metal. These serrations leave marks, which can easily be smoothed with a grinder or sander.

Instructional videos on the Internet can help you gain skill.

Form Correct Radius

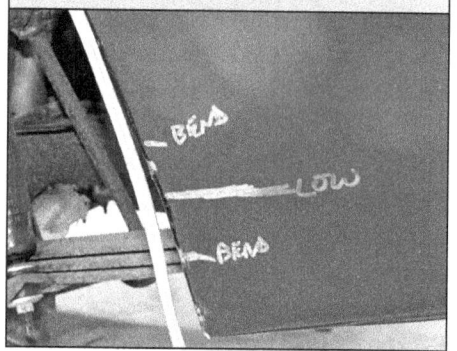

18 The replacement quarter patch does not have the slight concave roll in the lower portion, as does the stock panel. Although the roll may be slight, you need this roll for an accurate and faithful body profile. Using the shrinker/stretcher technique helps makes the slight bend necessary to achieve the correct body profile.

Use Factory Wheel Opening Molding for Reference

19 It is a good idea to use the factory wheel opening molding (if equipped) as a guide for the proper bend.

Create Flange on Quarter Panel

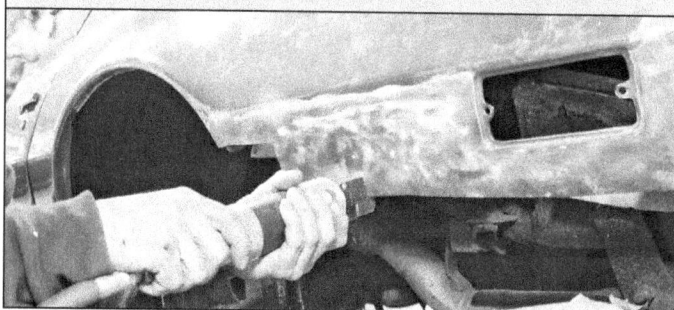

20 You need to create a recessed flange on the quarter panel so the patch panel can overlap the quarter panel and anchor it to the car. An air punch/flange tool is very easy to operate. Simply place the jaws of the tool on the edge of the existing quarter panel until it stops. Then press the button, and the flange is made. The jaws of the tool are fixed so you always get the same size of flange.

Create Flange on Quarter Panel (CONTINUED)

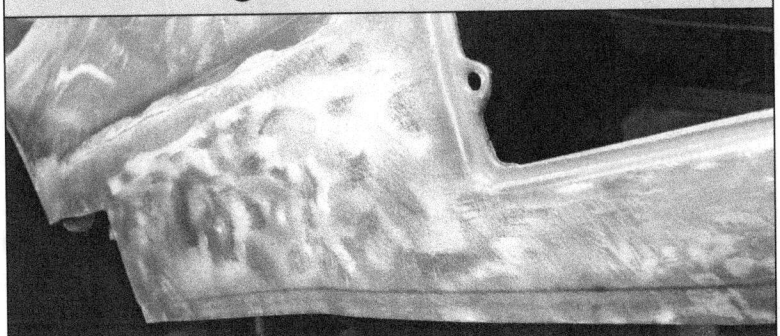

21 Carefully guide the air flange tool across the length of the quarter panel so you create one even flange surface area. Simply keep moving the flange tool over to the next spot after you have made the flange in that area until the entire area you want to flange is completed. You are now ready to final fit the patch panel.

Cut Patch Panel

22 In this photo, our veteran body technician trims the panel on a parts cart. I recommend using a workbench that affords you plenty of room. Make sure the patch panel is clamped or firmly held down on the bench. Position yourself so you have a clear sight line to the tape because you want the cut to be as straight as possible. Start from one end and methodically move the rotary across the trim panel until the cut is complete. The procedure is described in Step 3.

Prime Patch Panel

23 Treat the panel with a weld-through primer. The 3M product's quality is second to none and I always get consistent results. Place the panel over some newspaper or a spray cloth and evenly coat all the edges of the patch panel that will be welded. I typically apply two coats for thorough coverage. After the primer has been applied, use an air punch/flange tool to place spot weld holes 1 to 1.5 inches away from the edge and spaced 1 to 1.5 inches apart. These holes align with the flange area on the quarter panel and the spot welds hold the panel in place.

Tack Weld Patch Panel

24 Properly fit the patch panel in place using body clamps. Drill holes into the adjoining panel for spot welds Tack weld the panel starting at the corners. This is the same procedure used on fenders.

Rear Body Panel Sectioning

You need to section the rear body panel if the lower half has been previously rotted and poorly repaired. The upper half may be in good condition and structurally sound. Remember, you do not have to replace an entire panel just because you purchased it. This is especially true with structural panels. On this project, I was able to remove the lower section below the frame rail attachment point and leave the body structurally intact. This makes for a better repair.

Sometimes the entire panel may need replacement. Every car rusts differently depending on its care (or lack of care) and the environments to which it has been exposed over its lifetime.

I will section the panel just below the spot welds where the rear body panel ties into the trunk floor. This process is not exceptionally difficult, but it requires exact measurements and concentration.

You want to ensure that the part of the panel that remains on the car is solid. You should cut at least 1/2 to 1 inch beyond the edge of the corroded or rusted metal, so the panel serves as a solid foundation for the patch panel. Multiple measurements are critical so a proper cut is made. In the body industry, this is called sectioning, and it means you are only replacing a portion of the panel and not the entire panel.

When trimming a wide panel, leave a strip of metal toward the center to help assist with placing the panel. Once you have the panel where you want it, use a cutting wheel to lightly cut a groove into the new panel and existing panel to create alignment marks. This allows you to take the panel on and off for final trim but still line it up properly.

Tail Panel Installation

Inspect Trunk and Valance Area

1 The lower portion of a rear body panel is a common area for Firebirds to rust. The 1974 and later Firebirds tend to have more rust in this area because the sheet metal is hidden behind the rear bumper cover and moisture gets trapped behind the bumper cover. Often that area is not cleaned because it's not visible.

Determine Cut Line on Valance

2 This cut panel reveals prior body filler and rust. After determining where the solid metal starts, use a cutoff wheel to cut along your marked line to properly section the panel. You need to find clean, non-corroded metal so you can cut at least 1.5 inches into that solid metal surface.

Remove Rust from Valance

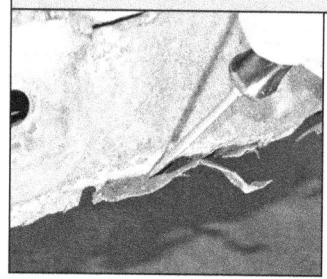

3 It's important to remove all the rusted sheet metal from an area; once metal has started rusting it doesn't stop until it's cut out and replaced with fresh sheet metal. You can use a cold chisel or screwdriver to knock off the rusted metal; a chisel often works the best. A hammer and chisel are typically required for tougher spots.

Inspect New Sheet-Metal Panel

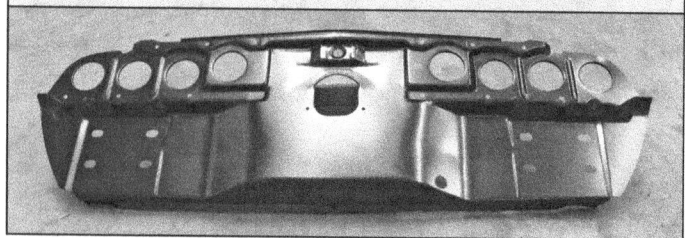

4 Here is the new replacement panel prior to being sectioned. It is important to measure multiple times before cutting the replacement panel. Several suppliers offer this rear body panel, including Tamraz Parts Warehouse (I bought one for $288, including shipping). If you trim the panel a bit longer it can incrementally be trimmed until a perfect fit is made rather than trying to add metal to fill the gaps.

Apply Rust Neutralizer

5 Once you have removed the panel, cleanup is needed. Use a rust neutralizer such as Mar-Hyde One-Step (PN 3509). It converts the rust into a black primer sealer.

CHAPTER 3

Neutralize Rust

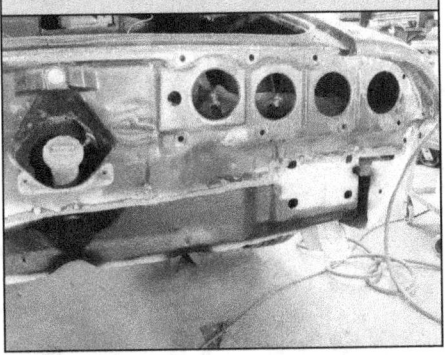

6 Apply rust neutralizer to the exposed metal on the original side and the back side of the new panel to help minimize corrosion.

Punch Spot Weld Holes in Rear Valance

7 Use an air punch tool for adding holes on the bottom and sides approximately 1 to 1.5 inches apart. Be sure to place the holes in the center of the flange for a neat and clean appearance but also so the panel has the best support and strength when attached. Find a large clean area of your shop to spray down the valance with weld-through primer. Apply the anti-heat compound to the existing part of the taillight panel (as you did when repairing fenders). Using the anti-heat compound reduces the possibility of warping the tail panel while welding.

Clamp Patch Panel in Place

8 Start clamping the panel in place and trim the edges as needed to make them fit as close to the original panel as possible. Make sure that the new valance is correctly aligned with the existing panel. Once it's tack welded in place, you would have to cut off or grind down the tack welds to realign it. Again, place the spot weld punch holes 1 to 1.5 inches apart. Use the body clamps as needed to hold the panel in place but allow enough room for welding.

Butt Weld Seams

9 Align the new lower body panel with the existing upper body panel. Tack weld a couple of corners along with the existing ear. Press along the line where the new panel meets the old to make sure there is no overlap. Here, I butt weld the two panels together. You want the seam to fit as flush as possible so you have less metal work to do and use less body filler later. You cannot plug weld the panel because there isn't a flange. You need to trim the panel in the middle. Make sure the MIG welder is set at the proper amp setting and the correct wire is being used. Make the actual welds start at the farthest point and work inward. Once enough of the panel has been welded the ear can be simply cut off.

Tack Weld Patch Panel

10 Tack weld on the outside of the panel and work your way to the center. Keep the body clamps in place until you have spot welded in the center of the panel. You do not want the panel to shift during this process. Place about a dozen spot welds at the outside of the panel on each side.

TRANS AM & FIREBIRD RESTORATION

BODYWORK PART I: BODY PANELS

Tack Weld Patch Panel (CONTINUED)

11 Remove the center ear that was used to anchor the lower panel to the upper panel. Place spot welds every 8 inches along the seam between the upper and lower valance panels (the panel is now securely welded in place). Remove the body clamps. When all the spot welds have been placed along the panel seam, start stitch welding between those seams. It's like connecting the dots.

This thin-gauge sheet metal can withstand a moderate amount of heat before it starts warping, and warpage must be avoided. Lay down a bead of weld between two spot welds and then move to the opposite end of the panel so you are spreading the heat. Apply air to the area of the panel that has been stitch welded and let it cool for a few minutes. This is the best way to avoiding warping the panels.

Smooth Out Welds

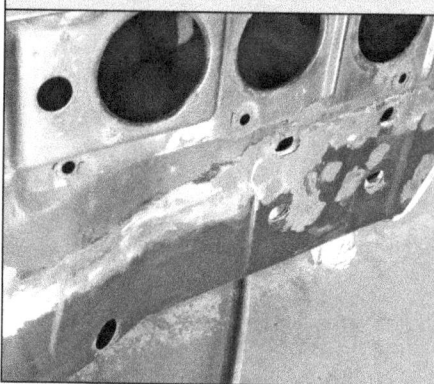

12 After the panel has cooled grind the welds smooth to finalize the metal work. A coarse 36-grit grinding disc on a DA sander is sufficient to remove the weld slag.

Patch Panel Fabrication

Sometimes you need to patch a small area on a panel, and it is not feasible to buy an entire panel just to cut a small piece out of it, nor is there a replacement patch panel available. You need good tin snips, a vise, a hammer, a marker, and 16-gauge sheet metal of sufficient size for the panel you intend to make. You also need something to form the metal against. For this project, I used a wheel-bearing race to create the correct radius for a patch panel. As long as you have something the same size of the radius of the curve you need, you will be fine. You need patience to make the panel, especially when forming the radius.

I ran into this very problem with a 1978 Firebird Formula W72 car. I had replaced the lower quarter panel with a patch panel, but that panel did not cover a particular area that required a patch. This was the edge of the quarter where the bumper resided below it and the taillight was just on the inner side of it. This area commonly rusts because the rear spoiler ends either have their sealant dry out or someone doesn't properly replace the sealer when reinstalling the spoiler end. It also can be due to the trunk lid leaking from a failed and misadjusted weatherstrip on the trunk lid.

Patch Panel Installation

Inspect Quarter Panel

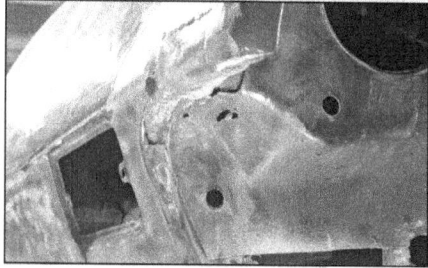

1 Here, the rear edge of the quarter panel near the front fascia has rusted through. As you can see, someone has already attempted a partial patch in this area but the new patch panel did not cover this area. Patch panel fabrication is easiest when you have something to copy, as in this case. You can use 18-gauge sheet metal to fabricate a patch panel for this area. To complete this procedure, use a vise, cutting shears, and metal-working hammer.

Cut Sheet-Metal Patch

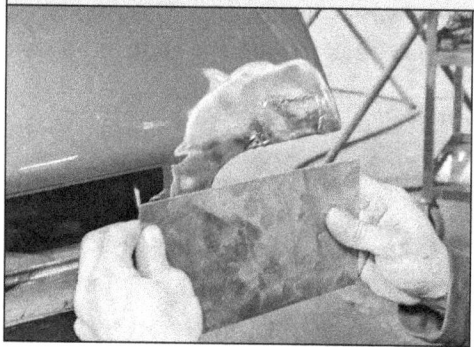

2 Use metal shears to cut a piece of sheet metal large enough to serve as a patch panel for the curved areas. A large patch panel is required for the curved profile of the quarter panel. And the patch panel needs to be stretched to fit this area. Compare the size of the new sheet metal to the actual work area to ensure the piece is large enough.

CHAPTER 3

Mark Sheet-Metal Patch

3 Place a sheet-metal patch on the side of the quarter panel and, with a Sharpie or other permanent marker, draw a solid line where you intend to cut. Use dotted lines for where you will be bending the metal.

Trim Sheet-Metal Patch

4 Because you are cutting such a small piece of 18-gauge sheet metal, you do not need air-powered shears. Use tip snips to trim along the traced line, but be careful not to trim off too much material.

Create Sheet-Metal Radius and Flange

5 To form the piece of sheet metal into a patch panel worthy of installation, you need a ball-peen hammer, vice, and dolly. If you bought a fairly complete metal forming tool kit, a dolly should be included. If not, you need to buy a dolly of the correct radius. Here, this wheel-bearing race was the ideal size for the radius on the panel, and it came from a front rotor wheel-bearing race on another Trans Am. You use it to help shape the panel. The wheel-bearing race is basically being used as a dolly.

6 Place the sheet metal and the wheel-bearing race into a vise so the lines are in the correct position. Stretching and forming sheet metal requires many small moves until the flat steel is correctly formed into the piece that can be welded onto the car. Strike the sheet metal with the ball end of a hammer repeatedly within the race. Slowly move and stretch the metal to form along the lines drawn. Moderate blows around the race area helps shape the metal slowly to make the curve you need. Take your time.

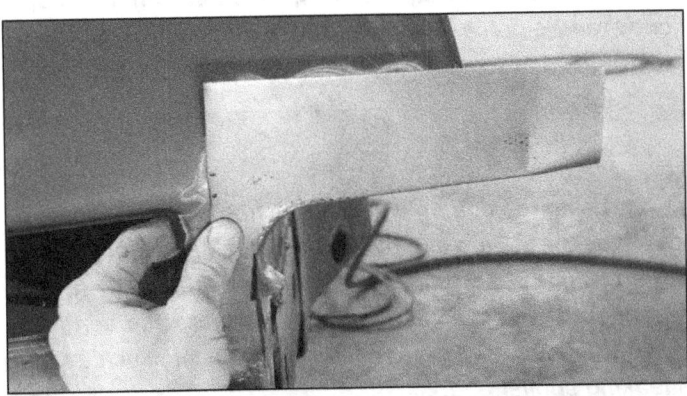

8 Place the patch panel in the vice along the second bend line. Place it back in vise once the panel fits properly to the quarter. (Here, the bearing race is used to form the radius of the patch panel.) Use a your metal working hammer to first form the radius. As you can see the radius does not extend beyond the bodyline. The metal around the radius has been worked so it's at about a 90-degree angle.

7 Once the curve has been made, check it against the body for fitment. You butt weld this piece onto the quarter panel (much the same as with the rear body panel). Trim and fit the panel as it gets closer to its final shape.

Create Sheet-Metal Radius and Flange (CONTINUED)

9 It may require multiple trips from the car to the vise to achieve proper fit. Be sure the patch panel is held in the vice at the bend line. Once you have established the radius curve, use the hammer to work the metal and stretch it to the top of the vice. The leading edge of the metal patch panel should align with the radius and form a 90-degree bend.

Test Fit Patch Panel

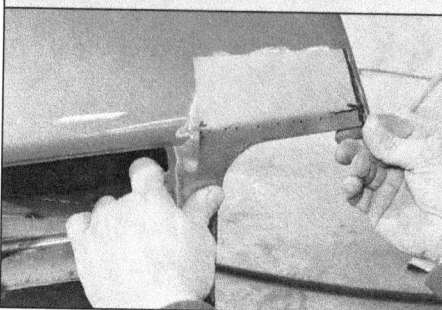

10 Be sure that the patch panel follows the contour of the quarter panel and properly aligns with the bumper. A properly fabricated patch requires much less body filler and makes for a much better repair. Often you need to compare the patch panel to the area and use tin snips or shears to trim it. Be patient. Don't take too much metal off at once or you will need to start over.

Test Fit Patch Panel

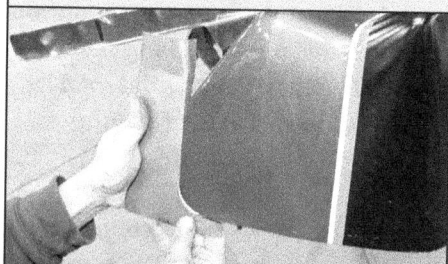

11 You always want the patch panel to align with adjacent panels or parts. When the car is completely assembled, the panel gap should be straight and a consistent 1/8 inch thick. It's very important to check the patch at this stage of the process. On this car, the rear bumper cover also resides in this area so the cover was also checked for proper radius.

Mark Cut Lines on Quarter Panel

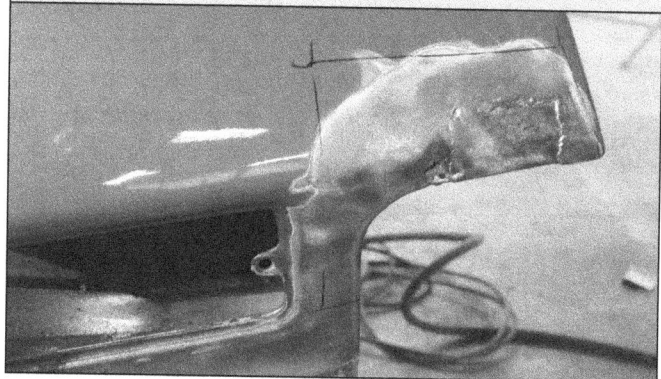

12 Once you've verified that the patch fits correctly and properly follows the body curve, it is time to prepare the body to accept the patch. Use the metal patch panel as a template for the cut on the quarter panel. Hold the patch panel in place and outline the profile against the quarter panel. You're now ready to use a cutoff wheel to remove the damaged sheet metal. It is very important to check every angle, curve, and contour to make sure the patch fits into the panel. Think of this as making a replacement piece for a jigsaw puzzle. Draw an outline on the body to prepare to cut the body for the patch. Draw the outline above the contour, and make the cut on the outside of the line so you can fine-tune the trim later.

Cut Rusted Metal from Quarter Panel

13 Using the cutting wheel, cut a horizontal line just below the top line by about an inch and along the other two lines to remove the panel. Once the cuts are made, grab the small metal panel with pliers and bend it down. This may reveal more hidden corrosion, such as from a leaking spoiler end.

CHAPTER 3

Remove Rust and Apply Rust Neutralizer

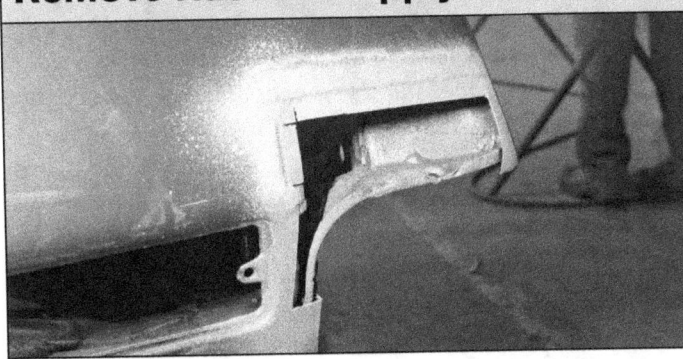

14 Use a wire brush or an 80-grit sanding wheel to remove surface rust, loose particles, and debris on the metal. Then apply a rust converter to neutralize the rust. Once the rust converter has dried, use a hammer to work the metal on the contour into a flange. Like other metal forming, you need to make a number of small moves so don't rush it. Spray some weld-through primer around the areas to be welded and inside the trunk area you just cleaned. This existing panel is only partially flanged.

Punch Tack Weld Holes and Prime

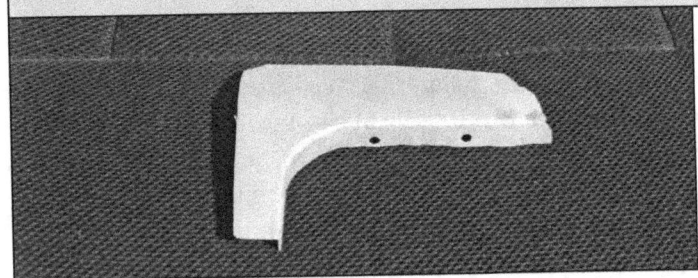

15 Punch the spot weld holes into the patch panel and spray the patch panel with primer. Punch holes only in the panel where it is being fitted, not on the other end. The whole point of the punched holes is to allow the spot welds to fill the hole and attach to the panel receiving the patch. This finished patch has the plug weld holes punched.

Fit Patch Panel on Quarter Panel

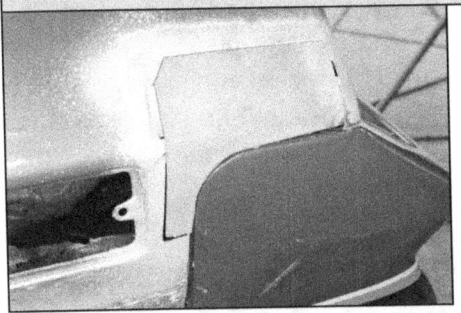

16 Re-install the bumper to check the fitment of the patch; this is a complex patch and the fit is critical. Properly align the patch in the quarter panel and make sure it accurately follows the contour of the bumper and the spacing remains consistent. Because this panel is so small and the area being patched is not very accessible you hold the patch in place and apply tack welds to the corners.

Tack Weld Patch Panel

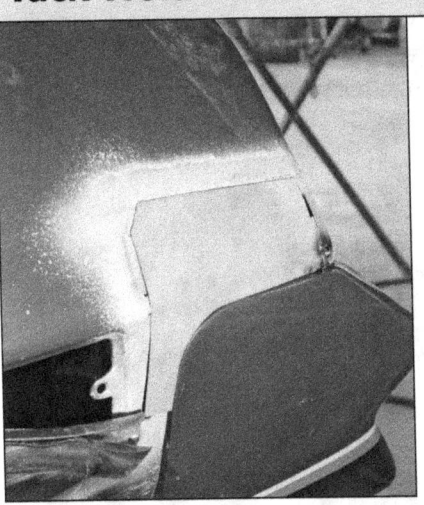

17 Fit the patch and use a little pressure from a screwdriver to adjust the panel to get the patch to fit better. When you have established the correct alignment, place a quick tack weld in the patch panel's corner to hold it in place.

Tack Weld Patch Panel (CONTINUED)

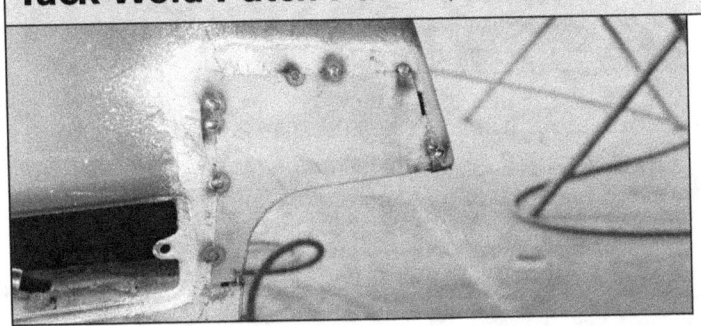

18 A tack weld in the corner holds the patch in place but pivots enough to allow further adjustments. This patch panel has been adjusted upward and there is a slight gap at the bottom, but a gap this small presents no problem. A bead of weld fills it in and can be ground down. After you are finished with the adjustments, remove the bumper and weld the panel.

Stitch Weld Patch Panel

19 *Stitch weld between all the tack welds so the panel is completely welded in place. This is a methodical process and you cannot weld the panel too quickly. Stitch weld between two spot welds on one side of the panel and quench with air. Let two or three minutes pass. Move to the opposite end of the panel and stitch weld between the two spot welds. And then again, use air to quench the bead. Then continue alternating until the entire panel is welded.*

Once the welding has been completed, allow the panel to cool for 30 minutes or so. By that time, the welding heat should be completely dissipated. At this time, the panel should be cool; now you can grind them smooth. Once you are finished, your result should look sort of like this. It almost looks as though nothing was ever done!

Fenders

Almost all Firebird second-generation fenders interchange among years. Although the earlier- and later-year fenders have some cosmetic differences that are not readily apparent, they do not affect the fit and function. The fenders can be found used or as reproductions.

The only important differences are at the front leading edge. Pontiac used two different brackets between 1970–1975 and 1976–1981 to provide mounting for the front lower valance on the earlier Firebirds and the bumper cover on the later years. These brackets are tack welded on at the front of the fender edge and easily removed with a small cutting wheel. Simply fit them onto the front of the fenders, clamp them in place, and tack weld them on.

This means that you can purchase a later fender to use on an earlier Firebird. This is especially helpful given the rarity of original or good used fenders because you now have an 11-year run of Firebirds to pick from. If you happen to locate an earlier fender and need to use it on a later Firebird, you can do that also.

Bear in mind that all Firebird, Firebird Esprit, and Formula fenders interchange with the exception of the 1971 fenders. Pontiac had a fake small vent placed above the Firebird nameplate on each fender in 1971. If you happen to find 1971 Firebird fenders, that vent opening can be closed off.

Trans Am fenders have a single air extractor opening in the side of the fender. All Trans Am years interchange, including the 1971, as they were not different.

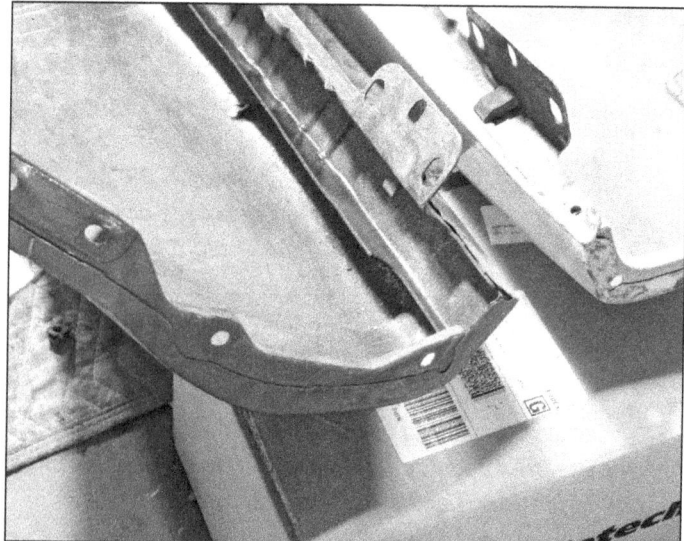

This is a 1978 driver-side original Firebird fender with the later front bracket. The front bumper cover can be mounted at the upper portion of the bracket.

This is the 1978 passenger-side fender that you spot welded the early bracket onto after removing the front bracket. The contours fit perfectly. The bracket has provisions for the lower valance; the 1975 and earlier models have the same bracket.

Fender Patch Preparation

Firebird fenders commonly rust just behind the front wheel near the attachment bolts on the underside. If your fender doesn't require replacement, but has some damage or rust, you can repair or patch it. A fender repair patch is available through Internet sources or The Parts Place. The patch is not very good quality as far as the shape of it, but it is of sufficient gauge to use as a last resort or for a good patch.

The procedure and technique for installing the patch can be performed with the fender installed. However, I recommend removing the fender to make for a better repair and to be able to treat the back side so the panel does not rust from the back side. The ears on the bottom of the fender where the attaching bolts are located also are prone to rust. The replacement patch panel also has the attachment ears.

Remove Front Fender

1 It's complicated to remove the front fenders on the Firebird because it has hidden bolts and other panels that tie into the fender. Rust commonly forms at the lower portion of the fender behind the front wheel. However, this particular 1978 Formula W72 in Martinique Blue has sustained an impact, which was not repaired properly. Although this is collision damage, the repair approach is the same as if the area were rusted.

Remove Headlamp Plugs

2 Open the hood and look between the bumper cover and the core support; you see the headlamp plugs. Reach down and separate the plugs from the headlamps. You also see the lower retainer bracket 1/2-inch bolt on each side behind the headlamps; it needs to be removed. Use a socket and ratchet and an extension to remove the bolts.

Hood Latch Support

3 From underneath the car, reach up and twist out the parking lamp sockets and let them dangle. Two upper 1/2-inch nuts and two lower 1/2-inch bolts on each side secure the front cover to the fenders. Remove the two 1/2-inch bolts that attach the center bumper brace to the hood latch support.

Remove Upper Cover Brackets to Radiator Support

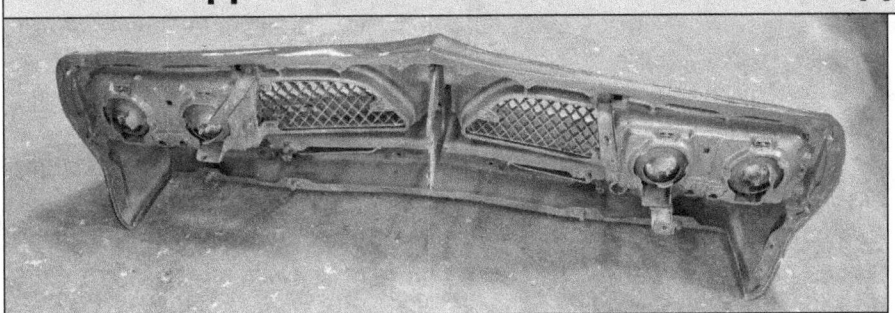

4 Remove the 1/2-inch bolts (one on each side) that hold the upper retainer on top of the radiator support.

Remove Front Bumper Braces

5 Remove the four 11/16-inch nuts on each side that attach the front bumper reinforcement to the braces. Remove the hood latch release handle bracket located on the driver's side of the bumper reinforcement; it is held in with a 1/2-inch bolt. Slide the front bumper cover assembly forward and place it in a safe place.

Measure Fender-to-Fender Distance

6 This Formula fender measurement is 54.75 inches in the front.

Measure Fender (CONTINUED)

7 The fender measurement is 57.50 inches at the rear using the base of the wipers and hood stops as points of reference.

Measure Width between Fenders

It is a good idea to measure the width between the fenders at the front and the rear to give yourself a baseline of where the fenders were. It makes reassembly much easier.

Add Tape around Hood Hinges

If you are reinstalling the hood without painting the underside, place masking tape on the hood around the hood hinges so you have a reference point for the hood alignment.

Disconnect Washer Hose Line

8 Disconnect the main washer hose line to the nozzle tee on the hood. Remove the hood hinge 9/16-inch bolts (two per side).

Remove Hood

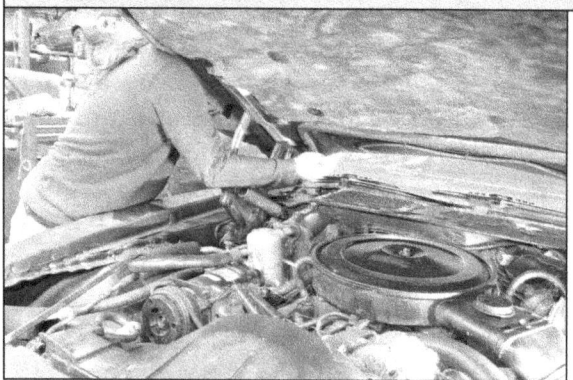

9 The hood is heavy and cumbersome; it can slide down and break the windshield or fall off and hurt someone if you attempt to remove it by yourself. Get a friend to help you. You need to be ready to catch and safely move the hood when the bolts have been removed. First, remove the two forward bolts and then place your shoulder underneath the hood and a hand on the backside to support the hood. Use a socket and ratchet to remove the rear two bolts to free the hood from the hinges. If you're positioned under the hood as described, you should have a firm grasp. Once removed, move it to a storage space to avoid damaging it.

CHAPTER 3

Part Removal

You must remove all smaller parts that affect correct fender removal. Pontiac was in the middle of changing from SAE nuts and bolts to metric during the year this Formula was built so you may find a mix of metric and SAE, all SAE, or all metric depending on when your particular Firebird was built. In my experience, 1976 and older Firebirds were all SAE, 1977–1979 were a mix, and later models were also a mix but more heavily metric.

Raise the vehicle and place jackstands under the front lower control arms so the body is supported by the suspension. Given the weakness of the subframe and having only four bolts attached to the unit body, it is not unusual to have the front sheet-metal flex when it's not supported by the suspension.

I remove the passenger-side fender in this example. The driver-side fender is not much different, except for some ancillary items attached to the wheelhouse.

Remove Radiator Overflow Bottle

1 *Use a ratchet and socket to remove the two 10-mm bolts that hold the radiator overflow bottle to the wheelhouse.*

Remove Wheelhouse Bolts

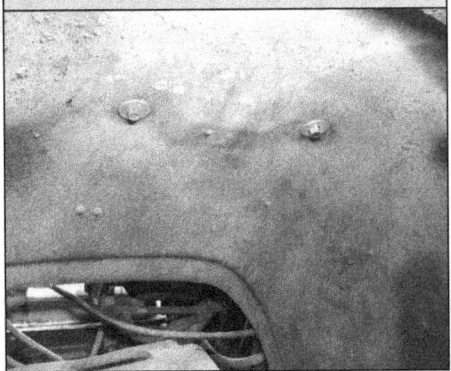

2 *Use a socket and ratchet to remove the two upper inner-wheelhouse 1/2-inch bolts and the two upper support-bar 1/2-inch bolts.*

Remove Side-Marker Lamp

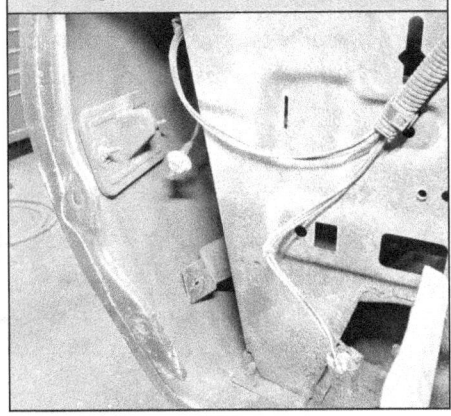

3 *Remove the side-marker lamp socket by twisting and pulling the bulb out.*

Remove Wheelhouse Bolts

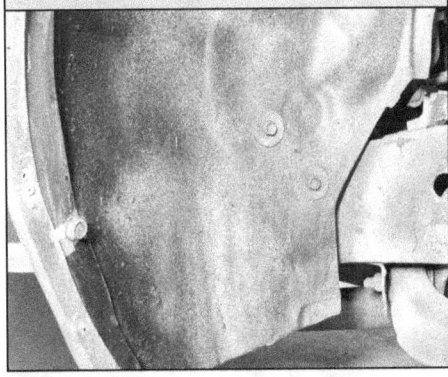

4 *Remove the two 1/2-inch rear wheelhouse support bolts. The wheelhouse may require a bit of wresting to remove it. It does not fall down when the bolts are removed.*

Remove Support Panel

5 *Once again, socket and ratchet are the preferred tools to remove the three 1/2-inch bolts that secure the small front wheelhouse filler panel to the radiator support panel.*

Remove Fender Hardware

6 *Remove the two lower forward 1/2-inch bolts that attach to the lower tie-bar of the radiator support.*

Remove Fender Hardware (CONTINUED)

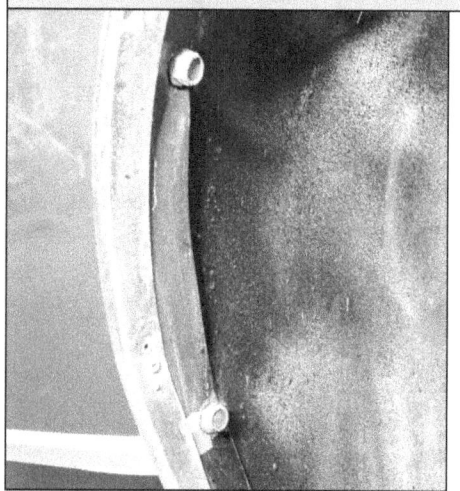  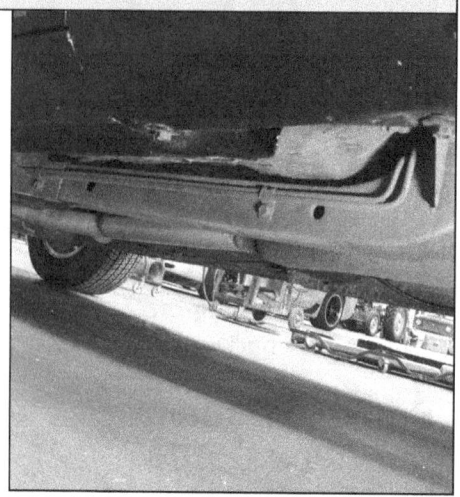

7 Remove the five 1/2-inch bolts that secure the fender to the wheelhouse, which are located around the wheel opening.

8 Remove one 9/16-inch bolt in upper rear of fender (located in the door opening).

9 Use a 9/16-inch socket and ratchet to remove two 9/16- and one 1/2-inch lower bolts behind the front wheel.

10 Use a 9/16-inch socket and ratchet to remove the 9/16-inch bolt on top of the fender, at the cowl by the windshield.

11 Remove two 1/2-inch bolts where the fender and the radiator support meet.

12 Locate the 9/16-inch bolt at the firewall where the back of the hood hinge is located.

Remove Fender Hardware CONTINUED

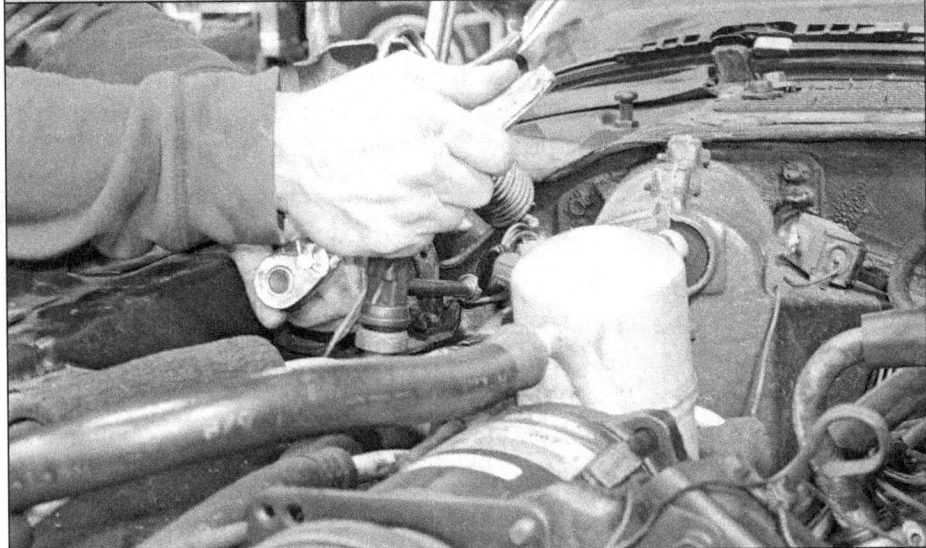

13 Use a 6-inch extension and deep well socket to remove this bolt.

Remove Fender

14 Because the bolts no longer secure the fender it can be separated from the chassis and other bodywork. After years of attachment to the car, it probably requires some wiggling to slide it off. Be careful when you wiggle the fender, and watch the top ear of the fender because you don't want to hit the windshield and crack it. The wheelhouse is loose.

Dent Removal

In this example, a smaller dent was filled without any attempt to pull it out. I will not be able to hammer and dolly that dent because it is located in front of the stiffener brace. I will use the Uni-Spotter, also known as a stud gun. The technique is quite simple.

The stud needs to be placed in the center of the dent. It may be necessary to attach additional studs around the circumference of the dent. Larger dents require the studs to be placed all around the dent. Each stud pulls on the dent as you work toward the center of the dent.

The stud gun is a tool used when access to the back of the dent is not possible. Before this invention, the common method was to drill a hole or a series of holes in the center and all around the dent. A screw was threaded in and a slide hammer attached. The slide portion of the hammer slid back with force to pull back the dent. The problem was that the area where the screw was threaded frequently created more damage and required additional labor to repair.

The Uni-Spotter works on the same principle but does not create additional damage or labor. The cost of a Uni-Spotter may be prohibitive, but your local rental shop may have one.

Using a Uni-Spotter is the proper way to repair a dent when you cannot access the back side of the panel. A small dent like this did not require the major amount of labor needed to remove and reinstall the fender to properly repair the dent.

Remove Body Filler

1 Use an abrasive paint-stripping disc to remove the paint. 3M offers a wide range of discs, such as the SandBlaster series, to quickly and safely remove the paint and underlying body filler. The 80-grit abrasive discs are often used to strip away the body filler. Once you work through the paint, the amount of body filler is revealed. Here it was quite substantial. Work the rotating disc back and fourth using moderate pressure and evenly strip the filler from the panel. Be careful not to grind one area for too long or the panel will warp.

Cut Out Dent in Fender

2 Use a straight edge and a Sharpie to precisely mark the cut-out line on the fender. Once the line has been drawn, use a pneumatic rotary tool with a 3-inch 80-grit wheel to cut out the affected area.

3 The damaged area has been completely removed.

Inspect Removed Panel

4 The lower part of this fender was in poor shape. The removed metal had a large amount of body filler in it so it was necessary to remove it.

Remove Paint

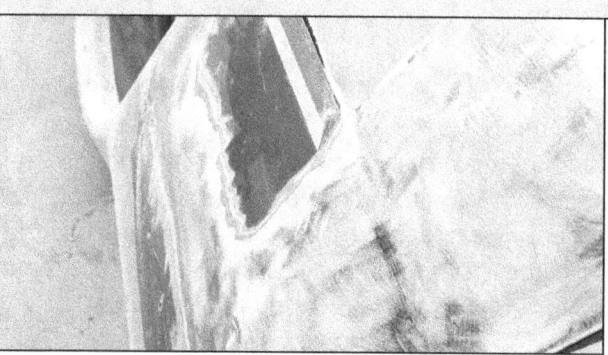

5 I used a 6-inch DA sander with 80-grit sandpaper to remove the paint and, in this case, the body filler. Use an orbital sander and apply even pressure as you work through the layers of paint.

Inspect Stripped Body Panel

6 Even after the entire half of the body panel has been stripped and the body filler has been removed, the panel still needs a lot of work. A dent needs to be pulled out and another part of the panel needs straightening. Even though I am going to cover the metalworking process and I am going to show how to use hammers, dollies, and dies, you should have a basic metalworking kit at your disposal. In addition, Automotive Sheet Metal Forming & Fabrication by Matt Joseph is a good resource for learning how to rework metal.

Weld Dent Rod to Panel

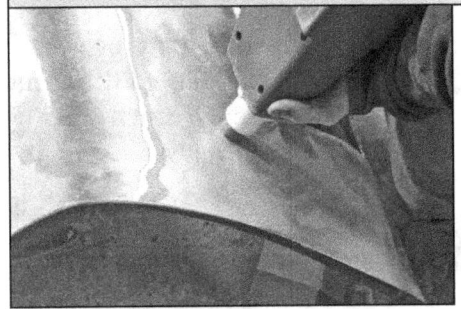 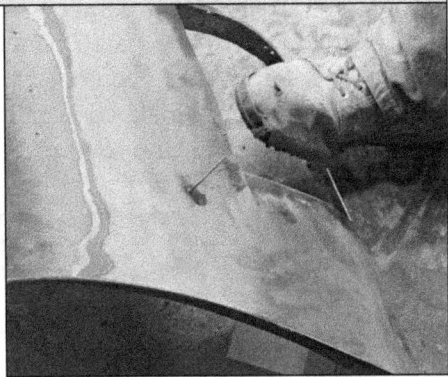

7 Insert a welding stud into a Uni-Spotter. Place the stud on the area of the dent you want to pull. Ensure the grounding element is flush against the panel and pull the trigger. There will be a glow when proper contact is made. The trigger only needs to be pressed for a second or two.

8 If the rod is firmly attached to the sheet metal, you can see the heat-affected zone. If the dent is larger, you many need to weld several dent rods to the dented area so you can pull it out evenly.

Insert Slide Hammer

9 Place the slide hammer over the stud.

Pull Dent Out

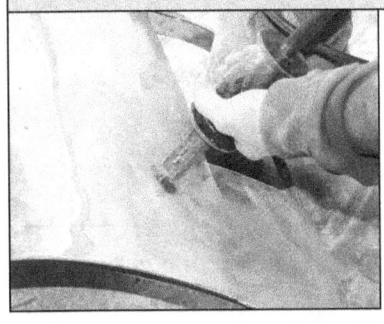

10 Glide the hammer up the shaft until it reaches the stop at the end. When it reaches the end, this force pulls the dent out of the panel. You can adjust the amount of force depending on the size of the dent. With a smaller dent, apply moderate force when sliding the hammer. Larger dents require more slide force. Slide the hammer back and forth until dent is pulled. Carefully examine the dented area to be sure the sheet metal in the dent aligns with the rest of panel. You may need to use several studs for larger dents, but the technique is the same.

Cut Off Rod Stud

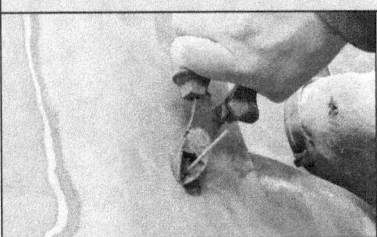

11 Use a wire cutter to simply cut off the stud just above its base.

Grind off Weld Bubble

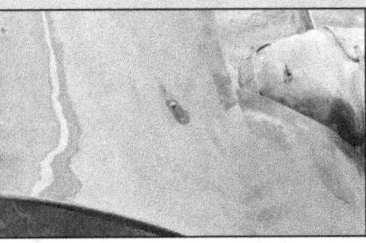

12 The base, or weld bubble, remaining on the fender needs to be ground off. Use an orbital sander with 80-grit paper.

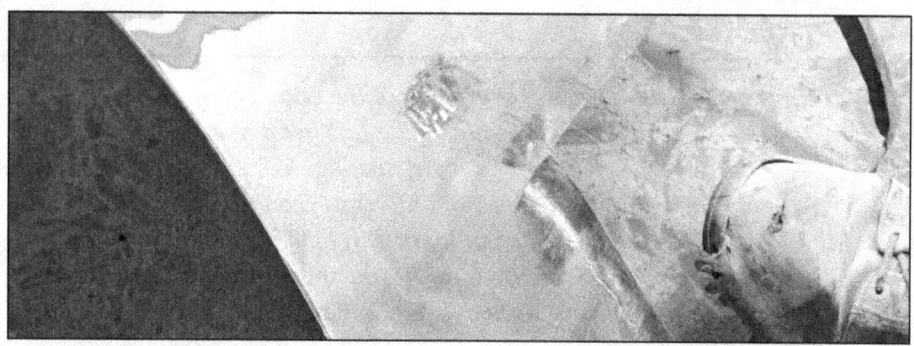

After grinding off the weld, you should see no evidence of the rod or the dent.

Fender Patch Installation

The patch for the fender is cut from the panel I purchased and fitted into the opening. The procedure is the same as for rear body panel repairs.

As with other patch-welding projects, you butt weld the patch panel into the fender. To do so you need to correctly align the panel, place tack welds on each corner, and then place several more tack welds on the sheet metal. After the tack welds have been placed on the panel, weld the entire seam of the panel by stitch welding between the tack welds.

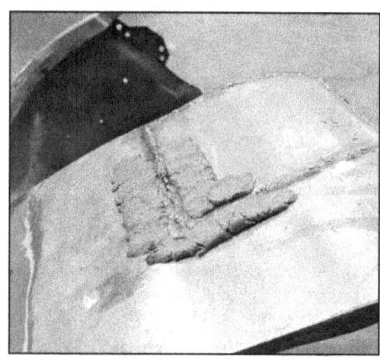

Stitch weld on one side of the panel, switch to the other side; continue alternating between sides to spread the heat around. You need to manage the welding heat to prevent warping the panel and creating other problems. You should place anti-heat compound on either side of the welding area on the sheet metal. You can also quench the weld with air to mitigate heat transfer. The compound helps prevent the 18-gauge sheet metal from warping the surrounding metal as it absorbs the heat.

When the entire patch panel has been stitch welded, remove the anti-heat compound. Use an 80-grit wheel on a rotary tool to grind the bead and make the joined panels flush. Once again, take your time when you do this. An abrasive wheel generates heat as it removes material so you don't want to warp the panel or take off too much metal.

1970–1973 Front End Removal

The 1970–1973 front end removal procedures are a bit different than the 1974–1981 models. Following is a brief overview.

Remove Front Endura Bumper

1 *The front Endura bumper is not bolted to the fenders. Instead two 3/4-inch nuts on each side hold it to a pair of bumper braces that bolt to the frame rail. The braces curve upward and the front bumper attaches with one 11/16-inch nut and bolt at the top and another 11/16-inch nut and bolt at the lower portion of the bumper.*

Remove Front Endura Bumper (CONTINUED)

2 The upper portion of the bumper is attached (with bushings) to the radiator support. To remove the bumper, use an open-end wrench and a socket/ratchet tool.

3 The 1970–1972 bumpers do not have the support structure of this 1973 model because the 1973 models had to pass new front crash standards for a 5-mph impact. Pontiac installed this support structure behind the new bumper so the Firebirds passed the crash standard. Although the bumpers appeared to be the same as the previous year, they were not. In addition, the grilles are set deeper. This is the first telltale sign of a 1973 Firebird.

4 The lower valance panel holds the two front park lamps with a chrome trim in the front. Remove the two Phillips-head screws on each side that retain the chrome trim. The parking lamp housing is also held in with the same screws.

5 Six 1/2-inch bolts on the bottom and three 1/2-inch bolts at the front hold the lower valance. One bolt is behind each park lamp, and the center bolt is visible unless a front license plate bracket is installed.

6 Although it is possible to remove the radiator support without removing the other fender, I recommend removing it as the reinstallation does not allow the fender to be on. Now you can go back to the radiator support removal, which is similar for all model years.

Engine Accessories and Related Component Removal

Remove Side-Marker Light

Remove Plastic Retainers

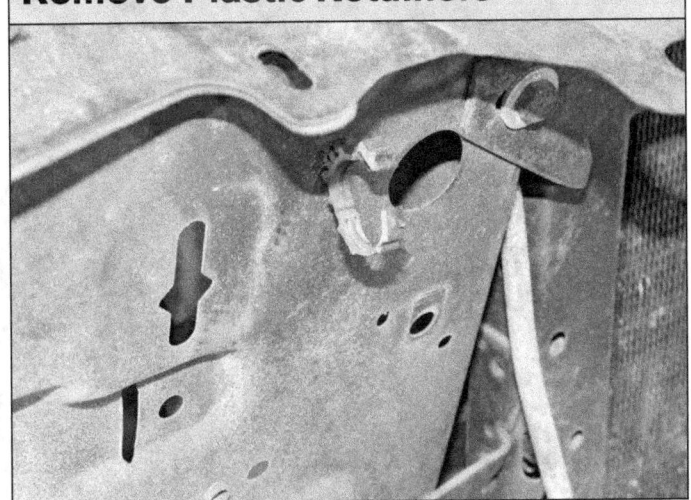

1 Remove the side-marker light 10-mm ground bolt located on each back side of the support.

2 Remove the seven wire harness plastic retainers, allowing the wire harness to fall out. This can easily be done with a flat-blade screwdriver.

BODYWORK PART I: BODY PANELS

Remove Wiring Harness and Battery

3 "Unthread" the wiring harness from the passenger's side to the driver's side. Use a 5/16-inch ratchet to remove the side terminals. Older models with a top post require a 7/16-inch wrench to loosen the terminals. If the car still has a battery hold-down bracket, remove it. This Firebird did not have one as it had long rusted away. Remove the upper radiator hose.

Remove Radiator Overflow Tank

4 Use pliers to remove the radiator overflow bottle hose spring clamp. Slide the hose off the radiator neck nipple. Remove the lower radiator hose. Disconnect the automatic transmission lines (if equipped) with a 1/2-inch line wrench. Remove the tank.

Remove A/C Condenser

5 If your Firebird is equipped with air conditioning, remove the four 1/2-inch bolts that hold the condenser to the support.

Disconnect A/C Condenser Lines

6 Disconnect the condenser lines leading to the evaporator using 5/8- and 3/4-inch wrenches.

Remove Carbon Canister Bolts

7 Remove the two 10-mm carbon canister bolts located on the passenger-side panel near the mount. Support the canister so you do not disconnect the hoses.

TRANS AM & FIREBIRD RESTORATION 65

Remove Cross-Support Bar

8 The cross-support bar is essentially a very long carriage bolt. To remove it, remove the 9/16-inch nut located on the driver's side. Two 3/4-inch nuts at the frame rail hold the bumper braces on each side. Remove them to remove the braces.

Remove Radiator Support Hardware

9 Remove the radiator support-mount hardware using 3/4-inch wrenches for the nut and bolt.

Remove Core Support and Components

10 Remove the two upper and two lower 1/2-inch bolts that attach the remaining fender to the support. Remove the battery tray 1/2-inch bolts and the three wheelhouse lower filler panel 1/2-inch bolts. Slide the radiator support assembly forward and off the frame rail.

Compare Old and New Core Support

11 Once you have the old support on the ground, compare it to the new support. Measure the mounting holes from center to center. Measure the width of the upper and lower tie bars to make sure they are the same.

12 Connect an A/C pressure gauge to the system to determine if it's charged. If it is, have it properly removed by a qualified shop. If A/C system was intact and not previously opened, tape off all openings once you disconnect the lines to prevent contamination, which could cause failure in the system.

13 Mark the driver-side and passenger-side bumper braces before you remove them. They may look different while on the car, but once removed, it is difficult to tell which is which. The last thing you want to do is to have to take everything apart when you are ready to install the front bumper.

BODYWORK PART I: BODY PANELS

14 Start removing the rest of the components from the old support. Once the parts have been removed, make sure you also remove the clips at the same time and install them onto the new support in the exact same location. Pay attention to which way the thread portion is facing (up or down), the direction the clip was installed, and whether the clips went on top or in between the metal panels. Not following the original orientation could cause headaches later and make rectifying them much more difficult later on. This also goes for any and all brackets still attached to the original support.

Remove Radiator Fan Shroud

15 Remove the radiator fan shroud's lower two 1/2-inch bolts and upper four upper 1/2-inch bolts. Lift off the shroud and place it to the side. Remove the lower radiator tabs, which hold 1/2-inch bolts.

Remove Radiator Cushions

16 Remove the radiator. Remove the old upper and lower cushions. Install the lower tabs and necessary clips onto the new support. Place the radiator and shroud into the new support.

Re-Install Hardware

17 Remove all other clips, brackets, and bolts, and transfer them to the new radiator.

18 Now, while the parts are removed, is a good time to clean, paint, and lubricate them for better performance and also so they look good when they are re-installed on the new support. Nuts and bolts work better and hold torque better when cleaned and lubricated.

19 Once reassembled, install the assembly back onto the subframe. It is a good idea to purchase new core support bushings because the originals most likely will have collapsed, shrunk, and cracked in 30-plus years.

Task List

For the front end, here are the components you need to remove:

- two 1/2-inch bolts from the hood pop-up spring
- three 1/2-inch hood latch bolts
- five 1/2-inch bolts for hood latch support
- two hood stops with an open-end 1/2-inch wrench
- five 10-mm bolts for the lower spoiler
- all of the wire retainers by popping them out of their holes

TRANS AM & FIREBIRD RESTORATION

CHAPTER 3

Basic Techniques

The following techniques are not meant to be quick or to rely on high-viscosity primers to fill body filler sanding scratches that were stopped at 220 grit or less. I am not saying that my techniques are the only way to perform quality bodywork, but they have served my thousands of customers and me well over the past 20 years.

Once the metalwork has been completed and is to your satisfaction, it is time to perform the bodywork stage. This can be extremely tedious and repetitive, and the urge to shortcut may be strong. But following these procedures will reward you with a beautiful and long-lasting repair that the paint job will reflect. It will be well worth the time and aching muscles.

These procedures are recommended for any body panel. The technique is the same no matter the shape of the panel. The labor costs can be quite high should you decide to have a professional shop perform the bodywork. An average body restoration without rust can average 500 to 800 hours.

All of the body materials described are available at any paint supply store. The body tools are available at any tool supply store. Air-powered tools can be rented if you do not want to purchase them. However, given the amount of time that you spend on bodywork, I recommend purchasing your own tools.

Manual tools include sanding blocks. You need a decent-quality DA air-powered sander. Long-board air sanders cost about the same or a bit more depending on what you buy and from whom. It is not unusual to spend $1,000 for a good set of body tools that allow you to complete all phases of bodywork.

You also need an air compressor capable of sustaining 60 psi over a period of 5 minutes. Generally a 15-hp or larger compressor is sufficient, but that depends on how large the storage tank is. Although I generally describe PPG products, you can source other manufacturers with similar products.

Sheet-Metal Stripping and Fiberglass Application

The first step is to use the DA sander with an 80-grit paper lightly over the bare metal to clean up the surface so it provides good adhesion for the epoxy sealer. Clean the bare metal with a product such as Prep-Sol. It evaporates quickly and removes any oils and contaminants that could create issues later on.

Use a short-strand fiberglass with resin. I recommend USC Duraglas. Unlike body filler, fiberglass is waterproof and provides a watertight barrier between the body filler and the surface. Using a 4-inch plastic spreader, mix the fiberglass and resin together on a nonporous mixing sheet. Spread the fiberglass using the spreader from one end of the repaired area in a side-to-side motion.

Apply Epoxy Primer to Fender

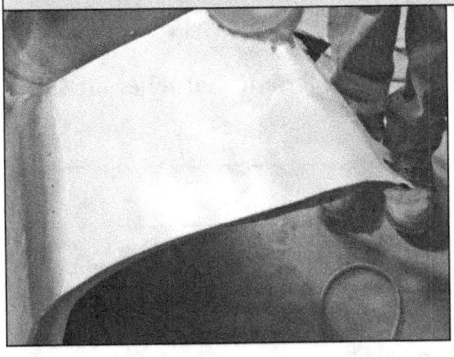

1 The stripped metal panel needs to be protected because in most environments, the bare metal panel accumulates some surface rust if not properly protected. Once you have inspected your work and the patch has been successfully completed, apply a primer coat. Next, apply a coat of epoxy primer to the bare metal surface. I use PPG DP50 without any reducer to seal the bare metal and crevices. Simply pour the DP50 into the canister of your primer gun, close the lid, and spray in light, even coats from side to side.

Apply Fiberglass to Fender

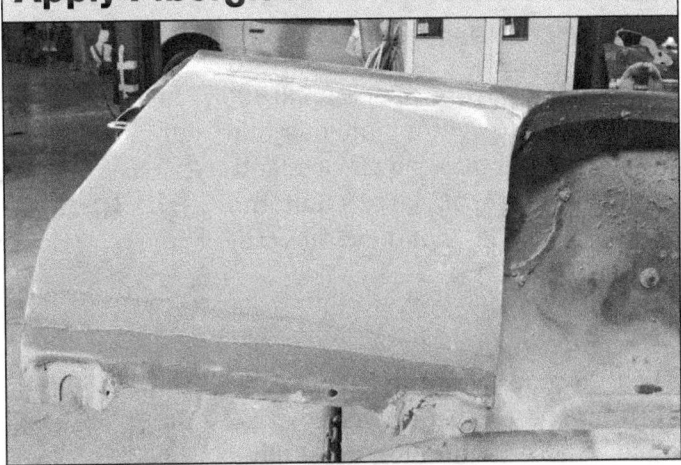

2 When applying fiberglass body filler, make sure you overlap the prior spread stroke by a small margin to ensure uniform coverage. I have used USC Duraglas body filler with excellent results for the past several years.

File High Spots

3 Let the fiberglass dry for at least 15 minutes at 75 degrees. Place a body file (also known as a cheese grater) on the ridgelines caused by overlapping the material at a 45-degree angle. With moderate pressure, slide the file back and forth. You want to remove any high spots and thicker material so you don't waste sandpaper when you are sanding.

4 As you use the file, stop from time to time and run your hand over the fiberglass to check for high or low spots in the material and to check the contours. If you cut through the material and see metal, you have a high spot. You need to tap down that spot with a body hammer or use a hammer and dolly to correct those areas and start the fiberglass process over again. Taking the time to get the metal panel as straight as possible reduces the amount of body filler needed to finish the repair. This is the first stage of the sanding process. Once you have finished knocking down the high spots, your panel should look something like this. All excess material has been removed.

Use Orbital Sander to Sand Fender

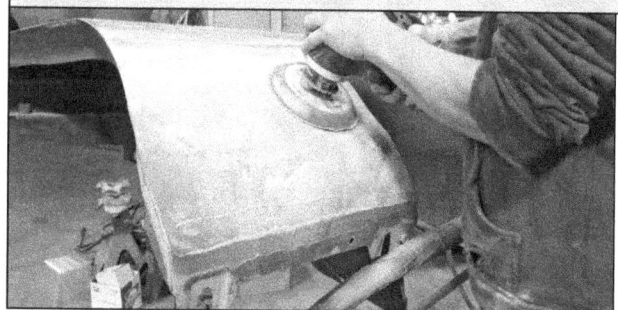

5 Use light hand pressure on a DA sander with 80-grit sandpaper to smooth and rough shape the panel so it conforms to the metal surface. Use a side-to-side motion to sand the fiberglass and thin the material. The process is not about speed, but about getting it right. It may take five minutes or an hour, depending on your skills.

Fiberglass Resin Application

The first pass of filler should be applied in a forceful manner so the filler is pressed into the crevices and pinholes on the panel. For a uniform surface it should not have any air pockets.

Apply two or three thin coats of filler rather than a single thick coat. The thin coats allow the filler to cure evenly. Let each coat dry for approximately 15 to 20 minutes, depending on the room temperature. Make sure the workshop is not too cold when doing bodywork. As with paint, it should be 50 degrees F or warmer when working. Also, it shouldn't be warmer than 80 degrees when you mix the filler and hardener and then apply it.

Fill in Low Spots

1 A darker area or gradated rings, indicates a low spot. Use a plastic scraper with body filler to fill in shallow low spots. Sand those spots with an orbital sander and 180- or 220-grit sandpaper. Deeper low spots require further metalwork.

Clean Surface Area of Panel

2 After you are satisfied with the shape and fiberglass coverage of your panel, use an air gun to blow out residue from the crevices in the fiberglass. Concentrate on any pinholes. Clean the area with Prep-Sol.

Stir, Select Resin and Add Hardener to Body Filler

3 Open the can of body filler. Use the best filler available because it is easier to work with and sand. I use Rage Gold body filler. Although it is not the least expensive body filler at $50 per gallon, it is one of the best-performing fillers I have used. Insert a paint mixing stick into the filler and, using an up and down motion, mix the material. Alternatively stir to extract excess air and thoroughly mix the ingredients for several minutes. The body filler settles at the bottom of the can so you need to thoroughly stir it. (To what degree it has settled at the bottom of the can depends on how long the can has been on the shelf at the store.) Once you have thoroughly mixed the filler, place a 4-inch blob on the mixing sheet. The hardener comes in a tube and you need to add a simple ribbon of hardener to the top of the filler that extends from one edge to the other. If there is not enough hardener added, then it will take too long for the filler to set up. If you add too much hardener, you will have very little time to apply and work in the filler.

Mix Hardener and Body Filler

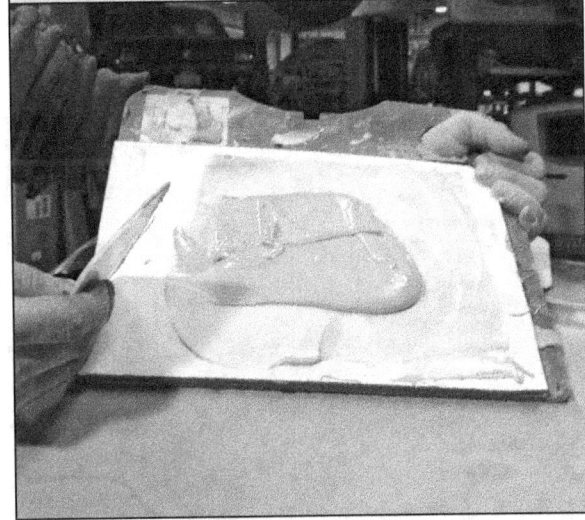

4 Once you add the hardener and mix it with the filler, you need to work quickly because the mixture starts to set up in four to five minutes at 75 to 80 degrees F and becomes unusable. Use a 4-inch plastic spreader and thoroughly mix the hardener and filler until you have a uniform color.

Apply First Coat of Body Filler

5 Using a 4-inch spreader (a 6-inch spreader can be used for larger panels), scoop some filler off the sheet. Spread the filler from end to end with some small overlap on each pass. Hold the spreader at about a 45-degree angle to the surface of the sheet metal and apply even pressure as you push the filler across the sheet metal. Try to use as little filler as possible. A coat should be no more than 1/4-inch thick, but try to keep the coat to about 1/8 inch.

Shaping and Sanding

Use a 120-grit sandpaper to lightly cut the top of the filler surface. Follow up with 180-grit to fully shape the bodywork. Run your hand over the panel repeatedly to check for consistency. Sand as needed to achieve the desired result. Once you are satisfied with the surface switch to 220-grit sandpaper and sand until the 180-grit scratches in the body filler are reduced. Keep running your hand over the bodywork to make sure the panel is staying consistent. Switch to 320-grit sandpaper and sand the body filler until all deep scratches are removed and the surface is smooth. When sanding reverse curves, use the curved softer block at a 45-degree angle on the curved areas.

Once you are satisfied with the surface, apply the DP50 epoxy primer mixed with reducer as specified in the directions to the bodywork area. The next step is to block sand the body to prepare it for paint, which is covered in Chapter 5.

File Body Filler

1 Allow the applied body filler to cure for 30 minutes; otherwise, you disturb the coat and have to start over. Once the coat has fully cured, use a body file to knock down any high spots and ridgelines left from the overlap process. Again, don't be too aggressive with the cheese grater.

Sand Body Filler

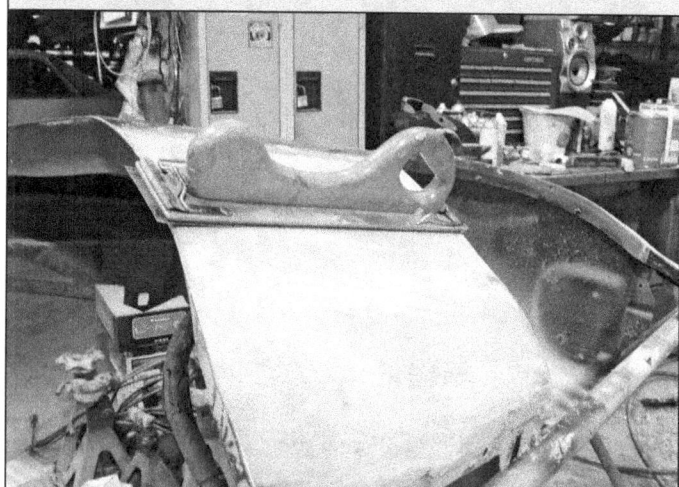

2 Use a long board sander with 120-grit sandpaper and a side-to-side motion. Apply a moderate amount of pressure to sand the filler. A long board sander allows for better control for shaping the panel, and making the surface consistent is critical. Sand until the surface has a uniform finish.

3 After the first pass of filler sanding, you may see bare metal or fiberglass. That indicates that high spots are still present. Tapping down the high spot area with a body hammer rectifies the issue. Here, minor low spots are still present. They will be taken care of in the next pass of filler.

Apply Second and Third Body Filler Coats

4 Using compressed air, blow out the area of residue for a clean surface and so the filler and panel are clean. Apply the second coat of filler as you applied the first coat. Again, give the panel 30 minutes for the filler to cure. Use a long board sander with 120-grit sandpaper to evenly sand the panel from edge to edge. You may experience some clumping of material on the sandpaper. Simply wipe the clumps off or blow them off with compressed air. Clean the surface again and apply a third coat of filler.

Finish Sanding Panel

5 The top should be relatively smooth at this point, and it's time for the final sanding step. Use a Dura-Block or similar fine sanding block to perform the final sanding. Work the sanding block from edge to edge and maintain surface uniformity. The flexible sanding block hugs curved surfaces and makes this finish sanding easier.

Verify Surface Straightness and Consistency

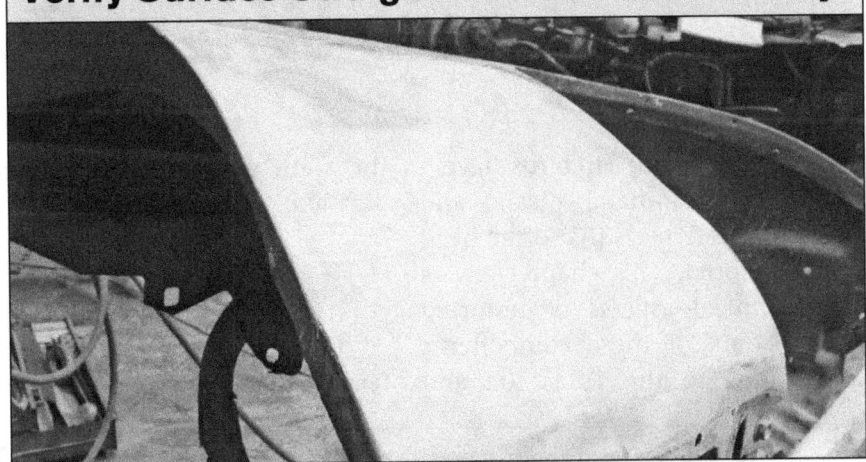

6 Check the surface with your hand to verify it is still consistent and smooth. It should be free of waves and any lumpiness. Running the palm of your hand lightly over the panel gives you an indication of its smoothness. If you feel a dip or a bump, be sure to investigate before proceeding.

Apply Finishing Putty

7 Once you have finished sanding the panel and verified that the surface does not have any significant flaw, it is time to apply icing, otherwise known as polyester finishing putty. As with filler, you apply a thin coat no thicker than 1/8 inch. The icing is used to feather the bodywork edges' small imperfections, pinholes, and persistent minor low spots. Once the icing has flashed, sand as described previously using 180-, 220-, and 320-grit sandpapers. Touch up spots as needed. The surface should be extremely smooth at this point.

CHAPTER 4

Bodywork Part II: Doors, Spoilers, Bumpers and Wheel Flares

Trans Ams and Firebirds have a variety of sheet-metal, plastic, and fiberglass body parts that often need to be restored. This chapter covers the technical aspects of restoring them. Some of these components are unique to the Trans Am and the steps to properly fit them are detailed.

Door Panel

Over the years, doors often suffer much use and abuse. Like other panels of the body, the doors have been exposed to the elements and often trap moisture. This leads to rust at the bottom of the door skin, which requires cutting out the affected area and grafting in a patch panel.

The front Endura bumper on this 1973 Super Duty 455 Formula has been restored. The process for restoring this bumper is shown and described later in this chapter.

TRANS AM & FIREBIRD RESTORATION

CHAPTER 4

Cutting and Patching a Door Skin

Inspect Door Panel

1 The sheet metal on this particular Firebird's door is in very good shape. Therefore, it does not require outer panel replacement. There is, however, evidence of small rust bubbles in the lower rear corners of the outer door panel. Second-generation Firebirds (as well as Camaros) tend to rust in this area and in the forward corners. Be sure to carefully inspect these areas, ascertain the condition, and determine whether or not repair is needed.

Strip Lower Corner of Door Panel

2 Use an orbital sander to evenly strip the paint off the outer door skin. You can use a DA sander with a 6-inch 80-grit sanding disc. It usually takes several minutes to remove the clear coat, paint coats, and primer. Once you sand down to the sheet metal, you see the reason for the bubbling. Someone had used body filler to simply fill in where rust had eaten away, and this does not provide a long-term solution. Filling rust with body filler does not stop rust. It just covers it up. When you see repairs such as this, you need to cut out the improperly filled area and install fresh sheet metal. It's the only reliable way to maintain body integrity and stop the rust.

Cut Outer Door Skin

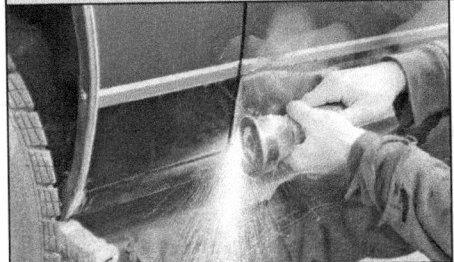

3 Use a magnet to see how much sheet metal remains in the affected area. If the area is pitted, it indicates rust beneath the sheet metal. Use a rotary tool with a 3-inch wheel to cut out the body filler and rusted metal. As described earlier, you need to figure out how far the rust extends and then go 1.5 inches beyond it to make sure you have solid metal. Use a Sharpie and masking tape to indicate your cut line.

Inspect Sheet Metal

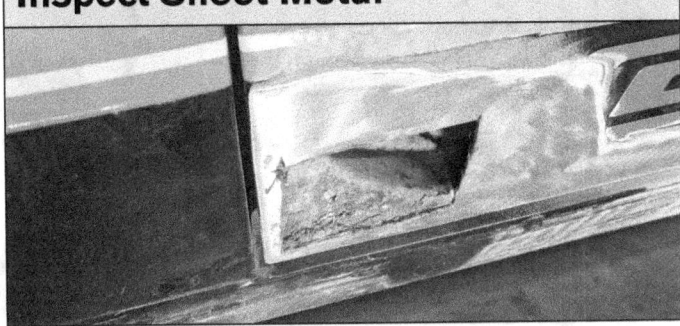

4 Once you remove the rusted area of the door skin (4 x 8 inches here) you can see where rust has started in the door shell. The rusting metal underneath the door skin must be treated so the door skin does not continue to rust from the inside.

Remove Rust and Spray on Neutralizer

5 Treat the rusted area with a rust neutralizer after cleaning the area and removing the loose particles with a wire brush. Once you have removed the top layer of rust, spray Rust Mort or a similar product on the rusted area inside the door. This product sprays on white and darkens as it sets.

BODYWORK PART II: DOORS, SPOILERS, BUMPERS AND WHEEL FLARES

Cut New Patch Panel

6 Use the old metal (top) as a rough guide to cut out the 18-gauge sheet metal patch panel (bottom). If the old sheet metal is left in the door skin, it will rust through in relatively short order.

Tack Weld Patch Panel to Door Skin

7 As with other patch panels, you butt weld it in place. It needs to fit flush with the door and cannot overlap the outer door skin. Make sure the welder is placed on a low-amp setting that's suitable for welding thin sheet metal. Place the patch panel in the proper position in the opening and use metal shears or tin snips to trim as needed for proper fit. Tack weld the four corners to hold the panel in place. Apply some anti-heat compound to avoid warping the panel from the welding heat.

Use Tape to Help with Welding

You can use a strip of masking tape to hold the panel in place when tack welding it. Remove the tape afterward.

Stitch Weld Patch Panel

8 Heat management is critical when stitch welding in a patch panel, particularly when the patch panel is small. You need to effectively quench the welds with air once you have welded it in. When laying down the stitch welds, start at the outermost points and work inward. No matter the size of the area it is important to follow these procedures.

Grind Stitch Welds

9 After stitch welding the patch panel, give it 30 minutes to cool. Use an 80-grit wheel to grind the stitch welds flush with the door panel. When using a grinding wheel, be careful not to apply too much heat because you can warp a panel by grinding aggressively.

Door Glass

The door glass on the Firebirds uses guides that attach to the door shell at the top under the door panel to guide the glass in the proper position as it rolls up and down. These guides are adjustable to control the glass. They also have pads that wear out, and when they do, the door glass is scratched. The scratches are vertical and limited toward the center of the glass. It is common to see the second-generation Firebird door glass scratched because most people are not aware of these pads until it is too late. The door glass is installed into the top of the window regulator, which moves up and down and folds in a scissor-like fashion.

TRANS AM & FIREBIRD RESTORATION

CHAPTER 4

Hardware Installation

When assembling the door glass and associated hardware take the opportunity to replace the glass hardware. The plastic rollers tend to seize or partially break off. This is often overlooked and can result in glass operation being compromised.

Auto Metal Direct sells this door window hardware kit for $175. It is available through other distributors also.

Remove Old Hardware

1 When replacing the hardware on an original window, you should remove one part at a time and replace it with the same part. It is best just to start at one end and work your way to the other end. There is no real secret in how to change the hardware other than removing it with an open-end wrench. Be careful to not overtighten the fasteners because too much pressure on old glass could shatter it. Use a 7/16-inch wrench to install the new fasteners. If you purchase new glass you do not have to remove the old hardware.

Install Window Lift Channel

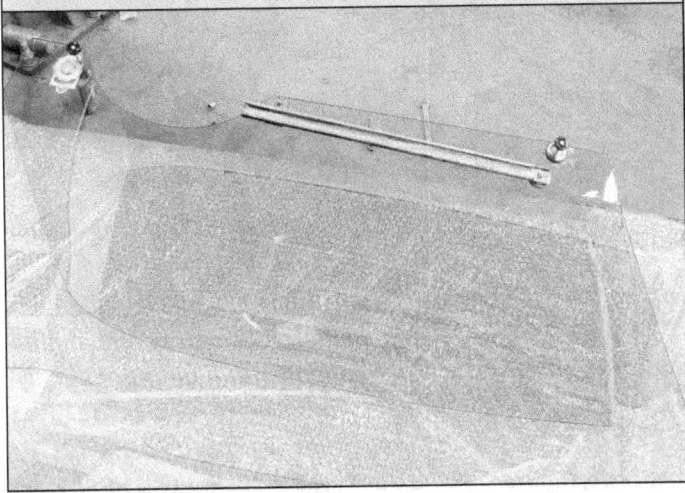

2 Once you have all the hardware installed, place the glass lift channel onto the studs to make sure it fits properly.

Inspect Window Actuator

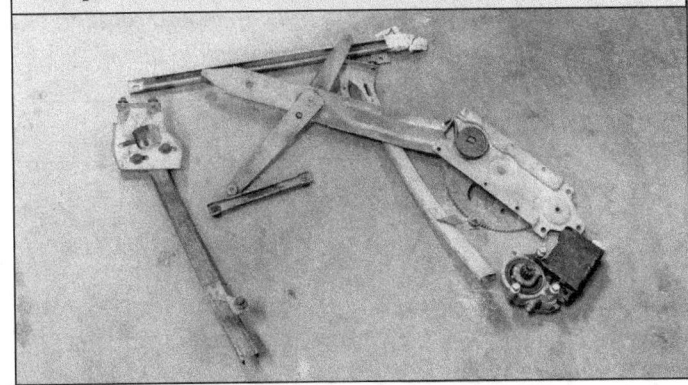

3 The window guides, regulator, and power window motor are shown here the way they should be installed in the door. If you have a manual window the setup is the same; it just does not have the motor. Make sure the regulator teeth are in good shape and that the arms move up and down easily.

Install Vertical Guides

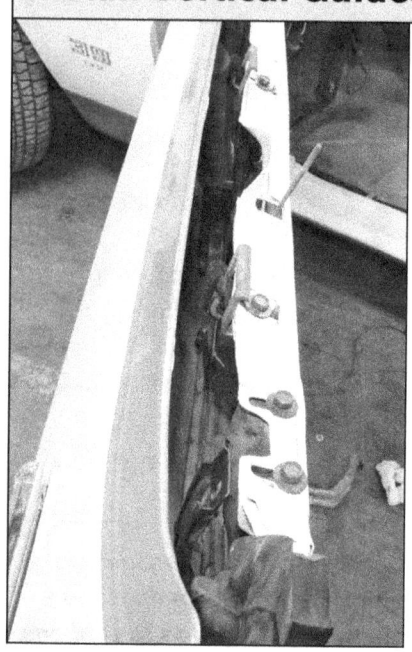

4 The front and rear vertical guides control the up and down motion of the glass. Use a ratchet and socket to install these guides. Two 7/16-inch bolts on top and one 7/16-inch bolt on the bottom hold the glass in place on each side. These bolts should be slightly less than snug once installed so you have some latitude for adjustment.

Install Horizontal Guide

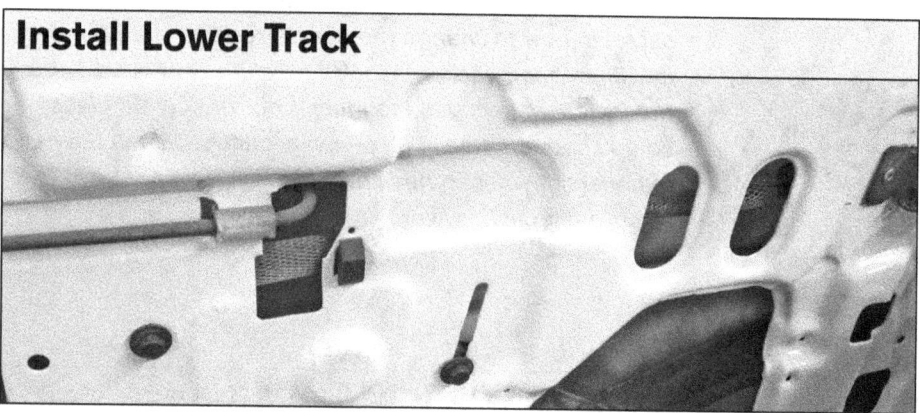

5 The smaller horizontal guide controls the back and forth motion of the glass and two 7/16-inch bolts hold it in place. When these are installed, they should be also left less than snug.

Install Lower Track

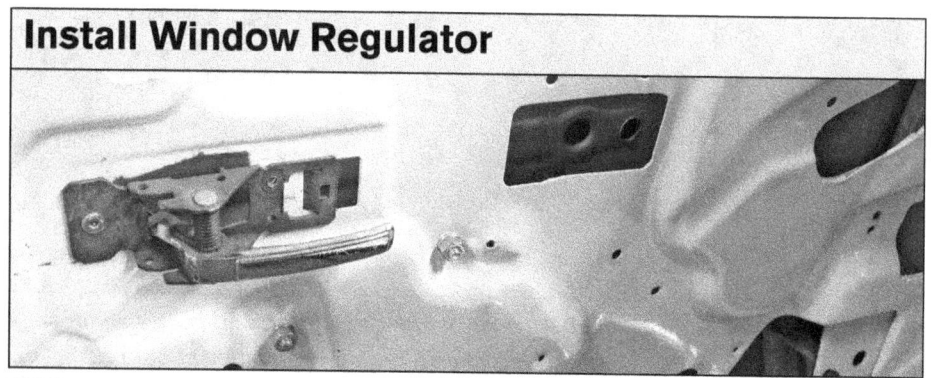

6 The short lower track controls tip in and rotation of the glass. Two 7/16-inch bolts hold the lower track in place.

Install Window Regulator

7 The factory riveted the window regulator to the doorframe. Unfortunately, rivets make it difficult to remove and service the regulator. You can replace these rivets with four 7/16-inch nuts and bolts. Three 7/16-inch bolts hold the power window motor to the doorframe.

Install Door Glass

8 Installing the glass requires patience, as it does not simply drop in. You need to remove the glass stop to properly position the glass in the door. Use a socket and ratchet to remove the lower glass stop. One 7/16-inch bolt holds it in the center bottom of the door.

Install Door Glass (CONTINUED)

9 It takes a fair amount of positioning and adjustment to get the glass properly situated with the hardware. First angle the front and rear rollers on the glass. Then, fit the glass into the front and rear vertical guides. It may be necessary to simultaneously tip the glass toward the front and outward to get the front roller in. Repeat for the rear. Once the rollers are in, do not let go of the glass. If you happen to lose grip on the glass, it will fall to the bottom of the door and possibly shatter.

Install Window Glass Stops

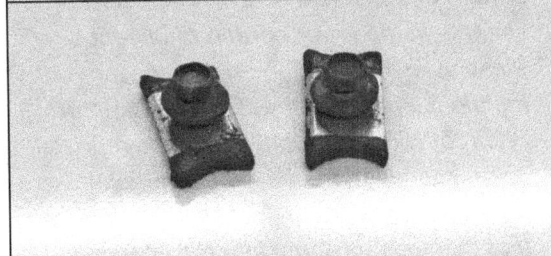

10 Once you have lowered the glass into the door, install the lift channel onto the studs and install one 7/16-inch nut in each end to secure the glass to the regulator. It may be necessary to raise and lower the window regulator slightly to gain access to the channel so you can attach it to the glass. Install the guide stops at the top of each vertical guide. A single 7/16-inch bolt attaches these stops to the doorframe. Their function is to prevent the glass from going too far up.

Install Door Glass Weatherstrip

11 While you still have the glass in the lowest position, install the outer door glass weatherstrip, otherwise known as a belt weatherstrip. Five short Phillips-head screws hold the weatherstrip to the door. Be sure to use the correct-length screws for this job. It's best to stick with the original screws. If you use screws that are too long, they dent the door panel from the inside.

Install Door Handle

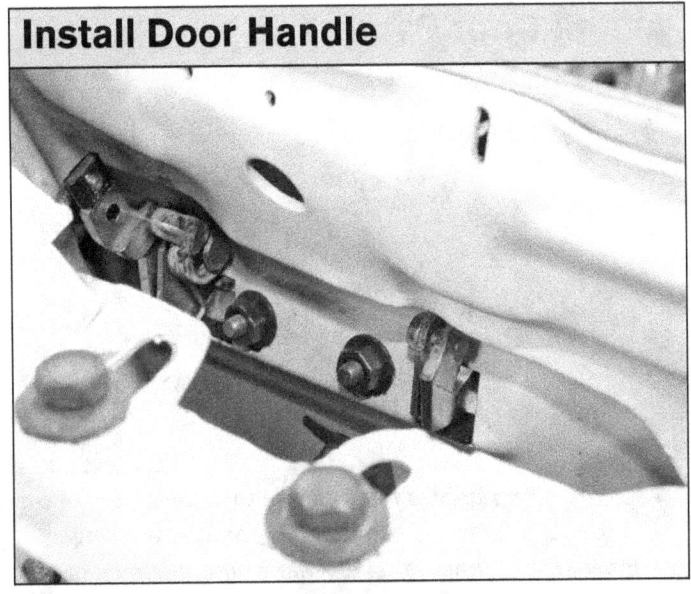

12 Slide the latch rod into the outer door handle. Use a wrench or socket and ratchet to secure the two 7/16-inch nuts that hold the latch in place.

Install Door Lock

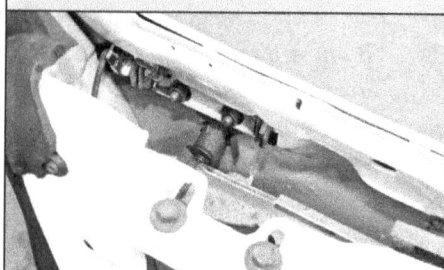

13 Install the door lock with a spring clip by sliding the clip between the ears on the lock and the door panel. Make sure the lock is properly positioned so that when the key is inserted the teeth are pointed downward.

Clean and Lube Window Parts

Clean the guides and all moving parts while the window is apart. Lubricate lightly with white lithium grease for smooth operation.

Interior Door Panel Installation

Install Water Shield onto Inner Door Shell

1 Plastic and wax paper water shields are typically available. You can slip either type of water shield over the door handle, in the center. Properly position the water shield and use butyl tape around the entire circumference of the shield. The bottom of the shield sets into a special channel in the lower portion of the door. Make sure the opening around the inner door handle is also sealed with butyl. Restorers often remove the shield and fail to re-install it. That can lead to serious damage because it guides the water to the lower channel and into the door shell, not into the interior.

Install Door Panel

2 The door panel is fairly simple to install. Most of the panel bottom clips in; the top portion hangs over the inner side of the door shell. Make sure the back of the door panel has all of the clips in the back side. Check the side of the door shell to make sure that no clips stayed in the hole when the panel was removed.

Install Armrest

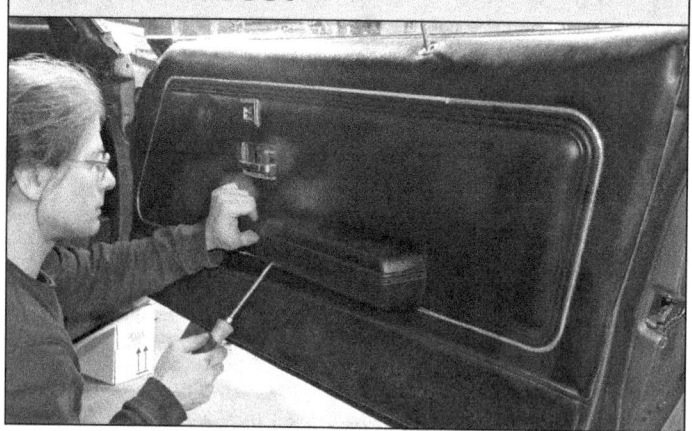

3 Use a No. 3 Phillips screwdriver to install the three Phillips-head screws through the armrest and into the door. Place the armrest against the door panel. Properly align the armrest with the fastener holes. Place the screw on the end of the screwdriver, slide the screw into one of the armrest openings, and tighten the screw.

CHAPTER 4

Use Door Panel Removal Tool

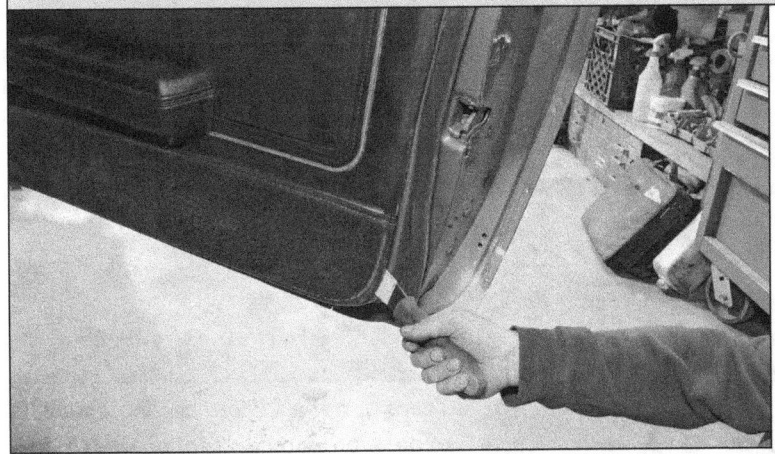

4 *This door panel removal tool is used to pop the door panel away from the door shell. It's important to use this tool so you prevent the door panel from ripping. Slide the tool between the door panel and door shell. The open end of the blade slides over the clip stud. Use the door shell as leverage and push against the door shell. This removes the clip from the retainer opening in the door panel and prevents the door panel backing from getting ripped. Once the back side of the panel is ripped the clip becomes almost impossible to function and hold the door panel in place.*

Endura Bumper

The Endura bumper is made of closed cell foam that was a relatively new product for Pontiac in the late 1960s and it was new to the 1970 Firebird. The Endura front bumper met mandated 5-mph crash standards, but the material and construction of the bumper requires specialized restoration. Pontiac first started using the energy-absorbing material when it fitted the Endura bumper on the 1968 Pontiac GTO. Although the bumper is beautiful, it has serious durability problems. The material has lasted far longer than anyone could have imagined.

The material is subjected to constant expansion and contraction, and deep fissure cracks result. Because the material is constantly in a state of flux, repairs are very difficult to make. I have dealt with these bumpers for 20-plus years, and fortunately the technology to repair the material has changed for the better. Although the repairs last longer, an owner must realize that repaired cracks eventually reappear. When you repair the bumper, you are not changing the original composition of the material. Make sure when you open your hood that you do not lean on the front bumper. It's fragile and you could damage it.

My opinions and techniques on the repair of these bumpers come from my experience as a restoration shop professional. This repair procedure greatly increases the longevity of the repair and keeps your Firebird looking its best. Over the years, I have developed this repair procedure and it has yielded the best results for my customers. But let me be clear, the repair does not stop the bumper from ever cracking again. When it cracks again depends on which region of the country you live in and how your Firebird is stored and used. As newer materials are developed, the procedures may change.

Bumper Prep and Crack Removal

The Endura front bumper is made of a urethane-type material that was originally designed to absorb a minor impact and retain its shape. It also satisfied the stylists because it eliminated the bulky and clumsy look of the typical chrome front bumper.

Although these bumpers were attractive and functional, they also proved to be somewhat fragile and not very durable. Over time, they started to crack. The metal support structure underneath the urethane bumper cover stops just before the edge. When a person places weight on the bumper (such as when peering into the engine compartment), the edge rolls down and creates half-circle cracks.

BODYWORK PART II: DOORS, SPOILERS, BUMPERS AND WHEEL FLARES

In my opinion, the front bumper on the 1970–1973 Firebirds is one of the most beautiful designs to come out of General Motors. However, they are also the most problematic to keep from cracking and the most misunderstood as to how to properly repair them.

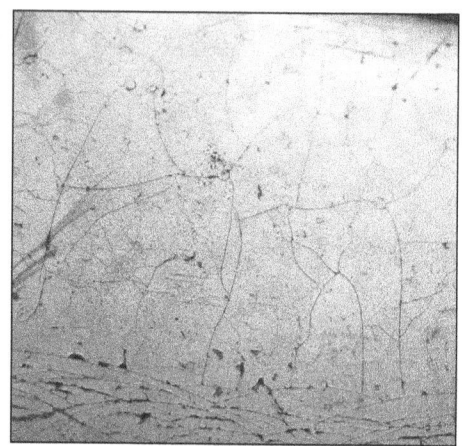

Years of hot and cold cycling caused expansion and contraction, plus the direct exposure to sunlight caused the bumper material to develop cracks running in various directions. Accident damage and minor impacts may also remove chunks of material.

Strip Paint Off Bumper

1 To repair these bumpers, you must use a DA sander to strip off the paint. The Endura bumper is made of a special material on which you cannot use a chemical stripper because the chemicals are absorbed into the Endura material. If chemicals are used you will never be able to keep the paint on your bumper properly. Use a light-grit sandpaper, such as a 320-grit, to avoid cutting into the bumper material.

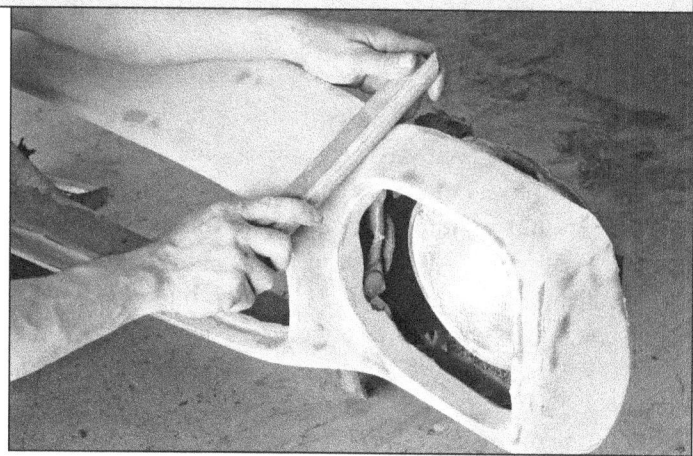

2 Apply light pressure to remove the layers of paint until you reach a gray surface. Hand sand around the grille openings and indentations where the DA sander cannot reach.

Inspect Endura Material for Cracks

3 Once the paint has been removed, you can see the cracks in the material. It is not uncommon to find additional cracks that were covered by the paint. Sometimes the cracks you see in the paint are just the paint separating as the material moves.

Remove Cracks in Endura Material

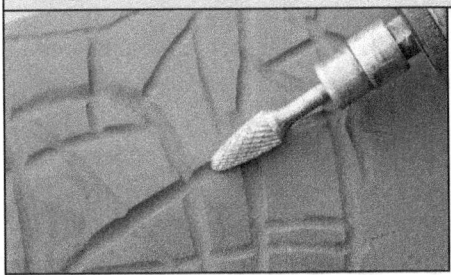

4 Use a carbide strawberry tip on a drill to gently remove a crack. You need to remove enough material so the carbide bit actually goes below the crack but not too far; you don't want to remove any more material than absolutely necessary. These cracks travel in any direction so you need to guide the bit along the crack line. Continue grinding along the crack until the crack is no longer visible. In some cases, it may be necessary to go down to the metal substructure, but that is very unusual. To the left, some cracks have been removed. To the right you can see some original cracks. Bear in mind that it takes a fair amount of time to carefully and completely remove all the cracks so be patient. It may take many hours, depending on the starting condition of the bumper.

Inspect Crack Removal Area

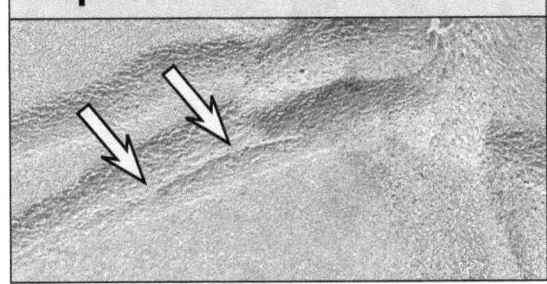

5 It is important to look closely at the removal area because some of the cracks are difficult to see. Inspect the bumper surface carefully as you perform the procedure. It may appear that the crack is gone but it is not. If a crack is not fully removed, the repair fails because the crack comes back much sooner. This photo shows the crack still remains and is difficult to see.

Bumper Crack Repair

Choose Replacement Compound

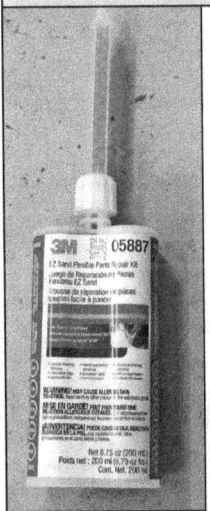

1 Once you are fully satisfied that all of the cracks have been eliminated, you can add new material. I use 3M EZ Sand Flexible Parts Repair (PN 05887) for repairing these bumpers. Although other repair products are on the market, this product has proven to be of exceptional quality and the repairs have lasted the longest. When you purchase this kit, it is necessary to purchase the mixing gun with it. The 3M repair kit has two chambers that mix into one when dispensed.

Apply Compound

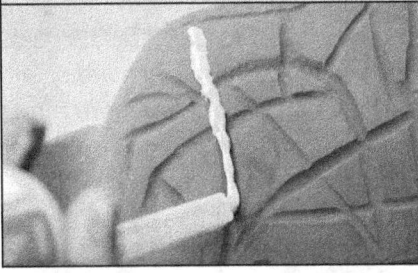

2 No tools, brushes, or plastic applicators are necessary. You can properly apply the compound to the channels using just your finger (and disposable nitrile or latex gloves). Run your finger over the bead to flatten it. Apply the compound between 60 and 80 degrees F to get the best bonding results.

Work Compound into Cracks

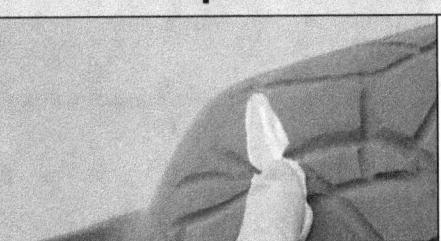

3 Each channel has a thin bead below the surface of the material, and you need to slowly build up channels until they reach the surface of the bumper. When applying compound, let every application thoroughly dry (not tacky) before repeating. It often takes 30 minutes at 70 degrees F. Do not expose the bumper to direct sunlight when performing this procedure because the bumper material absorbs heat and expands, which could potentially ruin the work.

Repeat this step exactly the same way until the repair material is slightly higher than the bumper material and is consistent throughout. This step could take days to finish, but it is very important that this step be followed precisely. If you add too much repair material or add it too quickly the material does not dry thoroughly or evenly in the cracks. It dries at a different rate. When it does dry, it could cause the upper repair material to sink and create low spots or new cracks, which undoes all the work.

BODYWORK PART II: DOORS, SPOILERS, BUMPERS AND WHEEL FLARES

Shop Temperature Control

Make sure your shop space is constantly maintained at an even temperature. This minimizes the expansion and contraction of the material on the bumper during the entire repair procedure.

Work Compound into Cracks (CONTINUED)

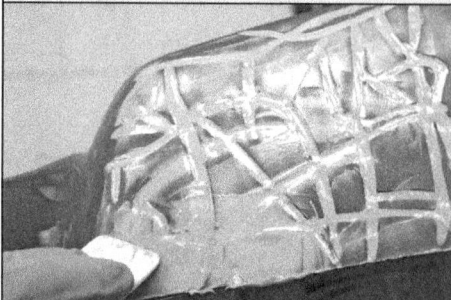

4 After all the cracks have been filled and the repair material has dried thoroughly, use a plastic applicator to apply more repair material over the entire bumper. The entire bumper needs to be thoroughly and liberally covered and then allowed to set and dry for 24 hours.

Sand Endura Bumper Surface

  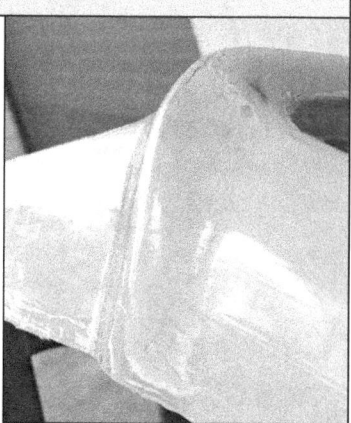

5 After the bumper has thoroughly dried, lightly sand the surface by hand or with an orbital sander. It's a critical stage and you need to be particularly careful because you don't want to remove too much material or break through to the Endura material itself. Use 220-grit paper and sand the entire exterior to knock down the repair material. You want to create one smooth and even surface that can be repainted.

Sand Endura Bumper Surface (CONTINUED)

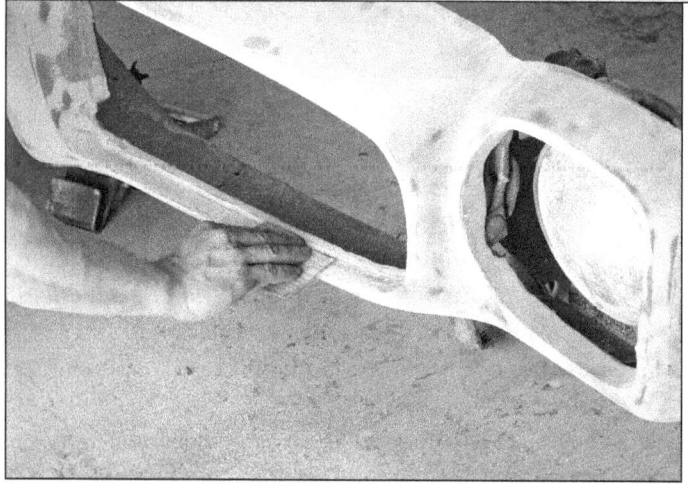 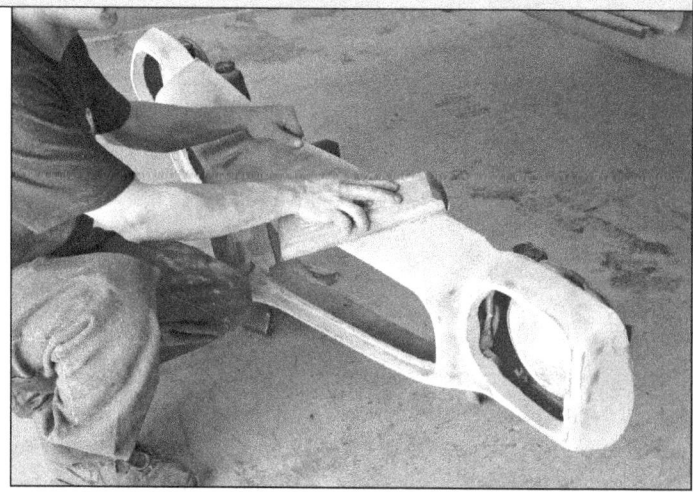

6 You have now sanded off the high spots and the bumper should be a light shade of gray. It is time to block and hand sand to make the bumper material smooth. Use 320-grit sandpaper and a Durablock rubber sanding block is helpful because it can flex and forms to the contours of the bumper. Once you have completed sanding the bumper it should be a fairly uniform color of light gray.

TRANS AM & FIREBIRD RESTORATION

Apply Guide Coat

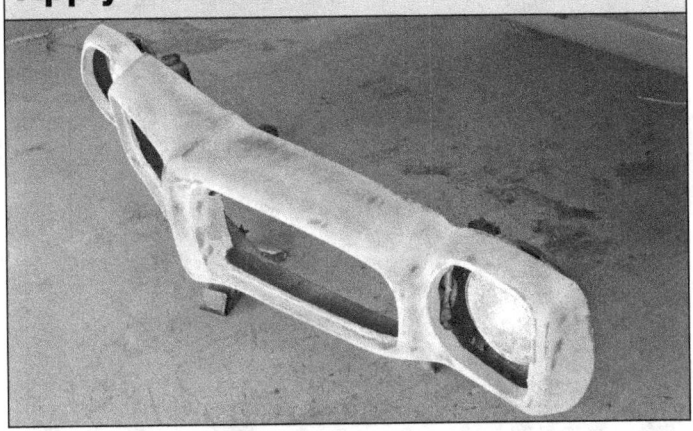

7 Spray a light mist of black paint over the bumper. This is referred to as a guide coat. This is simply a way to check your work for any low spots. Low spots retain the black paint while the rest of the bumper remains light gray.

Sand Low Spots

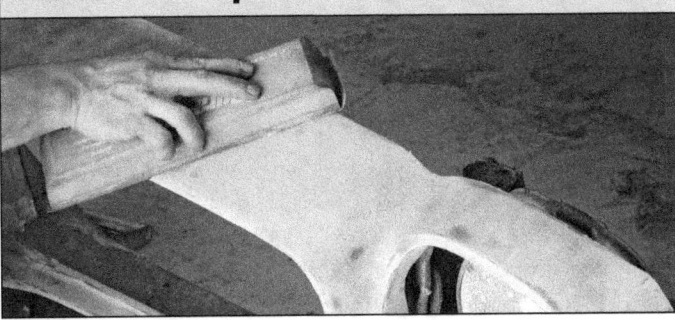

8 Continue sanding in preparation for final sanding. Use a block with 320-grit sandpaper so that your final sanding verifies the smoothness of the bumper and reveals any low spots by the black remaining behind. If you see low spots, add repair material to the low spots to make the surface smooth (as you did with the fender patch). Repeat the steps as necessary.

Apply Epoxy Primer

9 Once you have determined that the bumper is smooth and no low spots need to be filled in, sand the entire bumper again with 400-grit sandpaper. Do this lightly to smooth the surface so that it feels uniform and soft to the touch as you run your hand over it.

Next, apply epoxy primer with a flexible additive to the bumper. The flexible additive needs to be applied so the primer can expand and contract with the bumper and not crack. I have used PPG Universal Flexibilizer (PN DX814) and PPG epoxy primer (PN DP50LF) because they have produced excellent results. The mixing instructions are on the can and are specific to the temperature.

The later 1974 and up Firebirds have urethane bumper covers. The repair procedures use the same repair kits and techniques. The 1970–1973 front bumper is mounted loosely when spraying metallic colors. This keeps the metallic flow consistent on the top and the sides.

Spoilers and Flares

Trans Ams have additional exterior spoilers to help with aerodynamics, enhance visual appeal, and make the trim package instantly recognizable. The three-piece front spoiler, rear wheel spoilers, and a three-piece rear spoiler add to the muscular look of the Firebird.

Those are not the only exterior changes the Trans Am has over the Firebird and Formula. A shaker hood scoop and fender air extractors complete the Trans Am appearance package. The exterior spoilers and flares were made of the same type of plastic from 1970 to the 1978 model year. In 1979, spoilers and flares were changed to a urethane material, which made them fit much better. The same principle applies to adjusting them at the mounting points.

Correct reproduction wheel flares and spoilers are not available currently for 1979–1981 models. The repair procedures used for bumpers also apply to the 1979–1981 rear outer spoilers, wheel flares, and three-piece front spoiler. ∎

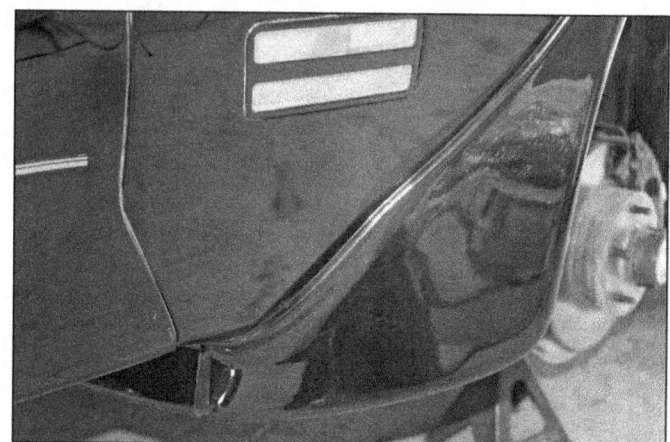

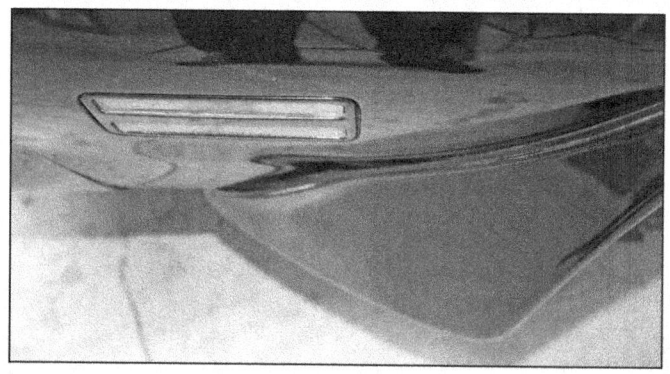

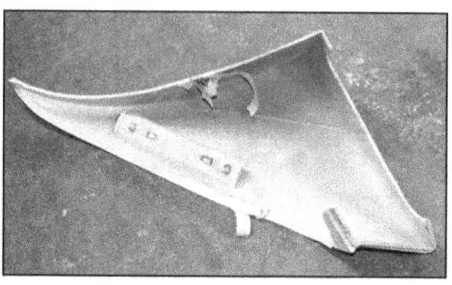

The 1979–1981 flares and rear spoiler attach the same way as the 1970–1978 versions. This example is a 1979 spoiler. It was taped off for the striping on the Macho Trans Am.

I concentrate on the 1970–1978 spoilers and flares for fitment. The front spoiler, wheel flares, and rear spoiler are difficult to fit so they are flush to the contours of the body and line up with one another. These usually do not fit very well from the factory, but you can tweak them a little to make them fit much better.

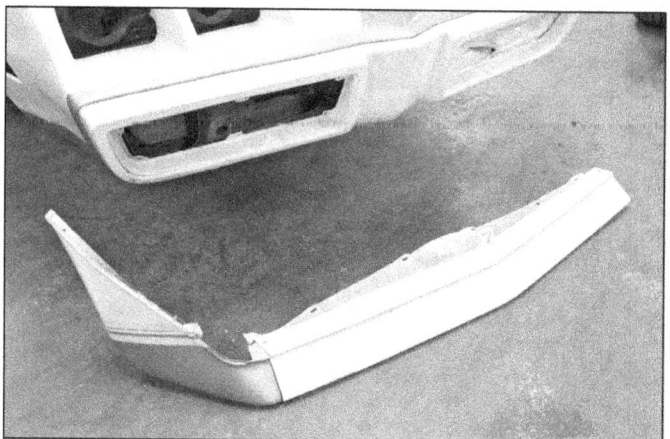

The 1979–1981 center front spoiler is different than the 1970–1978 models. It is a urethane piece that has one center attachment point and one hole on each end that bolts to the outer wheel flares. The rear part of the center spoiler attaches to the lower tie-bar of the radiator support.

CHAPTER 4

Rear Spoiler

The Firebird Formula rear spoiler was standard for some years and optional for other years. The rear spoiler was the only spoiler available for the Formula. The Trans Am rear spoiler was standard equipment and identical to the Formula's. It's crucial to follow these installation procedures so water and contaminants are not trapped between the spoiler and trunk lid. If the spoiler is incorrectly installed, the trunk lid and quarter panel can rust.

The rear spoiler is a three-piece fiberglass unit from 1970 through 1978. In 1979 through 1981, the outer ends of the rear spoiler were changed both in shape and in the material used. The later ends are more squared off on the quarter panel sides and the material changed from fiberglass to urethane. The two outer ends attach to the top of the quarter panel on each side while the center spoiler attaches to the trunk lid.

Rear Spoiler Sealing and Installation

One of the most notable and distinctive parts of the Trans Am styling package is the rear spoiler, as shown on this 1973 Trans Am. The rear spoiler is made of three pieces and constructed of fiberglass. To protect the rear bodywork and prevent rust from forming, the rear spoiler needs to be properly sealed to prevent moisture from seeping into the bodywork.

Place Caulk Strips Around Stud Holes

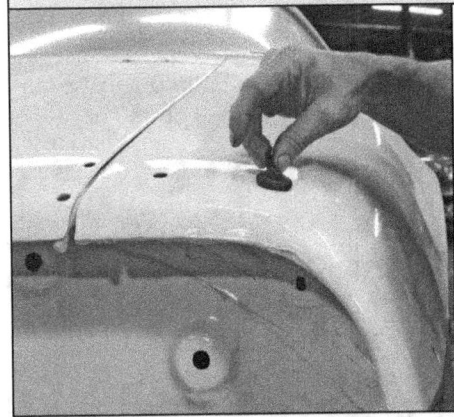

1 *This is an important step because the stud holes are larger than the studs. Lay a strip around the opening of the hole just at the edge.*

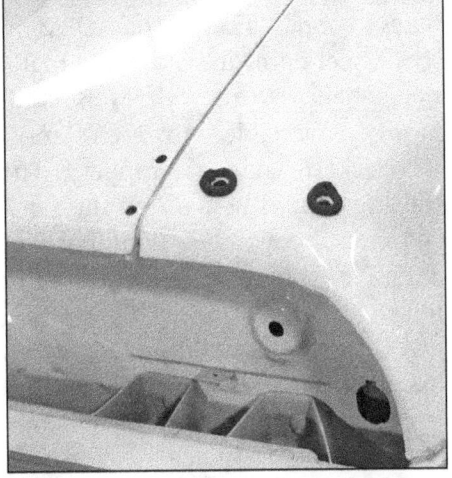

2 *The caulk strips should be about 1/4-inch high and completely surround the spoiler holes.*

Install Rear Spoiler

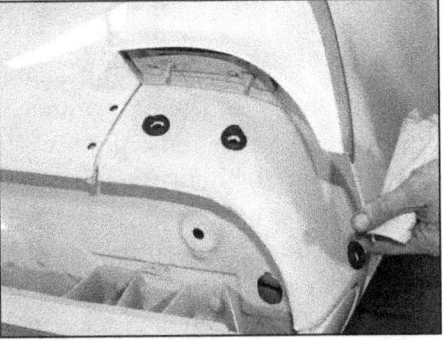

3 *Timing is important and you should apply caulk strips to the rear quarter panels as you install each spoiler part. These strips are very sticky and you don't want them to dry out. In addition, you do not want dirt to stick to the caulk.*

BODYWORK PART II: DOORS, SPOILERS, BUMPERS AND WHEEL FLARES

Align Rear Spoiler

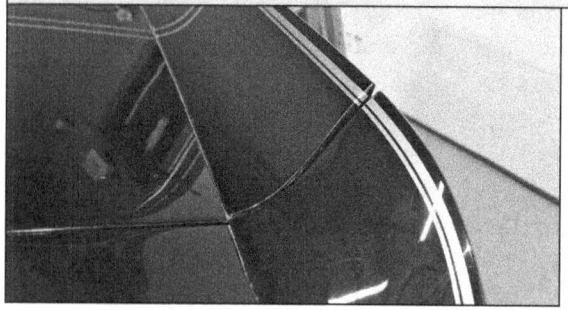

4 *You want all three pieces of the spoiler to align on the same plane. Several methods can be used to attain this alignment. In most cases, these spoilers align fairly closely from the factory but are rarely perfect.*

Align Rear Spoiler (CONTINUED)

5 *Most of the outer spoiler ends are at different angles when bolted in place. Placing double-sided body-molding tape on the edge props up the spoiler ends and makes the angle change to line up to the trunk-mounted spoiler. It is not visible once installed.*

Attach Center Spoiler

6 *A combination of bolts and nuts attach the center spoiler to the trunk lid. You can also place double-sided tape at the bottom of the center spoiler to adjust its angle and align it with the end spoilers. Washers can also be used on the ends between the spoiler attaching stud and the trunk lid to raise the end to match the height of the ends. It is important that all these nuts and bolts are tight but not overtightened because that causes the spoiler to distort or crack.*

Wheel Flares

Some replacement wheel flares do not come with the proper attaching points so you must modify the flares to attach them properly. It is important to make sure that excessive body filler from prior bodywork has not compromised the contours of your fenders and quarter panels or that the panel is bent, otherwise proper fitment of the flare is almost impossible. With the exception of gluing the support panels to the flares, these procedures are the same whether original flares or aftermarket flares with the supports already installed. You can use unsupported flares to obtain a better-than-OEM fit.

Wheel flares use a flexible material called welting, which is commonly available through most Pontiac aftermarket suppliers. The welting should be painted the same color as the flare. A light bead of adhesive should be applied prior to flare installation. This welting gives the flare a finished look when installed. To remove the front flare, jack up the front using the subframe rail and place a jackstand under the rail. Then remove the wheel. For best results, turn the wheel inward so you have ample room to work. Remove the screws that are on the edge of the flare just on the wheel opening edge of the fender.

The flares attach to the fender using these mounting holes.

TRANS AM & FIREBIRD RESTORATION

CHAPTER 4

Flare Restoration

Remove Wheelwell Flare

1 Remove the three bolts on a rectangular sheet-metal panel in the forward part of the wheelhouse to access the lower nut that retains the flare to the fender. Two are at the top of the panel and one is on the bottom just where it curves under. The upper nut for the flare must be accessed from the top side of the engine compartment. There is a gap between the wheelhouse panel and the radiator support for access.

Transfer Flare Support

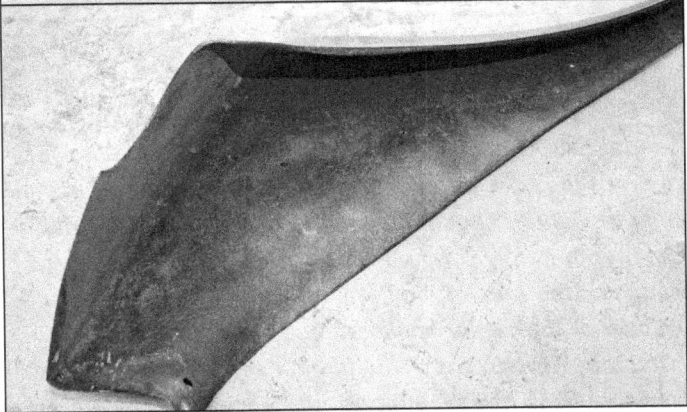

2 These aftermarket flares do not come with a center support.

3 The original center support needs to be removed and installed on the replacement flare.

Remove Support from Stock Flare

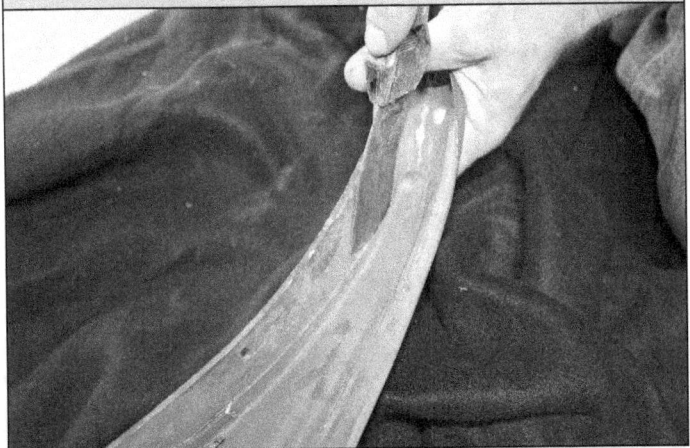

4 The original support is glued in; remove the support panel by using a putty knife to break the glue spots. You may also have to use a flat-blade screwdriver and a utility knife; apply minimal pressure because you do not want to break the support panel. It may splinter, but that is acceptable.

Cut Out Flare Support

5 If a putty knife or utility knife does not work, you may need to take more drastic measures. Use a Dremel or small electric rotary tool with a small cutoff wheel to loosen the support panel where it is sticking. The assembly glue was not done in a consistent manner so every flare comes apart a bit differently.

BODYWORK PART II: DOORS, SPOILERS, BUMPERS AND WHEEL FLARES

Trim Flare Support Panel

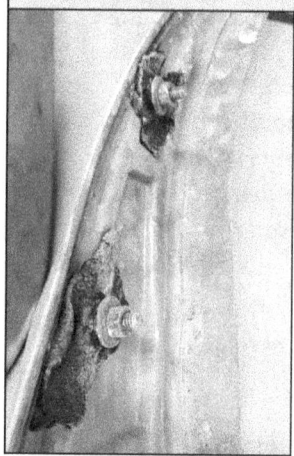

6 Once the support panel has been removed, trim the splintered edges so you have solid plastic. The support panel has two studs with threads and nuts.

Install Flare Support on Fender

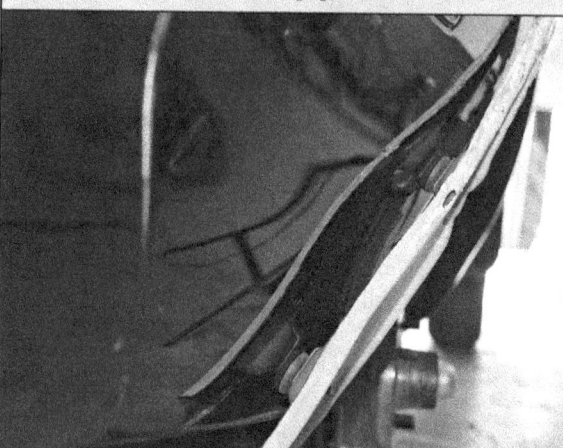

7 Install the support onto the fender using the studs and the two nuts. It is a good idea also to wedge a couple of rubber grommets between the fender and the support panel to give the panel enough height to mate to the flare.

Test Fit Flare to Fender

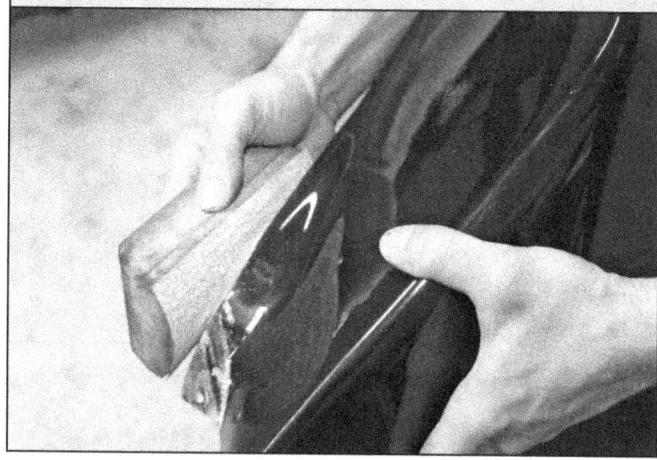

8 Place the flare against the fender over the support panel to check fitment. (Do not install the welting yet.) Any part of the flare that is preventing it from resting flush against the fender should be hand trimmed. Use 100-grit dry sandpaper to gently sand any edge that extends too far. In most cases, the area of the flare that transitions underneath the fender to the center spoiler needs to be trimmed.

You may have to check the fitment several times before achieving a flush fit. Be cautious and proceed slowly as you trim the panel. Remove a little material at a time rather than too much. Sanding off too much material creates a larger gap and requires difficult bodywork to get it back into shape.

Install Support Panel

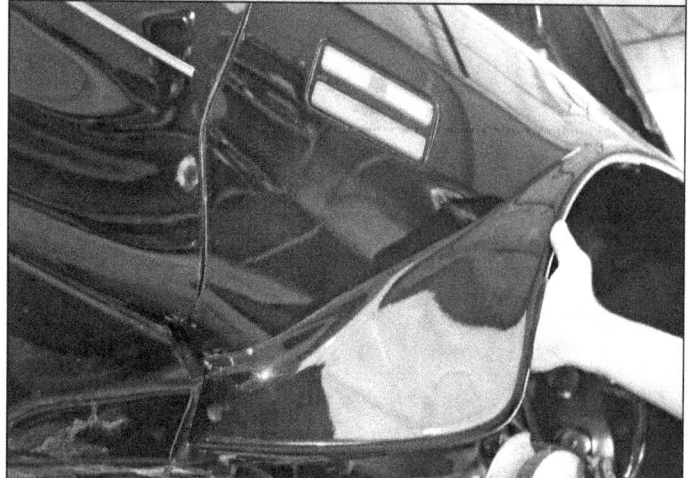

9 Once the flare fits flush along the leading edge from top to bottom, mate the support panel and flare together.

Protect Painted Flare Area

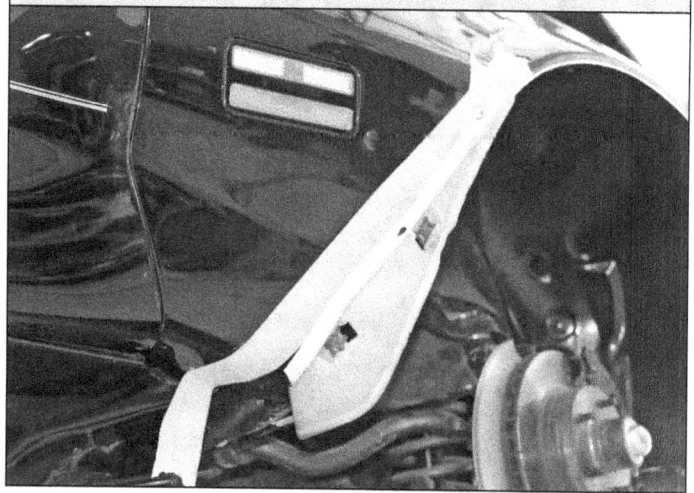

10 This is a good time to tape the fender where the flare edge will rest. This prevents scratching the paint if the Firebird is already painted.

TRANS AM & FIREBIRD RESTORATION

CHAPTER 4

Epoxy Support Panel to Flare

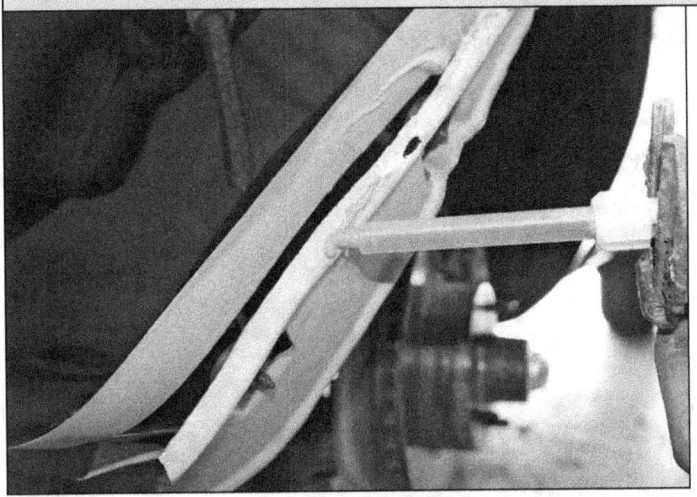
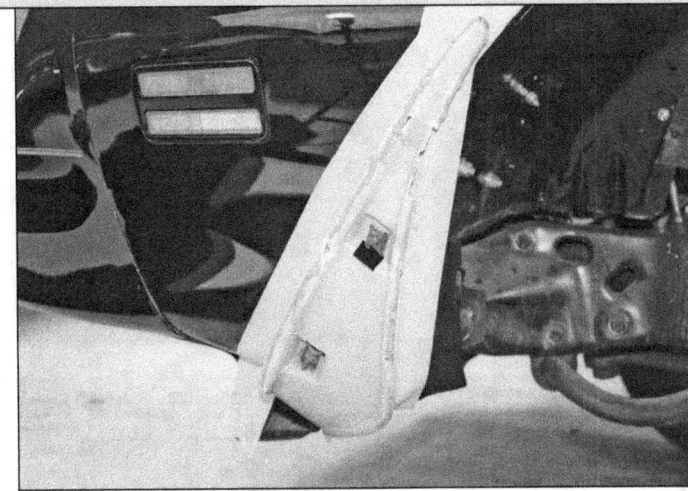

11 Apply a thick bead of epoxy around the edges of the support panel and place the flare over the support panel.

Re-install Fender Flare Screws

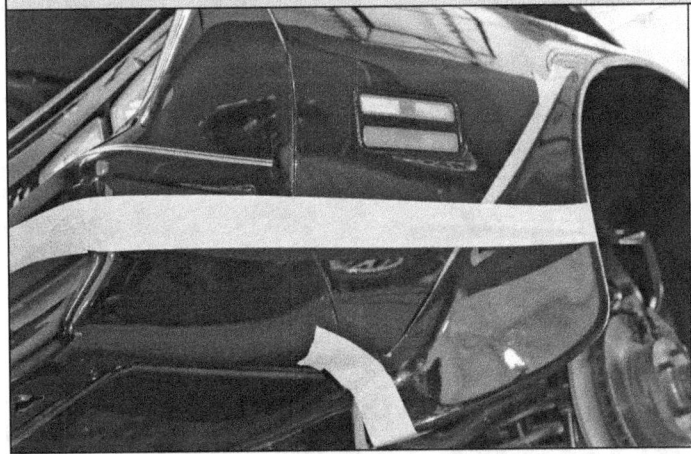

12 Re-install the screws in the wheel opening of the fender edge to hold the flare in place. Tape the flare in place from the bottom and from the fender around to the front. This holds the flare in place so the support bonds together with the flare in the proper position.

Allow Panels to Cure

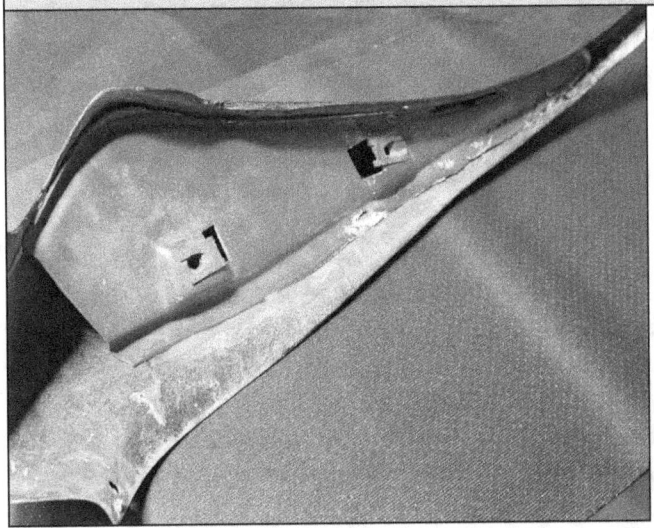

13 It takes approximately 20 minutes for the epoxy to cure at 70 degrees F. If your room is colder or warmer the curing times vary. Colder temperatures dramatically increase the drying time. It is also important that the parts are at the same temperature as the room where you are working. If you live in a cold climate plan for everything to be in the same room at least 12 hours prior.

The same goes for the glue. I do not recommend doing this project when the temperature is below 55 degrees F in your work area. The chemical bond may not last as long. Make sure you read all the cautions about working in a well-ventilated area and skin contact precautions. After about 45 minutes to 1 hour (in a 70-degree room) remove the retaining tape, screws, and attachment nuts, and gently remove the flare.

Apply Additional Epoxy to Front Flare

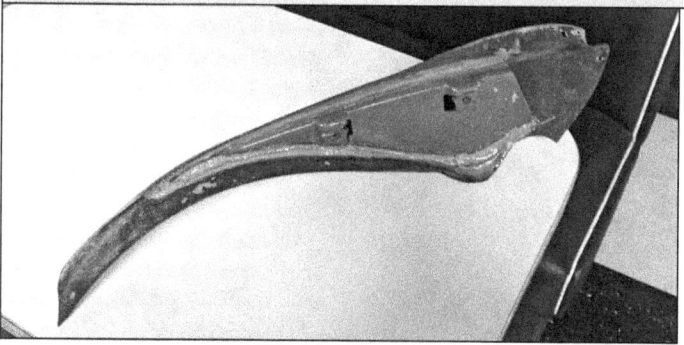

14 Run additional 3M glue around the outside edge of the support panel where it meets the flare. This fills in areas that may have been missed and gives the flare additional strength. Let dry 30 minutes at 70 degrees F.

Apply Additional Epoxy to Rear Flare

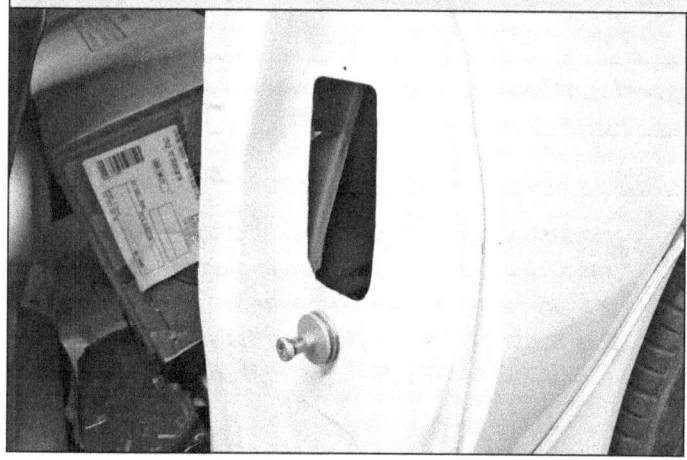
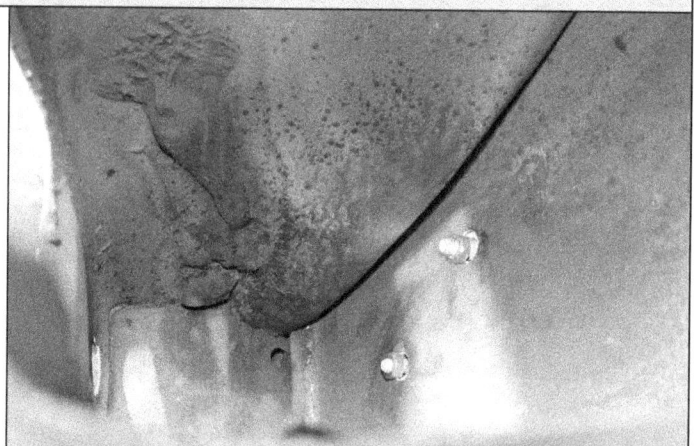

15 Repeat this same procedure for the rear flare. These attachment nuts are accessed through the door opening vent on the lock pillar.

Center Spoiler Fitment

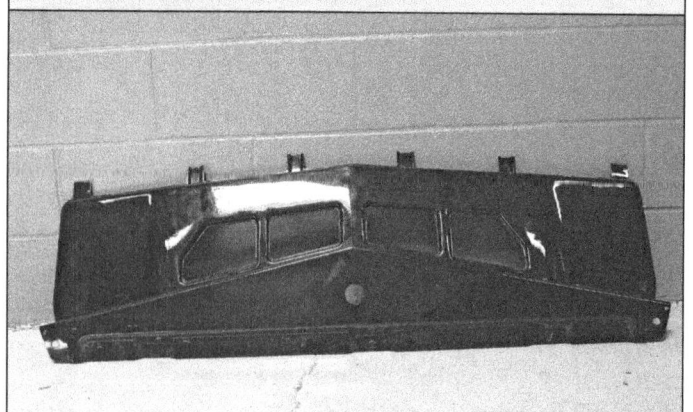

16 The front center spoiler on 1970–1978 Firebirds is also critical for proper fitment of the outer wheel flares. The front center spoiler is really a larger under-bumper filler panel with the spoiler molded in. It rarely fits square and flush with the other parts. Therefore, some adjustment is usually required.

Straighten Lower Tie-Bar

17 You can check front spoiler fitment in a couple of ways. The tabs on the front part of the panel slide into the front lower part of the bumper; the rear portion attaches to the lower tie-bar of the radiator support. Often drivers have hit parking blocks, curbs, or other road obstacles and have damaged the lower part of the radiator support. Straightening the lower tie-bar of the radiator support is not difficult. Usually, a large dead-blow or ball-peen hammer can be used to straighten the tie-bar so the spoiler panel can fit flush.

CHAPTER 4

Straighten Lower Tie-Bar (CONTINUED)

18 Large channel lock pliers can also be used to straighten the edges of the tie-bar so the panel sits flush.

Adjust Spoiler Center Section

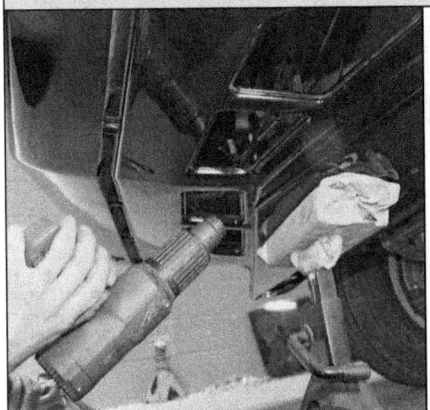

19 If the spoiler panel does not fit properly, you can use a heat gun to apply heat to the center section of the panel. Use a jack and blocks to make the panel conform better. Place a jackstand and wood blocks in the center of the spoiler panel. Apply pressure to the area so the panel moves into the correct position.

Once the spoiler panel fits correctly, aim the heat gun in the same area as the wood blocks. Be careful to not get too close, as you do not want to overheat the panel. When the panel relaxes a bit, remove the heat gun. Let it cool for 5 to 10 minutes and then slowly remove the wood blocks and jackstand. If the panel is in the correct position, you are done. If not, repeat as needed. Then simply bolt the panel into place. This procedure is not damaging to the panel or the paint if you take your time.

Panel Alignment

Aligning the fender is important. It is a strong indicator of the quality of the restoration. Attention to detail separates a mediocre restoration from a top-quality restoration. A second-generation F-Body car with accurate and consistent body panel alignment presents well, is satisfying to the owner, and will be well judged in competition.

Many panels depend upon the proper alignment of the fenders. The hood, front bumper, and doors all rely on the fenders being in their proper position. Otherwise, at a minimum, the gaps are not straight and even. Worse case is when the panels interfere with each other and cause damage and impair their function.

Start the alignment process by checking the height of the door top edge compared to the top of the fender closest to the windshield. Add or remove shims as needed to the top cowl panel bolt to raise or lower the fender to meet the door top edge. Snug the bolts as you go.

Every time you make an adjustment, you need to check all other alignment points because the one change you make could possibly affect the other parts of the fender. If the fender needs to come out at the side upper portion to be on the same plane as the door, you may need to shim the fender bolt located in the door opening at the base of the A-pillar.

The wheelhouse provides stability to the fender and affects how the lower portion lines up. Leave the bolts slightly loose. Open the door slowly again to check the clearance to the fender.

Visually check the door-to-fender gap. Stand in front and look for a uniform and consistent line. Once you are satisfied with the rear portion of the fender, it is time to move to the front.

Install the bolts to the upper radiator support and the fender attachment bracket. Tighten the wheelhouse bolts and snug the front upper and lower fender bolts where they attach to the upper and lower tie bars of the radiator support.

Install the hood hinge and hood so that you can check the hood-to-fender gap. Loosen the upper and/or lower front bolts attached to the radiator support to move the fender out as necessary to achieve a consistent gap. If you feel you need to rotate the fender out at the top, you can loosen the top bolts and push it out. The same goes for loosening the lower bolts while the upper bolts stay snug so you can move the line around on the lower portion of the fender.

Aligning a panel can be very time-consuming and frustrating. Depending on your skill and patience (and some luck), you could spend several minutes to many hours getting that gap where you want it. It is not uncommon to have one part where you want the line to be only to find another line moved in the process. Once you finally have the panel where you want it, tighten all the bolts securely.

Gap Checking

Install Front Fender

1 Place the fender slightly forward of the wheel and slide it rearward until the rear part is resting on the cowl. Be careful not to hit the windshield or it may crack. If necessary, gently pull out the lower rear portion of the fender to clear the cowl.

Install Front Fender (CONTINUED)

2 Secure the fender with bolts at the corners except where the fender attaches to the upper tie-bar of the radiator support. Only tighten the bolts enough so that the panel can still move slightly with minimal resistance. Place a larger size punch into the top of the radiator support upper tie-bar through the fender attachment hole. This allows the fender to move when aligning it.

Check Body Panel Gaps

3 Inspect the door-to-fender top line as well as the door-to-fender gap. Because this was a fender previously removed from this car it aligns much easier. If you have a used fender, an NOS fender, or a reproduction fender the alignment technique may be more tedious and time consuming to achieve a good fit. The procedures are the same.

Check Body Panel Gaps (CONTINUED)

4 Look down the side of the door and the fender where the two meet. Check how the side of the fender meets up to the door both on the upper and lower curves. Check the middle body contour line. All should be flush and even.

5 Run your hand over the door-to-fender gap to make sure that the two panels are on the same plane. This verifies what your eyes see.

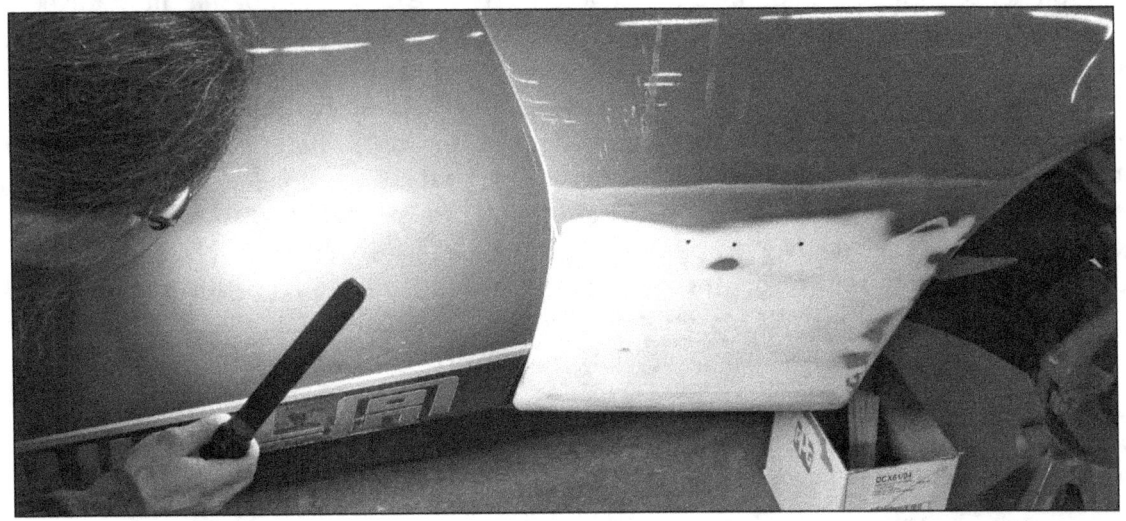

6 Carefully open the door to verify that the door clears the fender with enough room to allow for body movement.

7 At the base of the back of the front fender, move the bottom in or out as needed so the lower portion of the fender and door are on the same plane. You may need to add or remove shims so the curve and clearances are correct. In this particular case I had removed excess filler from the lower portion of the fender and that required additional alignment for proper fit. Remember to check the bodyline to make sure it is not higher or lower than the door line. Snug the bolts once you have the rear portion situated.

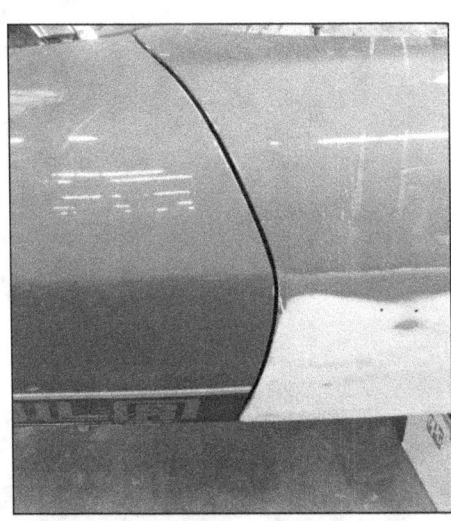

8 Now that the fender is aligned the door to fender gap is consistent.

CHAPTER 5

PAINTING

One of the first things you notice about a car is its paint job. Your car is often judged, whether informally or formally, by the quality of its paint. And therefore, a high-quality paint job enhances all the bodywork that lies beneath it as well as the entire restoration. And, of course, the reverse is true. A substandard or flawed paint job diminishes the quality of a restoration, establishes a poor impression of the car, and negatively affects its value.

The big difference among paint jobs is the body prep time and amount of sanding and buffing required to give the clear coat and paint the deepest shine. The amount of labor involved often has the biggest impact on the overall cost of the paint job. As most car owners can attest, painting a car is one of the most, if not *the* most, expensive stages in a restoration project. And while many variables exist, such as prep time, paint type, paint process, sanding and buffing, shop rate, and more, you should expect to spend $3,000 to $7,000 for good daily-driver paint job. But this isn't a definitive range for a paint job; a concours or high-level paint job can cost $20,000 or more.

You want to do everything possible to ensure your Firebird or Trans Am receives the highest-quality paint job within your budget. To attain the best results, you should rely on a qualified professional restoration shop to prep, shoot, and buff your car. The following are some things to consider if you want to paint your Firebird yourself.

Painting is not as simple as it appears. If something appears to be done easily by someone who does it for a living, it usually is not. Having a professional shop spray your car may not be as expensive as you may think if you have done all the prep work. If the shop makes a mistake, it will rectify it at its expense. If you make a mistake, it is all on you. Repairing a paint job is not easily done. This is a critical decision you have to make.

This 1973 Trans Am is in a paint booth. Prep work and taping off the car is a tedious process.

TRANS AM & FIREBIRD RESTORATION

CHAPTER 5

Although you can perform a competent-quality paint job at home, you have to battle against contamination. A restoration shop has a professional paint booth; you probably do not. Constructing a temporary paint booth in your garage is an option, but it does not produce the same results. When you paint at home, you need to do everything in your power to avoid contamination and drips, runs, orange peel, or other problems.

As with the various levels of restoration, there are as many grades of paint jobs as there are types of paint. First and foremost, you need to determine how you will use your car. Second, you need to determine your budget so you can allocate the money for a particular type of paint job. And third, you need to know where the car will be parked. Will it be in a climate-controlled garage or outside and exposed to the elements?

If it's a daily driver, weekend car, or a car that sees regular use, most people opt for a urethane paint job because it resists abrasion and sun damage and is far more durable than the original lacquer paint. And any of these paints can be matched to the factory color code so it appears as a factory original color.

Environmental Laws and Safety Considerations

Local and federal laws may prohibit you from painting your car in your own residential garage. You would be wise to not only check with your local law enforcement, but also the state environmental authorities. If the law allows you to paint at your residence, you need to take every precaution to protect yourself, your neighbors, and all property.

Equipment and Materials

If you want a quality paint job, the first thing on your list is to have some sort of sealed enclosed space with an opening for intake and exhaust with the appropriate filters. You also need an air compressor capable of sustaining at least 50 PSI over a period of 10 minutes. A compressor that starts and stops while spraying makes your paint job inconsistent, especially when spraying metallic paints.

Other materials you'll need include the following:

- High-volume low-pressure (HVLP) spray gun for color and clear coats
- HVLP spray gun for priming
- Desiccant inline filter for the air hose
- Proper full-face respirators (I recommend a fresh air supply system)
- Disposable paint suits
- Mixing cups
- Paint stirrers
- Paint masking tape
- Painting paper
- Plastic sheeting
- Sanding block
- Sandpaper
- Safe method to dispose of unused materials and used materials
- Large Class B fire extinguisher (not the one in your car)
- Explosion-proof lighting
- Explosion-proof fan(s)
- Clean, hard surface

If you come to the conclusion you cannot properly ventilate the painting booth and control overspray, have no shame in relying on a professional shop with a commercial booth and the necessary equipment. Painting is an expensive and exacting process that involves using hazardous chemicals. Bottom line: You must control the paint, and overspray cannot be allowed to fly into the open air and leave your property.

Do not ignore this advice! Paint overspray may blow into your neighbors' yards and houses and can color anything in its path. Eliminate any possibility of paint mist floating about and overspray covering their house exteriors, cars, and anything else. Imagine what could happen if a cloud of overspray traveled into a neighbor's yard and a child breathed in the paint or fumes. That kind of exposure is most likely not covered by your homeowner's insurance; it would be deemed an illegal act. Additionally, if the state environmental police issues you a ticket, those fines could easily exceed $10,000.

Most painting products are combustible and you could seriously injure yourself or others, or worse. You also have the possibility of breathing the toxic fumes. At a minimum, you could get sick or, at the very worst, die. The long-term effect for exposure to paint fumes is not fully known. The hydrocarbons, solids, solvents, and other chemicals that are used in the mixing and manufacturing of these primers and paints can cause damage to your lungs and other parts of your body, not to mention anyone in the vicinity. In my opinion, it is simply not worth it to save a few bucks.

Paint Job Types

Now that you have decided whether to paint the car yourself or have a shop handle it, it is time to decide what level of paint job you want. The levels run from a driver-quality to top-level paint job. This is not to say that there is any difference in how your car is restored and prepped for paint. Every decision made from the time you start disassembling your car to performing metalwork and bodywork to priming affects the finished product. Paint reflects all the work done prior to the actual painting.

I have always said that you can do the proper bodywork and prep and apply a lesser-quality paint and the results look fantastic. However, if you do not follow the proper procedures and take shortcuts when performing bodywork and sanding, a high-quality paint will not yield good results. The correct prep is an absolute necessity. It is obvious when looking at a restored car whether the prep was done correctly or not. Under budgeting a restoration or attempting shortcuts usually results in a vehicle that is diminished in value. A well-done restoration usually returns some percentage of the investment when it's time to sell.

The three types of paint jobs are driver-quality, concours-level, and top-level. These represent a wide range of paint qualities and financial investment. You need to determine the type of paint job that's best for your restoration project.

Driver Quality

The term driver-quality is usually reserved for any paint that is one color covering the entire car and is consistent throughout. The type of restoration can affect the type of paint you choose. Enamels are the least durable and do not shine much. Lacquers are not available in their original formulations. The modern base/clear systems are urethane with lacquer origins. The most commonly used systems are base/clears because they offer original paint color replication (for the majority of colors) and ease of repair when damaged or scratched. Enamels are the least expensive and can be purchased for as little as $25 per gallon. The cost of a base/clear system can run in excess of $1,000. The cost of paint materials is usually tied to the quality of the materials. The prep and labor to apply the paint is the same no matter the type of paint. It really does not make much sense to use low-quality paint materials. A Maaco-type paint job or inexpensive collision shop respray is an example of a driver-quality paint job. It's meant to protect the sheet metal more than it is meant to showcase the car. This type of respray is usually done with all the bumpers and trim installed, or what is commonly known in the industry as a "tape and shoot."

A single-stage paint in Starlight Black covers this 1978 Trans Am.

These types of paint jobs could be single-stage (meaning no clear on top of the color) or clear coat. Paint material costs vary, but expect to pay $600 to $1,000 in materials for this type of paint. Believe it or not, reds and greens cost more than any other color.

Concours Level

This level of paint is needed to meet points judging criteria for restored cars competing in an original or concours-type show. This paint replicates the original finishes and sheen (or lack thereof) that an original car had. Most of the paints applied to Firebirds were single-stage lacquers and enamels that had little shine and varying degrees of orange peel throughout. These paints were also hit or miss in their applications.

A concours paint job attempts to replicate the paint so it appears as original; it also replicates all of the mistakes and faults common to the assembly plant where the car was built. This paint job takes much more time and expertise because special techniques must be used

CHAPTER 5

Concours-level paints replicate original finishes such as on this 1977 Special Edition Trans Am. This type replicates the original finishes and sheen (or lack thereof) that an original car would have had. Most of the paints applied to Firebirds were single-stage lacquers and enamels that had little shine and varying degrees of orange peel throughout. These paints were also hit or miss in their applications. A concours paint job is meant to replicate the paint to appear as original and that includes replicating all the mistakes and faults common to the particular assembly plant. This paint job takes much more time and expertise because certain techniques must be used to make the paint appear factory original.

This 1974 Super Duty Trans Am has Show Quality Paint. Achieving a top-level paint job requires many levels of prep starting in the finishing of the body work process. You start by block sanding the body to make sure the panels are arrow straight and the contours are perfect then you finish sanding with a 400-grit paper. Afterward you apply a primer coat and sand the body again using 600-grit wet sandpaper. Next, you apply a base coat of color and wet sand the color coat with a 1500- to 2000-grit sandpaper and then follow up with multiple layers of clear coat. The process continues as you wet sand the clear coat starting with 800-grit and transition to finer and finer sand paper in wet sanding until the desired surface finish is achieved. You progress from 1000-, 1500-, 2000-, 2500- to 3000-grits and ultimately the finish is smooth as glass. Power polishing two successive times is required with compound, finesse mid-level compound, and then finish with a hand polishing yields outstanding results.

to make the paint appear factory original.

Those techniques are generally secrets that are closely guarded by individual painters. However, most of the time, you can practice on old body panels until you feel you have the technique down and the results you want. Generally, the technique involves increasing the air pressure and adjusting the distance that you hold the spray gun from the body. The type of paint you use also can affect your technique. Obtaining the factory orange peel is best done by experience and practice.

If you really want the paint job to replicate the factory paint as closely as possible, you should take the car to a professional shop. A car owner typically selects this type of paint job for entering a national points judging contest or a concours d'elegance. You can expect to spend roughly the same amount in materials as the driver-quality job. Most of these paint job types do not involve clear coat because General Motors did not use clear coat until late 1981 and 1982. Bear in mind that if your car has a metallic single-stage paint, it cannot be wet sanded and polished because that will ruin the metallic flake and create a distorted and dull paint.

Top Level

I define a top-level paint job as "show-quality paint." However, this term has been widely misused and does not mean what most people think it means. This refers to a level of paint job that has a deep shine to it and is nearly flawless. Obviously, this term is correct as used here. In this case, the show is not judging a vehicle based on its originality. Instead a car's paint is judged on its

PAINTING

quality, which is far better than the original paint job.

Achieving a top-level paint job requires many levels of prep, starting with the finishing of the bodywork process. You begin by block sanding the body to make sure the panels are arrow-straight and the contours are perfect; finish sanding with a 400-grit paper. Afterward, apply a primer coat and sand the body again using 600-grit wet sandpaper. Next, apply a base coat of color and wet sand the color coat with a 1500- to 2000-grit sandpaper, and then follow with multiple layers of clear coat.

The process continues as you wet sand the clear coat; start with 800-grit and follow through with successive wet sandings of 1000-, 1500-, 2000-, 2500-, and 3000-grit papers to smooth the finish out like glass. Then power polish with compound, finesse it with midlevel compound, and finally finish with hand polishing. This will yield outstanding results.

This kind of sanding and finish treatment is labor and time intensive, but it's essential to attain the best finish possible. This means that the entire Firebird required an additional 9 full sandings over the entire body. For a Trans Am, at least 11 additional parts require the same sandings.

Now, add in the two entire vehicle power polishings, plus a hand-applied glaze. This all translates into dollars.

Choosing Your Paint Job Type

Before you order any materials or perform any work, you need to decide on the type of paint job you want for your project. Of course, your budget and the intended use of the car largely dictate the type of paint you select. For obvious reasons, the person applying paint to the vehicle needs to know whether driver-quality or concours-level paints should be used.

This decision is even more important with top-level paint. The painter has to apply four or five coats of color rather than the normal three because wet sanding removes material; you do not want to cut through the color to the primer.

The power polishings also remove material, especially because of the intense heat that is built up. A burn from a power polisher can require the entire panel to be repainted. The paint material costs associated with this type of base coat/clear coat paint can run $1,500 to $2,500, depending on the system you use. PPG, Glasurit, Dupont, and Sikkens are all good-quality paint systems. Custom paints can run more than $5,000 in materials only for pearl or candy paint.

All of these paint job types require skill to apply, and it's no mystery why body shops have trained professionals to shoot cars. An amateur can spend a lot of money for materials, and if you do not have the aptitude to use the paint guns, booth features, and other materials, you do not wind up with a top-quality paint job. Even if you manage to measure and mix the paint and clear correctly, you need the knowledge and experience to apply the paint.

Another reason to use a professional is that if the shop makes a mistake, or you are not happy with the results, you have recourse that does not cost you additional money. If *you* make a mistake, you are on your own. I can tell you that paint is not where you want a mistake to happen. Repairing your own paint job mistakes are the most time consuming and difficult to overcome.

Another factor in choosing the type of paint job is how you plan to use the Firebird. If you put a top-level paint job on the car, you may be a lot more stressed about using it for anything other than shows. A door ding, paint chip, or careless scratch can result in an expensive repair.

A concours-type paint job probably resigns the Firebird to a life of enclosed trailers and climate-controlled garages and high stress at shows. A driver-quality paint job may not look the best, but it places a much lower stress level on you because it's a moderate investment and doesn't require constant vigilance and protection.

I believe that you need to be happy with the visual aspect of your Firebird every time you look at it whether it is in a garage or outside in a parking lot. Just remember: Paint can always be repaired. It is really not worth getting so stressed about something happening to your Firebird that you cannot enjoy your time with it.

Painting at Home

If you decide to paint at home, you can take steps to prepare the area. The first is to create your own temporary paint booth. You need to make it as clean as possible before and during the painting process; otherwise, the contaminants in the booth area get into the paint, and this necessitates touch-up painting.

If you have limited space, you will most likely cause dust or debris to get into the paint job, and that may be a good enough reason to have a shop paint it. You may also inadvertently brush up against the body with the air hose or your clothes. Mount as much lighting as possible all around

CHAPTER 5

and in both high and low spots to eliminate shadows.

Create Your Own Paint Booth

For a home paint booth you need at least 250 feet of heavy-duty, thick-mil clear plastic sheeting. The sheeting should hang from the ceiling to the floor on all four sides. You also need to cover the floor. The space you create with the sheeting needs to be at least 2 feet larger in every direction than the car to allow for proper movement while painting.

Once you have hung the plastic, tape off the entire area with a high-quality duct tape. You want the only airflow to come through the opening you create. Any outside contaminants are sucked in through any open areas if not properly taped. You are actually creating a vacuum chamber.

An explosion-proof fan should be mounted in an opening in the plastic wall opposite to where the air is drawn into the booth. This fan must be a sufficient size to move the air rapidly. The way to tell if you have enough airflow is to feel for the air moving when you stand in the middle of the booth. Place a high-quality charcoal filter before and after the fan to clean the air. These filters greatly diminish the smell so you don't disturb the neighbors.

The opposite end of the booth requires a fresh air source with filters on both sides of the opening. These are ordinary paint booth filters. If your paint booth is in the garage, you can open the garage door high enough for the filters to stand in the opening. Be sure to tape all around the filters and outer openings to keep the incoming air directed through the filters. You want any air coming into the booth and exiting the booth to be channeled through those filters. Make sure you have a large Class B fire extinguisher in the booth with you.

Of course, you could also rent booth space at a body shop for a weekend when the shop is closed. That way you can perform the work yourself without creating your own paint booth.

Safety and Cleanliness

A high-quality paint job requires meticulous work, correct handling of harmful chemicals, skilled application, and adherence to safety protocols. But that does not necessarily mean you cannot do it at home: it does mean that applying automotive paint comes with a substantial responsibility.

You also need to recognize that painting is difficult to do correctly. To do it professionally requires a commercial paint booth and a great deal of equipment. For most paint types (enamel, lacquer, polyurethane), the materials are hazardous and expensive to manufacture. In addition, a large amount of preparation work is required for a quality outcome, but it also takes the mastery of several different operations, all of which are essential to a high-quality result.

Where the car is painted, or more specifically, its painting environment, has an enormous impact on the outcome, or quality level, of the paint job. Will it be a high-tech paint booth with state-of-the-art temperature and humidity control and filters for dust and overspray, or a damp and dusty cement-floor garage? Regardless of how well you clean the garage, some errant dust or debris can get into the paint at the most inopportune moment. As such, if you follow all the procedures and take all the precautions, you can complete a decent paint job at home, but you won't achieve the same results as a pro in a commercial paint booth.

Selecting the Right Shop

On the surface, it may seem that a body shop and a restoration shop are similar because they both repair car bodies, but there is a huge distinction between the two. Most people are not aware of the differences between these types of shops.

Body Shop

Most body shops primarily repair modern cars that have been involved in collisions. Collision customers depend on their vehicles for daily driving and therefore are not concerned about a factory-correct level of repair or restoration. In addition, insurance companies dictate how much they pay for repairs, how long it should take, and what type of parts are to be used. As such, these shops are focused on efficiency so that the vehicle gets back on the road as quickly as possible.

I know a very busy and successful shop owner who is proud of the fact that he can deliver a car to the customer 1½ hours after painting. Taking your Firebird to this type of shop is rife with perils because its business philosophy, focus, and priorities are not suited to classic car restoration.

In many cases, a collision shop takes on a restoration for filler work during slow times. That usually means that your Firebird has many different people working on the body during any slow periods. It is difficult to maintain a high degree of quality when that happens. One technician may feel that the technician before him did not do the job the way he would have done it. Then another technician may not care at all; he just wants to get it done and employs the methods used in the collision industry, which can mean shortcuts.

Most collision shops do not know how to properly deal with rust and fabrication. They may just apply body filler over the rust.

This is not to say that all collision shops are not capable of performing a quality job on your vehicle. It is just not their business model.

Restoration Shop

A restoration shop is dedicated to restoring classic cars to their original condition or to a customer's specific requirements. As such, a restoration shop has a completely different approach and philosophy toward completing bodywork than does a collision shop. A restoration shop's business model does not involve repairing daily-driver vehicles. A genuine restoration shop is set up to accommodate a wide range of restoration projects, and the planning and execution of the work is to achieve high-quality results that meet the customer's expectations.

Do Your Research

When it comes to selecting a shop to perform bodywork on your Firebird, you need to do your research, visit the shop, and speak to former customers. And you're far better off choosing a Pontiac specialist that has restored many cars. A shop that specializes in muscle cars requires some degree of learning curve. A shop that specializes in second-generation Chevrolet Camaros, for example, may have less of a learning curve. However, certain body pieces, the interior, and most of the mechanicals on a Firebird are not familiar. In particular, Firebirds were equipped with the Endura bumper material and the Pontiac engine.

Choosing a shop that has the experience with Firebirds can also reduce the overall costs because shop workers are not learning how to take your car apart and put it back together. They know all the weak spots and problematic areas; they have the experience to repair them properly.

Some unique examples for Firebirds are the 1970–1973 Endura bumper and the fitment of the flares and spoilers on the Trans Am. If the shop has no experience with these, how can you expect your car to be restored correctly? A collision shop probably doesn't have the knowledge to properly repair the Endura bumper and likely employs some other method that does not last.

A professional restoration shop should be a full-service facility. Such a shop has the required tools and machines to properly restore your car, such as a paint booth, MIG welders, and rotisserie. All Firebirds and Trans Ams have their eccentricities and you need a knowledgeable shop to properly restore them.

A direct conversation is the best way to find out whether the shop you are considering does quality work or not. Visit the shop to watch an actual restoration in progress. This will give you information you need to make a decision.

Visit Car Shows

The best way to locate a good shop is to attend car shows. When you see a car that you like and that looks great (especially a Firebird), talk to the owner. Find out where the restoration was done and how the owner's experience was with that shop. If the car was purchased restored, does the owner know who did the restoration? Are there any problems with the quality of the work? Any paint bubbles indicating issues with the bodywork?

I suggest that you do not consult only Internet forums to find a shop; the information can be unreliable and is not verifiable.

Choose Your Involvement

Paint and preparation may not be your strengths, or maybe you just do not want to do that work. You certainly have options, as there are so many other necessary aspects of a restoration that you can perform. Removing and installing trim can be done with care. Removing the interior and re-installing it afterward also may be within your abilities. Mechanical work, such as working on the engine, transmission, rear axle, brakes, steering, suspension and wiring, may be more suited to your skill set. In addition, many car guys already have the tools and facilities or can acquire the tools and learn the necessary skills to complete many mechanical restoration procedures.

You could also act as your own general contractor by subcontracting out the various parts of the restoration. Disassembling and reassembling the vehicle is entirely possible by most mechanically inclined people. Sending the body to a restoration shop, the engine to a machine shop, the transmission to a transmission shop, the rear axle to a mechanic shop, and the seats to an interior shop all are easily done once you have selected competent players and are comfortable with them.

CHAPTER 5

After the body work has been completed, your car should look very similar to this. At this stage use a sanding block because hand sanding can leave indentations from the curvature of your fingers that you will not see until the car is painted.

You could even do all of this but have the restoration shop disassemble and reassemble the car. You can decide how you want the restoration to be done.

Panel Sanding and Cleaning

Before you actually paint the car, the bodywork must be properly completed so the paint has the best foundation for adhesion. Bodywork finishing requires meticulous work and a lot of verification because once you've sprayed the body it's too late to fix underlying problems. The last sanding is at the 320-grit stage, the prep for paint actually starts.

You want to make sure the panels are as straight as possible. Try to complete the work on a particular panel before you take a break or stop for the day so you can keep progressing and not have to repeat the same sanding procedure. Consistency is key in this phase and every phase going forward. Be prepared for a lot of sanding as well as sore fingers, hands, and arms.

Prior bodywork should have used minimal filler. Today's body filler is exceptional in quality and nothing like the old lead, which is no longer available in its original form. However, as with any product, if it is not used as directed, it is doomed to fail.

At this stage, you should obtain a sanding block because hand sanding can leave indentations from the curvature of your fingers; you won't see them until the car is painted. Obtain good-quality 400-grit sandpaper, such as that made by Norton or 3M, and start sanding at one end of the vehicle. You need a good-quality spray bottle filled with water to spray on the panel as you sand. It is important to keep the panel liberally wet because you do not want to generate heat.

It is necessary to sand each panel in a forward-to-backward motion of 18- to 24-inch sweeps with light pressure on the panel. Do not worry about the actual measuring of the stroke you use; just use what feels comfortable. You do not want to sand in short strokes because that makes the panel potentially uneven. When you think you have completed a panel, run your hand over the surface feeling for any inconsistencies.

Once you are satisfied with the feel of the panel, wet a cloth with "DuPont Prep-Sol or PPG's Wax and Grease Remover (PN DX330). Apply it liberally to the panel and, before it evaporates, look down the side of the panel for any waves. You are finished with this stage on that panel if you don't see any waves.

Repeat this step for each panel. It is best to work methodically. For example, start on the right front fender, move to the right door, the right rear quarter panel, the trunk lid, and so on. On the larger panels, such as the roof, trunk lid, and hood, it might be more beneficial to apply the solvent on half of the panel at a time.

After all of the panels are sanded, it is time to clean the car thoroughly. All sanding residue must be removed not only from the panels but also from the edges, inside the engine compartment, inside the trunk, and inside the passenger compartments. Pay attention to the underside of the panels and the wheels and tires.

Contamination from missed debris is your enemy when it's time to spray primer and paint. You want to make sure the body is as clean as possible. If you run into some rough-edge issues, use a red Scotch-Brite pad to knock them down. Open the doors and get into the fender edges. Every nook and cranny must be cleaned. Using compressed air also greatly helps to vacate unseen contaminants. This step should not be rushed, as cleanliness is critical.

Masking

The next step is to mask off everything on the car that you do not want primed. Removing primer overspray takes far longer than masking and creates more issues than taking your time to tape off the car properly. Using a good-quality tape is of paramount importance.

Make sure that the edges of the masking tape are stuck down completely to prevent primer and paint bleed through. The tape should

PAINTING

be 1/2-inch wide in most cases unless you are using masking paper for the larger areas such as glass, the trunk compartment, and the engine compartment openings. (It is acceptable to use a single-edge razor blade to trim the edges before priming). Make a practice of running your finger over every piece of applied tape to make sure it is stuck properly. Having bleed-through could require a re-prime or repaint of that missed area.

Do not forget the underside of the vehicle. Overspray on the subframe, floors, and suspension components requires substantial work to get them back into clean condition. Tape from the back side of the rocker panel lip with the masking paper on the floor. This helps prevent overspray.

A proper tape job can be a full-day affair so don't rush the process or underestimate the amount of time you need.

Paint Type and System

The cost of paint materials, the time to apply the materials, and the type of restoration are the primary

Solvent-Based versus Waterborne Paints

Here is a brief run-down on the pros and cons of the common paint types.

Lacquer

For a number of years, GM used lacquer to finish its cars. Replicating original paint finishes can be difficult because many early Firebirds used lacquers, and the modern lacquers have different formulations. The original lacquers are essentially obsolete thanks to high lead content, cost of materials, and state bans because of the hazardous materials. Lacquer paints require maintenance polishing from time to time to maintain their gloss. In addition, this paint lacks UV–ray resistance and has low chemical tolerance.

Enamel

Acrylic enamels are inexpensive. This type of paint was popular in the 1960s but did not shine well. Although the application process is not difficult, enamels can take 24 to 48 hours to dry fully. Extended drying times can lead to contamination by flying and crawling insects (they get stuck or, at best, leave a trail). Dust and other types of debris can possibly end up in your paint. Enamels do not wet sand well either.

Enamels also chip easily. The application process requires higher pressures, and the paint material attaches to everything, including the painter. The life expectancy for enamel is less than 10 years under optimal conditions. Although you can purchase a gallon of enamel for as little as $25, this is not the time to start minimizing costs.

Urethane

Urethane paints became commonplace in the mid- to late 1980s. They are easier to apply and can be used either in single-stage or two-stage systems. Urethanes are much more durable and can last for more than 20 years. This type requires a catalyst; a full paint job can set up and dry in as little as two hours. However, the catalyst contains isocyanates, which are absorbed through your skin and lungs.

Water-Borne Paint

I do not think waterborne is a better system than solvent-based paints, except to your health. An experienced professional can do an excellent job with waterborne systems.

The equipment and booth setup needed for waterbornes is different than for a solvent-based paint. Color matching becomes much more difficult as waterborne tends to appear grayish. I do not recommend spraying it without the isocyanate, because the durability suffers. Waterbornes are difficult to touch up.

At this time, I do not recommend this system for the inexperienced painter or for an at-home paint job. ■

factors to consider when making a decision on paint type. Several types of solvent-based paint are currently available, including lacquer, enamel, and urethane. You can also choose a waterborne paint. Each paint type has benefits and drawbacks, so be sure to choose the best paint type for your project.

The type of restoration you are contemplating also can affect your paint type decision. Enamels are the least expensive but the least durable and do not have much shine. Lacquers are not available in their original formulations.

The base/clear coat systems use urethane with lacquer origins and are the most commonly used paint systems. Base/clear systems offer original paint color replication (for the majority of colors) and ease of repair when damaged or scratched. These paints are offered in one- or two-stage systems. A two-stage system needs an activator to dry while a one-stage system does not.

A one-stage system is the easiest to use and can be a suitable choice for a beginner. You need to mix the paint often with a thinning agent to attain the correct ratio for the spray gun, and then you can simply apply the paint. One-stage paints contain the color coat and do not need a clear coat. However, in many cases, one-stage paints don't provide the shine and luster for as long as a two-stage system.

Two-stage products contain a base coat and require a clear coat. In addition, a hardener is added to the paint to set up and dry. In most cases, you are better off choosing a two-stage paint product with a base coat and clear coat applications because the clear coat provides vital paint surface protection so your Firebird's paint job lasts for many years. If your car is a solid color, you may go with single-stage paint. However, if you use a metallic color, I recommend using a two-stage system. It is not feasible to wet sand a single-stage metallic paint because it can distort the metallic color. And I think that metallic looks best under clear coat.

As a professional restorer, I have found that clear coating solid blacks and whites is not necessary. If you do, the color tends to appear a bit hazy. The exception is with two-tone colors, such as on the Macho Trans Am. I always use clear coat on metallic paint finishes.

Paint formulations have continued to improve over the years so your Firebird will receive a paint job that's far superior in quality to the original paint. Although I am not advocating any particular brand of paint, some companies have earned a solid reputation for high-quality paint. PPG, House of Kolor, DuPont, and 3M are a few of the top brands available.

As with most aspects of car restoration, you get what you pay for, and painting a car is a sizable investment. The cost of the paint materials is usually tied to the quality of the materials. Don't cut corners; buy the highest-quality paint you can afford. The prep and labor to apply the paint is the same regardless of the type of paint you are using. Currently, the most popular paints are acrylic enamels and urethane paints, but other options are certainly available.

Prime Time

After the car is properly taped, you apply primer. I recommend a high-quality primer, such as PPG DP50LF, because it is a light-sanding epoxy primer.

Just prior to spraying the primer, wipe down the body with Prep-Sol to make sure all contaminants are removed. The oils from your fingers can create areas where the primer does not stick; this is known as lift. Anywhere that your fingers and body came in contact with the car body while taping may not become apparent until well after the car is painted and assembled. Yes, it is critical that the body be clean!

The clear coat has been applied to this Macho Trans Am in the booth.

PAINTING

After the primer is dry, sand with a Dura-Block sanding block and 600-grit wet sandpaper. The 600-grit makes the panel really smooth to the touch. Be sure the body has no imperfections. The paint job makes every imperfection very visible if the block sanding process is not done properly. You need a can or two of black spray enamel for the guide coat. Spray a mist of black all over the primed areas.

Reapply black spray enamel and sand the panel again to make sure it is arrow-straight. This process can be extremely time consuming, but it makes a huge difference to the finished product. This is where the amount of work that went into the restoration shows because the results are stunning.

The primer application process is really quite simple. Apply light coats and do not try to cover or hide all of the bodywork in one pass. After about three light coats, you should start seeing a uniform gray color throughout. On the fourth and then fifth coats, the application should be a bit thicker. You will block sand the primer so make sure that you have enough material to work with.

Let it dry thoroughly. Leave the tape and paper on for the block sanding process.

You block sand as before, panel-by-panel. As you complete each panel, you will see if you cut through the primer or if black paint is left behind. If you sand through the primer, bare metal or bodywork is evident, which means you have a high spot. The high spot has to be knocked down either by more sanding or performing metalwork to level the area.

If you see black paint, you have a low spot. That requires using spot putty or icing to level out the low spot.

Whether you have corrected a low or high spot, it is necessary to finish sand the areas and reapply primer.

Color Coat Process

Now that all the preparation is done and the primer has been block sanded, it is time to start seeing the results of all your hard work. This and

If you decided to use a base/clear system, you need to choose driver-quality or top-level application. The processes are similar with the exception of sanding between the color and clear coat for the top-level job. If you choose a driver-quality paint job, once the color coat is finished, you can go straight through to clear coat.

Mix the paint in a measuring cup according to the instructions on the can. Remember that the shop air temperature affects paint. Using proper equipment such as respirators, a fresh air system, and proper ventilation all affect the outcome of your paint job.

CHAPTER 5

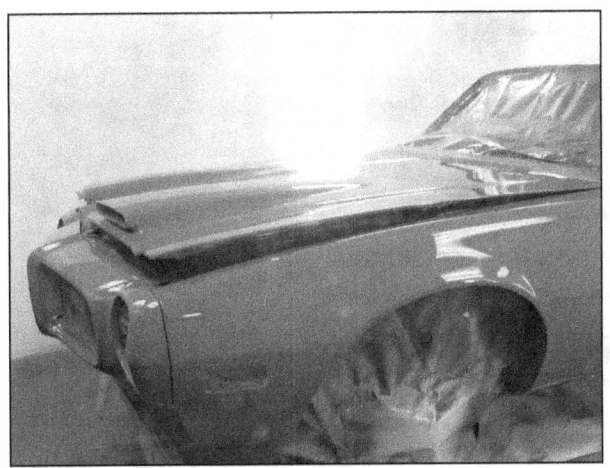

Once the clear is applied anything left over in the color is sealed in. The clear process is pretty much the same as the color coat process. I commonly use a PPG product (DBU 2021) that costs more than $400 without the chemical additives. The clear is mixed in a plastic measuring cup and is subject to ambient temperature.

The spray techniques include applying a very light coat on the first pass. The second and third coats are applied a little heavier after allowing sufficient time to dry. This is known as "flash." The average time to allow the paint to flash between coats is 15 minutes at 70 degrees. (If the temperature is warmer or colder you need to adjust according to information in the product literature.) The fourth coat should be applied the heaviest. This coat receives many wet sandings and polishings.

When you are sanding you are removing material. When you are polishing you are heating the material so you need enough material present to not burn through the clear.

If you want a top-level paint job you lay on a fourth coat of clear a bit heavier because of the wet sandings to come. It is common for the final coat of clear to run. These runs are not a problem as they sand out in the wet sanding process.

After the paint has dried sufficiently it is time to wet sand. I generally wait several days after painting in warm weather. I often put the car outside in the sun and allow it to bake naturally. In colder temperatures I advise waiting at least a couple of months before starting the wet sanding process. You begin at with 1000-grit. Using the same type of Durablock as before wet sand each panel while keeping the panel and paper wet during the entire process. It is a messy job. Do not wet sand without using the block as the curves of your fingers will make indentations in the paint that you will not see until after the car is polished. I do not advocate using power wet sanders because you can't "feel" the surface as you sand. I also believe that they lead to inconsistent sanding that makes the paint job look splotchy.

After you have completed the 1000-grit stage, clean the car thoroughly. Make sure all of the sanding sludge in the cracks, crevices, and gaps are completely removed. Once that sludge dries it acts like concrete. You do not want to be chipping away concretelike slabs on your beautiful new paint job.

The next step is to start all over with 1500-grit wet sandpaper and a block. Repeat the entire process. Depending on the level of shine you are after you can stop here for most driver-quality paint jobs. If you are looking for the deepest shine possible then continue with 2000-grit sandpaper and a block. Repeat the process. Next is to use the same techniques with 3000-grit. If you want to go further use a 5000-grit sandpaper. Repeat the process. Clean the car extremely well after this as you do not want any sanding residue during your polishing processes.

every succeeding step require skill and patience because any mistake will be obvious and could potentially require the process to be redone. Because you should have already decided what paint you want, the next step is to make your car ready for the first coat of paint. If you chose a single-stage paint, there is really nothing else to do once you are ready to spray.

Every paint manufacturer has its own set of instructions and they should be followed to the letter. These companies spend millions of dollars to develop these products and the instructions are created by engineers who know how these chemicals react at every step of the process: from the time you mix them to the time they have dried on your car.

Using an HVLP spray gun greatly reduces the amount of material used and actually directs more material onto the car than into the air. Generally speaking, you should not use more than 2 quarts of color, and you should only need to spray three or four color coats.

The only exception is the 1978 Solar Gold cars, as that color does not cover as well. Solar Gold can require substantially more material because of its composition. Trans Am models use at least a quart more because of the flares, scoops, and spoilers.

Clear Coat Process

Before applying the clear coat, check the base (color) coat before spraying, even if you are not sanding the color coat as you would for a top-level paint job. This is the time to check for any bugs, hair, dust, runs, or any other contaminants before applying clear. These problems can be sanded out once the base coat has dried after 15 minutes or so (depending on booth temperature) and, if necessary, resprayed.

However, once the clear coat is applied, the color is sealed.

The clear coat process is very similar to the color coat process. Following is an overview of this process and techniques.

Apply a very light coat on the first pass. Allow this coat to dry, or flash.

The average paint flash time between coats is 15 minutes at 70 degrees F. If your temperature is warmer or colder, you need to adjust accordingly. (Information in the paint literature explains how to adjust specific flash times.)

Apply the second and third coats a little heavier.

The fourth coat should be the heaviest. This is the coat that receives many wet sandings and polishings. When you are sanding, you are removing material. When you are polishing, you are heating the material so you need enough material to not burn through the clear.

For a top-level paint job, I lay on the fourth coat of clear even a bit heavier. It is common for the final coat of clear to run. These runs are not a problem as they sand out in the wet-sanding process.

After the fourth layer has dried sufficiently, it is time to wet sand.

You have the option of stopping at 1500- or 2000-grit paper depending on how deep you want your paint to look. Darker colors benefit more from really fine grits, whereas light colors do not.

Wet Sanding

Once the clear coat has thoroughly dried (at least 72 hours) you can begin wet sanding. If you are going for a driver-quality result you may have to only lightly sand the clear to remove any dust or imperfections in the paint. If you are going for a top-level paint job you will wet sand multiple times.

The procedure is the same as previously outlined. You must start with a coarser grit (800) and move to finer grits at each stage.

I generally wait several days after painting when the weather is warm. I often put the car outside in the sun and allow it to bake naturally. In colder temperatures, I advise waiting at least a couple of months before starting the wet sanding process.

Again using a Dura-Block, sand each panel while keeping the panel and the paper wet during the entire process. It is a messy job. Do not wet sand without using the block because the curve of your fingers make indentations in the paint that you will not see until after the car is polished.

I do not advocate using power wet sanders because you cannot feel the surface as you sand. I also believe they lead to inconsistent sanding, which makes the paint job look splotchy.

After you have completed the 1000-grit stage, clean the car thoroughly. Make sure all of the sanding sludge in the cracks, crevices, and gaps is completely cleaned out. Once that sludge dries, it's like concrete. You do not want to be chipping away concrete-like slabs on your beautiful new paint job.

The next step is to repeat the sanding process with 1500-grit wet sandpaper and a block.

Depending on the level of shine you want, you can stop here for most driver-quality paint jobs. If you want the deepest shine possible, sand again with 2000-grit sandpaper and a block.

If you want a top-level or concours paint job the next step is to repeat the process with 3000-grit paper using the same techniques. If you want to go even further, sand again with a 5000-grit sandpaper.

Cleaning the car extremely well after the complete sanding process is critical. You do not want any sanding residue when you begin the polishing process.

Polishing and Hand Glazing

Once you have completed the wet sandings to the necessary grit level, it is time to polish the paint finish. Polishing requires skill and you need to follow a process.

Starting with the coarsest-grit compound, you must be sure that you don't allow the polisher to stay in one place too long, and do not exert too much pressure on it. Both are key to a successful polish. A wool pad is also necessary for this step.

As in every previous step, working panel by panel is the way to go. Polishing the top of the car is far easier because you don't have to fight against the weight of the polishing machine. The sides create interesting challenges thanks to all of the Firebird's curves. Holding a 14-pound machine on its side while applying some pressure and getting to every angled surface but not burning through the paint requires tenacity.

After polishing make sure the body dries thoroughly, and then remove the tape and masking paper so the edges can dry.

Finally, you hand-glaze the body. Use a product such as 3M Imperial Hand Glaze (PN 05990). As the name suggests, this is applied by hand. Use the same panel-by-panel approach. With a soft cloth or foam pad, apply the glaze with some force. Then, using a microfiber cloth, remove the glaze as you complete each panel. Do not apply the glaze in direct sunlight.

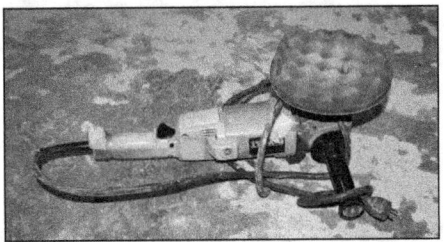

A good-quality polisher is a must to properly complete the paint job. These are obtainable at almost any tool supply store. The polisher is a heavy piece of equipment and requires guidance so it does not burn through the paint. Although the weight of the polisher is not a factor for the top surfaces, it makes polishing the curved side panels much more difficult. Be sure the pressure is consistent for an even shine.

Once you have finished polishing the paint, it is time to thoroughly clean the body, especially the crevices. When these compounds harden, they are like concrete and are difficult to remove.

After the initial compounding, change to a foam waffle pad such as this 3M pad (PN 05723). Use a polish such as 3M Perfect It Ultra Fine Machine Polish (PN 06068).

Once you are finished, the results of this process are evident. With a high-quality paint job, you can see the reflections of the scenery as if you were looking in a mirror. Another test is to look at your face in the paint, and if you can see every detail, that's good. Any other type of paint job would have orange peel and lower reflections.

CHAPTER 6

ENGINE REBUILDING

Pontiac installed a variety of engines in Firebird and Trans Am models over their 11-year production run: everything from the anemic Chevrolet inline 6-cylinder all the way up to the powerhouse 400 Ram Air III and IV as well as 455 Super Duty engines. The 403-ci Oldsmobile engines were slotted inside these cars also. Firebirds and Trans Ams fitted with the special high-performance engines command the highest values, but certainly the more common Firebird and Trans Am V-8 cars are worth rebuilding.

Pontiac made some of the best V-8 street engines from the muscle car era. Most V-8 engines in Firebirds and Trans Ams spooled out a lot of torque so they were ideally set up for street driving. And it was one of the reasons that Pontiac created such a well-rounded and fun driving package.

Through the Years

Most of the Firebirds being restored today are the performance versions of the Formula and Trans Am. Over the years, many different engines were slotted into the second-generation Pontiac F-Body. The early years saw only Pontiac engines in the 400- and 455-ci sizes. In 1977 the 403 Oldsmobile engine appeared, wheezing its 185 hp. Although technically a big-block engine, the 185 hp was about the same as a base engine in a Corvette. Coupled with a 2.56:1 rear axle ratio and weighing more than 3,800 pounds, it wasn't much of a stoplight performer!

The 301 light-cast engine was introduced as an effort to increase the fuel economy standards. The turbo version of the 301 was introduced in 1980 after the 400 was discontinued in 1979.

The 305 Chevrolet engine was made available in 1980 and 1981 as a performance engine. With a long oil

The engine is being moved into position for installation. This W72 400-ci engine has 9.5:1 and produces more than 350 hp at the rear wheels. Use care when moving the engine into position so you don't damage any vital components or the firewall. When performing the work, it's best to have someone move the engine hoist and lower the engine while another person steadies and guides the engine into position at the motor mounts.

CHAPTER 6

This 1979 Trans Am engine compartment contains an optional L37 301-ci V-8. If you wanted a 4-speed manual transmission, you had to get the L37 or the 400-ci engine. The 301 was a credit option, and that means you received a deduction (or credit) off the sticker price for ordering it. In 1979, Pontiac produced 1,530 Trans Ams with the L37 301 engine, 4-speed, and T-Top CC1 option.

fill neck in front of it, the Oldsmobile engine is easily identifiable.

Originally, the factory labeled the shaker as a T/A 6.6 when equipped with the Pontiac 400 engine, and when equipped with the 403 Oldsmobile engine, the shaker received a 6.6 Litre decal. Over the years, the replacement decals were changed so you cannot believe the shaker callout. The VIN designation of K is the 403 Oldsmobile engine while Z designates the 400 Pontiac engine.

Rebuilding an Oldsmobile engine versus rebuilding a Pontiac engine is not really that different as far as a machine shop is concerned. There are no real differences whether you are rebuilding a Ram Air III, IV, SD 455, or base 400 engine. Rebuild kits are available from most performance retailers, including Jegs or Summit Racing.

Rebuilding the 301 Turbo is difficult as hardly any parts are available. Performance upgrade parts are almost nonexistent. Rebuild kits for the 301 and the 301 Turbo are difficult to find, if you can find them at all.

Squeezing performance out of the 403 is certainly possible. Mondello Performance sells the necessary parts to wake up the 403 and make it run like some of its 455 cousins did back in the day.

Bear in mind that all of the engines during the Firebird's run can benefit from port matching, carburetor tuning, distributor advance, and exhaust sizing improvements. This is true whether you have a Pontiac 301, 400, 455, SD 455, Chevrolet 305, or even an Oldsmobile 403. Even more gains can be made if keeping the stock appearance under the hood is not the priority. Numerous performance parts are available for the Pontiac engines (except the 301), Oldsmobile, and, as you probably are well aware, the Chevrolet engine.

The 455 Oldsmobile engine bolts in right in place of the 403; the 350 Chevrolet engine bolts in right in where the 305 resides.

By 1981, performance was all but gone. The Trans Am and the Corvette were the top contenders when you looked at performance numbers. The second-generation Firebird was still portly and Pontiac's attempts at weight loss were not working out too well. By comparison, the four-door Bonneville weighed 100 pounds less in 1981.

Engine Identification

Many Pontiac engines have lived demanding and less-than-ideal lives. Whether because of abuse, neglect, or internal component failure, many Firebirds and Trans Ams do not have their original engines. Some engines were yanked in favor of service replacement blocks, but you can't simply assume that your car has its original block. You need to identify the engine so you can formulate a rebuild plan. Each engine has certain individual aspects that are different and need to be taken into account.

For example, look at the rear edge of the block to locate the block casting number. The date code for the Pontiac V-8s is found at the back of the block near the driver-side cylinder bank and distributor hole. The block casting number is found behind the passenger-side cylinder bank at the rear of the block.

All engines installed in the Firebird have a block code. The block code tells you the engine and

ENGINE REBUILDING

application. You cannot, however, let these codes be the sole determining factor as to whether you have the correct engine in your Firebird. These codes were reused every year. For example, a 1970 YZ code is a 400-ci Ram Air III 345-hp engine, but in 1972 the YZ code designated a 400-ci 2-barrel 200-hp engine. Definitely a big difference!

Deciphering a Pontiac engine means you need to look at several numbers. The casting number is on the passenger's side of the block, on the back side. The date code and last two numbers of the year are near the distributor opening. The block code is on the front, below the passenger's side of the head. The VIN, located on the engine pad near the lower pulley is the final check.

Because a number of restamps exist, it is important to piece together all of the information to make sure everything is accurate. The block code is a two-digit number until 1979 on Pontiac engines (three-digits after 1979). Immediately above the code is the engine unit number, which is either six or seven characters. Remember, these numbers have nothing to do with the VIN. Block codes beginning with "W" are manual transmission vehicles and "Y" codes are for automatics. However, there are always exceptions to this rule.

In 1970, Pontiac revised the motor-mount bosses in the Firebird blocks to have five mounting holes; not all of them were tapped. The exception is the 1978 and 1979 400 blocks. They did not have the rear part of the motor mount openings at all.

The Firebirds that came equipped with the 403 Oldsmobile engine have the VIN and casting number in a different location. The VIN is located on the driver's side of the block front just below the head and behind the power steering. The casting number is on the top of the engine just behind the oil filler tube. In 1979 the Olds engine code was placed on the driver-side rocker cover on a bar-coded label.

Rebuilding Considerations

Few other engines enjoyed more interchangeability than the Pontiac V-8. Heads, intakes, internals, and exhaust manifolds swap between the 350, 400, and 455 with relative ease, but that also means a lot of engines have a lot of non-original parts on them. Before you endeavor to rebuild your Pontiac engine, you need to honestly and accurately assess your mechanical ability, workshop space, and necessary tools.

Most mechanically inclined car owners can competently rebuild an engine. Certainly, if it's your first and you take a thorough and methodical approach, you can rebuild the engine yourself. Of course, the machining work, crank straightening, or any other necessary machine work needs to be handled by a qualified machine shop. But don't kid yourself; it takes exceptional attention to detail and procedures must be followed methodically.

You must take the type of engine into consideration before you decide to do the rebuild yourself. Rare collector engines deserve professional rebuilds by shops. In my estimation, a professional should rebuild exceptionally rare and valuable engines, such as the 400 RA III, 400 RAIV, and 455 Super Duty. If you're a skilled engine builder and you've rebuilt several Pontiac V-8 engines (Firebirds, GTOs, or other Pontiacs), you have the experience and the knowledge to tackle virtually any engine-rebuilding project.

The engine in your Pontiac Firebird or Trans Am may not be original. When engines failed under warranty in a Firebird or Trans Am, service replacement engines were installed in their place. That means the block numbers do not match the VIN numbers.

Many Firebird and Trans Am V-8 cars were driven very aggressively through the years; after all, they were muscle cars. When these cars were used and abused, engines could be over-revved, worn out, or just neglected, which led to an engine failure. When this was the case, many of the engines were swapped out for something non-original.

You need to properly identify the engine under the hood before you start the rebuilding process. Once you have accurately identified the engine, you should conduct a thorough inspection and then evaluate your ability to meet the requirements of the engine-building process.

Crate Engine

Rebuilding the stock or existing Firebird or Trans Am engine is not the only option. If the car is going to be a rarely driven show car, and you have a numbers-matching engine, you should have the engine rebuilt and installed.

On the other hand, you can select a complete long-block crate engine that comes with a warranty. It's an excellent option if you're restoring a car as a weekend or daily driver and you don't want to pile up miles on the original engine. You can put the

CHAPTER 6

Firebird and Trans Am Engine Codes

1970 Pontiac 400
Manual
- WW   Ram Air IV, 370 hp, round-port heads
- WS   Ram Air III, 345 hp
- WT   330 hp

Automatic
- XP   Ram Air IV, 370 hp, round-port heads
- YS   330 hp
- YZ   Ram Air III, 345 hp

1971 Pontiac 400
Manual
- WT   300 hp, 3-speed
- WK   300 hp, 4-speed

Automatic
- XX   180 hp, 2-barrel
- YS   300 hp

1971 Pontiac 455
Manual
- WL   335 hp, HO round-port heads with 3-speed
- WC   335 hp, HO round-port heads with 4-speed

Automatic
- YC   325 hp
- YE   335 hp, round-port heads

1972 Pontiac 400
Manual
- WK   250 hp

Automatic
- YX   200 hp, 2-barrel
- YZ   200 hp, 2-barrel
- ZX   200 hp, 2-barrel, California
- YS   250 hp
- YT   250 hp

1972 455 HO
Manual
- WD   300 hp
- WM   300 hp

Automatic
- YE   300 hp
- YB   300 hp

1973 Pontiac 400
Manual
- WP   230 hp, unitized distributor
- WS   230 hp
- Y6   230 hp
- YG   230 hp

Automatic
- YZ   170 hp, 2-barrel, High Altitude
- ZK   170 hp, 2-barrel, California
- ZX   170 hp, 2-barrel, California
- YX   185 hp, 2-barrel
- X4   185 hp, 2-barrel
- X3   185 hp, 2-barrel
- W5   185 hp, 2-barrel
- Y3   230 hp, Unitized distributor
- YS   230 hp
- XX   230 hp
- XK   230 hp
- XN   230 hp

1973 Pontiac 455
Manual
- WW   250 hp
- WT   250 hp
- ZZ   250 hp
- ZE   250 hp

Automatic
- YK   250 hp, High Altitude
- YD   250 hp
- YC   250 hp
- YA   250 hp
- X7   250 hp
- XM   250 hp
- XE   250 hp
- XL   250 hp

1973 Pontiac 455 Super Duty
Manual
- ZJ   290 hp

Automatic
- XD   290 hp

1974 Pontiac 400
Manual
- Y3   225 hp
- WT   225 hp
- WR   225 hp

Automatic
- YF   2-barrel, 175 hp unless with dual exhaust, 190 hp
- YH   2-barrel, 175 hp unless with dual exhaust, 190 hp
- AD   2-barrel, 175 hp unless with dual exhaust, 190 hp
- AH   175 hp, unless with dual exhaust, 190 hp
- ZJ   AIR 2-barrel, 175 hp unless with dual exhaust, 190 hp
- ZK   2-barrel, 175 hp unless with dual exhaust, 190 hp
- YL   200 hp
- YM   200 hp
- YT   200 hp
- YZ   200 hp
- A3   200 hp
- AT   200 hp
- ZS   200 hp
- ZT   200 hp

1974 455
Automatic
- Y9   250 hp
- A4   250 hp
- Z4   250 hp
- YY   250 hp
- AU   250 hp
- ZU   250 hp
- YW   250 hp
- ZW   250 hp

112 TRANS AM & FIREBIRD RESTORATION

ENGINE REBUILDING

1974 455 Super Duty
Manual
W8   290 hp

Automatic
Y8   290 hp

1975 Pontiac 400
Manual
WT   185 hp

Automatic
YS   185 hp

1975 455
Manual
WX   200 hp

1976 Pontiac 400
Manual
WT   185 hp

Automatic
YS   185 hp
YZ   185 hp
XZ   185 hp, AIR

1976 455
Manual
WX   200 hp

1977 Pontiac 400
Manual
WA   200 hp, W72

Automatic
XA   180 hp
Y6   200 hp, W72

1977 Oldsmobile 403
U2   185 hp, High Altitude
U3   185 hp, High Altitude
VA   185 hp
VB   185 hp

1978 Pontiac 400
Manual
WC   220 hp, W72

Automatic
YA   180 hp
YU   180 hp
X7   220 hp, W72

1978 403 Oldsmobile
U2   185 hp, High Altitude
U3   185 hp, High Altitude
U5   185 hp, High Altitude
U6   185 hp, High Altitude
VJ   185 hp
VK   185 hp
VL   185 hp
VN   185 hp

1979 Pontiac 400
Manual
PWH   220 hp W72

1979 403 Oldsmobile
QE   185 hp
QJ   185 hp
QL   185 hp
TB   185 hp, California
TD   185 hp, California
TE   185 hp, California

1979 Pontiac 301
Manual
PWB   150 hp
PWA   150 hp

1979 Pontiac 301
Automatic
PX7   135 hp, 2-barrel
PXF   135 hp, 2-barrel
PX9   135 hp, 2-barrel
PXH   135 hp, 2-barrel
PXP   135 hp, 2-barrel
PXR   135 hp, 2-barrel
PXL   150 hp
PXS   150 hp
PXN   150 hp
PXT   150 hp
PXU   150 hp
PX4   150 hp
PX6   150 hp
PXW   150 hp

1980 Pontiac 301
4-Barrel Automatic
XT   140 hp
XW   140 hp
X3   140 hp
X9   140 hp
XN   140 hp
YN   155 hp, W72
YR   155 hp, W72

1980 Pontiac Turbocharged 301
YL   210 hp

1980 Chevrolet 305
Automatic
CEC   150 hp
CEL   150 hp
CEM   150 hp
CMM   150 hp
CEH   150 hp
CMR   150 hp

1981 Pontiac 301
4-Barrel Automatic
WBD   150 hp
WBJ   150 hp

1981 Pontiac 301
Turbocharged Automatic
WBO   200 hp

1981 Chevrolet 305
Manual
DHZ   145 hp, 49-state emissions
DHU   145 hp, California

original or stock engine on an engine stand and store it in your garage. And at a later date, it can be rebuilt and re-installed in the car.

When to Rebuild

Sometimes it's readily apparent that the engine needs to be rebuilt and sometimes it's not. Obvious evidence is blue smoke from the exhaust, knocking sounds, white smoke from the exhaust, or a seized engine. All are signs that a rebuild is necessary. Having a shop perform a compression test or leak-down test can also determine whether your engine needs a rebuild.

Sometimes an engine runs perfectly well but has low compression because it is worn out and is simply in need of an overhaul. Rebuilding an engine requires expertise and specialty tools that cost beyond what a quality engine rebuild would cost. Pontiac engines are best built by shops that specialize in Pontiacs because of their unique characteristics.

If you choose to have a professional shop rebuild your Pontiac or Oldsmobile V-8 in your Firebird, you also receive a warranty on your rebuild, which can be invaluable should there be a failure. Failures do occur and not always due to the shop's work. Parts today are sometimes of dubious quality and bad batches do occur. If a small part fails and causes a failure, the machine shop bears the responsibility. Even a small part failure can have catastrophic consequences. Some things are just worth paying for.

Because all Pontiac engines look pretty much the same, it is important to be able to identify the particular engine that is in your Firebird. However, do not rely solely on the casting

Firebird and Trans Am Block Casting Numbers

9799914	1970 Ram Air III
9799915	1970 Ram Air IV
483677	1971 and 1972 455 HO
481988	1971, 1972, 1973, and 1974 400
485428	1973 and 1974 base 455
490132	1973 and 1974 455 Super Duty
488986/500557	1975 400
500557	1976 400
500813	1975 and 1976 455
568577	1977–1979 400
481988	1978 and 1979 W72 400

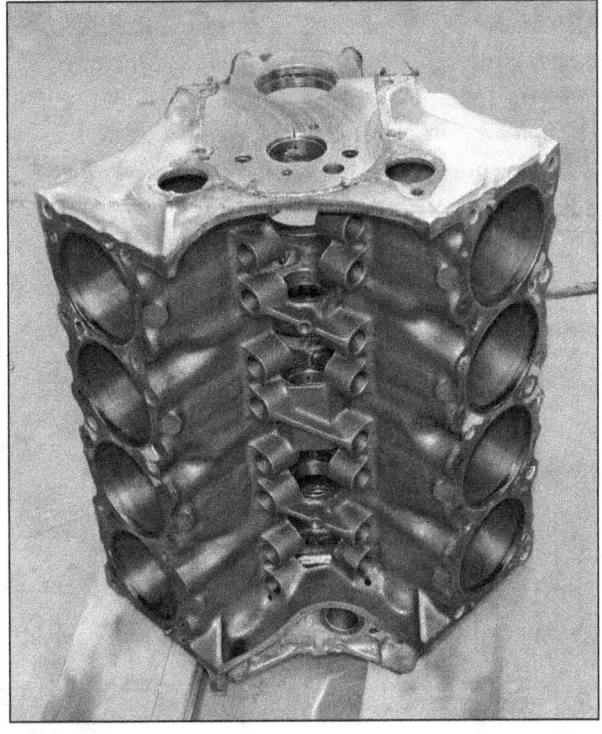

This Ram Air III 400 block has been dismantled and prepared for the machine shop to start the rebuilding process. The Ram Air III engine was used for the 1970 model year only.

Rebuilding Source Material

Several books are available that explain the rebuilding process in detail. Rocky Rotella's *How to Rebuild Pontiac V-8s* explains each crucial step of the rebuild process so you can confidently rebuild your own engine. It focuses on a stock rebuild with upgraded aftermarket parts.

If you're planning to build a high-performance Pontiac V-8 engine, Rocky Rotella has also written *How to Build Max-Performance Pontiac V-8s*. It's an excellent resource if you're going to build a high-performance street engine.

ENGINE REBUILDING

Pontiac engines have their displacement cast into the side of the block as this 428 shows. The 428 was never available in the Firebird lineup.

This casting indicates a 455 block, which had a long and illustrious life in Firebirds and Trans Ams. Pontiac installed the 7-liter engine from 1971 to 1976.

The Turbocharged 301 is a lightweight cast engine, which was not particularly durable. Most other Pontiac engines do not interchange their parts with this engine. The parts availability for the 301 is almost nonexistent. Before you embark on an engine rebuild, I advise you to locate as many common rebuild parts as possible. This will shorten the shop time while they wait for parts.

I also suggest you find a piston manufacturer that is willing to custom build a set of pistons in advance for you. It is not far-fetched to think that your 301 will need pistons. The only question is what size overbore will your engine require? The machine shop will not be able to give you that answer until disassembly at a minimum, but you may have to wait until they bore the block.

At the midway point in the rebuild process, you need to remove the rotating assembly and cam from the block. The main bearing caps need to measured and inspected for oil starvation and excessive wear or any damage. The connecting rods can be Magnafluxed and reused, but if you're going through the rebuild process, I recommend installing new rods. The crankshaft journals should be measured with a micrometer to see if they are within spec or need machining. And the crank needs to be measured for run out.

The intake, valley pan, and valvecovers have been removed so you can see the valley and valvetrain. Also visible are the stamped-steel standard-ratio roller rockers. This is another subtle upgrade that fits under the stock valvecovers. Roller rockers provide less resistance, which means that the engine has less friction. Less friction means more horsepower. Using a roller cam, roller timing chain, and roller rocker arms are all upgrades that are not visible when assembled.

CHAPTER 6

When you remove the rotating assembly from the block, you need to closely inspect the block for core shift, cracks on the deck area, and any cracks or damage around the lifter area. The piston and rod in this particular case seems to be in good shape so the engine didn't suffer catastrophic damage. However, the cylinder bore has some scuffing and scoring.

The rod bearings and caps attach at the rear of the crankshaft. The rear main seal also is installed here.

This engine has been professionally rebuilt. It has been flipped over on the engine stand, and the windage tray and oil pump have been installed.

Parts Sources

Maintaining the stock exterior appearance of the engine, yet increasing the performance, can be done in a number of ways. Many engine rebuilders specialize in Pontiac engines, including RaceKrafters in Lancaster, Pennsylvania; Butler Performance in Lawrenceburg, Tennessee; and Spotts Performance in Hatfield, Pennsylvania. Pontiac specialty machine shops can greatly enhance the performance by doing as little work as increasing the compression ratio to as much work as installing stroker crankshaft kits to increase the displacement and torque. Pontiacs respond really well from having the heads ported and polished, along with the intake manifold and exhaust ports. The ability to breathe is paramount, especially in a Pontiac engine.

When it comes to heads, several manufacturers offer excellent-quality products for Pontiac V-8s. SD Performance offers a cast-iron CNC-ported head. The company has developed many custom programs to effectively CNC port nearly every D-port Pontiac head.

Kauffman Racing Equipment also makes a fine D-port aluminum cylinder head for the street market. These particular heads are suitable for D-port exhaust headers, and the port volume is somewhat small so the heads retain port velocity for excellent street torque characteristics.

Edelbrock offers cylinder heads for virtually every engine platform. It also offers high-flow Pontiac aluminum cylinder heads. According to Edelbrock, they are patterned after the Ram Air IV heads. These Edelbrock heads are fitted with 2.11/1.66-inch valves, rated to 0.575-inch valve lift and for a flat-tappet cam setup.

Butler Performance also offers a selection of mildly ported Edelbrock heads for Pontiac. These heads deliver exceptional street performance because they are dialed into a particular engine specification and requirement. ∎

ENGINE REBUILDING

number as proof of having the original engine simply because the numbers match. The block casting number is just the first step to verification. It is located on the passenger's side of the block behind the right head.

The basic Pontiac block is a robust piece of iron. The block has the same exterior dimensions whether it is a 326, 350, 389, 400, 428, or a 455. The bore (size of the piston holes in the block) and stroke (crankshaft) determine the cubic-inch displacement. Almost all parts interchange among the different engines. For example, you can install 400 6X heads on a 350 and vice versa. The 1970 and up Firebird engines received a different motor-mounting boss.

Original Appearance Is Key

Pontiac engines really were not much about flash but more about the performance. Restoring the engine requires attention to detail.

Color Matters

Pontiac changed the color of the engines several times. The 1970 Ram Air III and IV engines had chromed valvecovers. The later 1977–1979 W72 engines used poorly chromed valvecovers. The SD 455 engines used engine-colored valvecovers and only added a decal to the left side of the valvecover behind the oil filler cap.

The 1971–1973s used Pontiac Blue non-metallic. Late 1973 and 1974s used Pontiac Blue. The 1975–1977s used Pontiac Blue Metallic, and the 1978–1981s used GM Corporate Blue. All of these paints are available from Ames Performance Engineering.

Numbers Matter

Making the decision to rebuild your engine rather than replace it depends on several factors. Because Pontiac no longer exists, there are no factory-fresh crate engines that other manufacturers support. Instead you have to rely on specialty rebuilders or the aftermarket, which produces blocks and heads of varying sizes and configurations.

If your Firebird has a numbers-matching engine, it would be wise to rebuild it. If you are planning to drive your Firebird and run it hard, it may be a good idea to consider storing the numbers-matching engine and purchase another Pontiac engine to rebuild. Or you can go the resto-mod route by installing a Chevrolet or LS engine.

Internals

The scope of this book does not cover resto-mods. Numerous options are available for building an engine internally for performance enhancements, but that can still remain stock appearing from the outside. Stroker kits are a popular upgrade that increase power but maintain anonymity.

Rebuild versus Upgrade

If your Firebird does not have its original engine, you have to decide if you want a correct engine or an upgrade. A correct engine is the original-displacement engine with the correctly coded block and heads that originally came with your car. In addition, the engine component dates must fall within the two to three months before the build date of your car. It may show a different VIN or be a service replacement block, but other than that, it would be the same engine originally installed in your car.

Any other type of replacement engine is not considered a numbers-matching engine. It is not uncommon to find stroker 400-ci or 455 engines residing in Firebird engine compartments.

Procedure Overview

The whole process of rebuilding an engine is time consuming and tedious. The good news is that most of the attaching hardware is rarely rusted because oil leaks through the years have kept everything well lubricated. Removing the radiator and fan components is covered in Chapter 13 so I will continue from there.

It is necessary to disconnect all wires that attach to the engine. All hoses must be disconnected. Engine oil should be drained, but the oil filter left in place. Remove the A/C compressor (if equipped) and put it to the side. Remove the power steering pump and the steering box hoses.

Disconnect the fuel line feed at the fuel pump and plug it to prevent gas spillage. Disconnect the head pipes at the exhaust manifolds. Remove the motor-mount bolts. Remove the transmission bellhousing bolts. If equipped with an automatic transmission, remove the inspection plate and remove the torque converter bolts.

Now the engine is ready to remove. Using an engine crane, attach a chain to the front eye on the water pump and to the rear of the intake manifold. This is not the only way to attach the engine to the crane; suitable locations may be available at the front and rear of the engine. Another alternative is to use a plate that is designed to bolt to the intake manifold where the carburetor attaches.

Lift the engine using the engine crane jack. It may be necessary to pull the engine forward to clear the transmission input shaft. An alternative process is to remove the transmission before removing the engine.

TRANS AM & FIREBIRD RESTORATION

CHAPTER 6

Remove Engine

1 *Removal of the engine is not a difficult process, but it takes some time and work. Before you start, disconnect the battery and place it in storage. You will find many connectors to disconnect: coolant hoses, transmission lines, engine accessories, vacuum lines, fuel lines, and the transmission. I recommend removing or at least disconnecting the transmission when removing the engine. Removing the engine with the transmission attached is much more difficult, increases the opportunity for damages to the car and the transmission, and usually is very messy.*

Remove Linkage

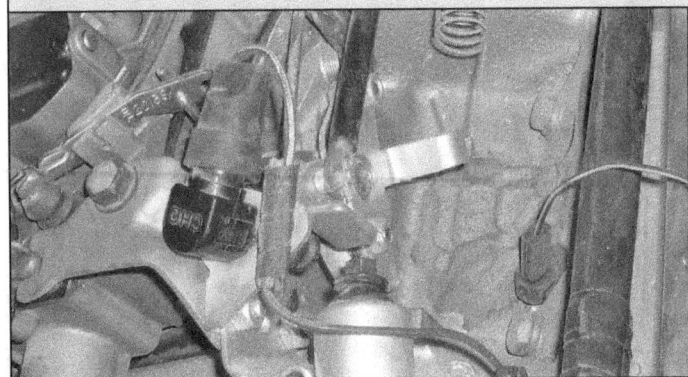

2 *Disconnect throttle linkage, kick-down linkage (if equipped), and shaker solenoid actuator if equipped). The throttle linkage is held on with a washer and cotter pin. The kick-down linkage pops off at the end and is held in at the retaining bracket with a spring clip. Use long-nose pliers to compress the spring clips and then push the cable through the bracket. Remove the shaker solenoid actuator with an open-end wrench. It has a single connector to disconnect from the harness.*

Use Engine Stand

3 *Install the engine onto an engine stand while you're rebuilding it.*

Use Engine Dolly

4 *Once the SD 455 is removed, it's ready to be placed on a four-wheel engine dolly. You can find one through the Internet for less than $100.*

ENGINE REBUILDING

Send Engine to Machine Shop

5 If you want the machine shop to mill the heads and port match, you need to send the intake and exhaust manifolds; they need to match each port to create a smoother flow of air. Whenever a head is milled, it sits lower, which, in turn, makes the intake manifold not sit properly on the head-mating surface unless it is also modified. Pontiac engines make their power in the head so spending the money to have the heads ported and polished is well worth it. Late 1970s 6x heads can be made to flow as well as Super Duty heads.

Paint Engine

6 Pontiac engines were painted many different shades of blue throughout the years. The stock Pontiac blue was used to paint this 400 in a booth. This is more of a custom application than the traditional rattle-can approach. The paint used is an automotive-grade base coat/clear coat just like that used on the body panels.

Clean and Paint Hardware

7 Before the engine is reinstalled, clean and repaint the hardware that was removed. This particular engine is a W72 numbers-matching 400 engine out of a 1979 Trans Am. The engine has been rebuilt, the compression raised to 9.5:1, and the heads and aftermarket Edelbrock intake have been ported and polished along with adding 1.65:1 Harland rockers. This allowed the 220-hp powerplant to make more than 350 hp at the rear wheels on the dyno. The use of this type of rocker arm usually necessitates the taller valvecovers.

Once the engine is back from the machine shop, it requires a degreasing to prep it for paint. The engine may appear clean, but it has a film of oil from the processes involved in rebuilding and reassembly.

Once you have cleaned the surface and removed all oil residue, use a high-temperature primer. Pay particular attention to the center exhaust ports; paint burns here first because of the configuration of the port. You

CHAPTER 6

Install Manual Transmission Components

8 If you have a manual transmission, it is a good idea to install the flywheel, clutch, clutch fork, throwout bearing, and bellhousing before reinstalling. Tubular ceramic-coated headers are a great benefit for achieving additional power. Ceramic coatings help reduce the engine compartment underhood temperatures. Headers can add as much as 40 hp to the rear wheels when connected to a proper exhaust system. I highly recommend Doug's headers as they fit well to clear all of the 4-speed linkages and have provisions for air-conditioning brackets.

Install Engine

9 This engine has been placed on a hoist and rolled into position. Installing the engine is much easier as a two-person project so I recommend having someone operate the engine hoist while another person guides the engine into place and aligns the motor mounts. Be careful and be patient. You don't want the engine to swing too much and bang up the firewall, power steering pump, brake booster, or any other parts.

10 In many cases, you need to move the engine into position inch by inch. Once you have it in position and have the motor-mount bolts threaded, you can start connecting the throttle linkage, coolant hoses, electrical harness, and all the other parts.

can use either automotive-grade paint applied in a booth or rattle-can paint.

The key to removal and installation of your engine is patience and organization. Take pictures of where things are connected prior to removing them. You may not get your engine back from the rebuilder for months and you may not remember every item, especially to how hoses and wires were routed.

I recommend replacing all hoses, mounts, and clamps now. One failure could cause internal damage to the engine or, at a minimum, a mess that is not easy to clean up.

CHAPTER 7

TRANSMISSION REBUILDING

With the right equipment, you can certainly rebuild your Firebird's transmission in your garage. But a professional-caliber rebuild requires specialized tools. You need an arbor press, and you must follow a detailed and comprehensive process.

It may be evident that your automatic or a manual transmission needs rebuilding because common transmission problems are typically easy to spot. They exhibit any number of problems, such as sloppy shifting, slow engagement into gear, leaking from various orifices, and hanging up in gear. Rebuilding the transmission, along with replacing the torque converter, is the only choice to remedy these ailments.

Manual Transmissions

Manual transmissions require specialized tools and knowledge. The Muncie M-20, -21, and -22 were available in the Firebird lineup, but the M-22 is very rare option. Pontiac designated the M-21 on the build sheet, but in many cases, it was actually the BorgWarner Super T-10, which was phased in sometime in the mid-1970s.

Manual transmissions usually require rebuilding after exceptionally high miles and extreme use, such as racing. When rebuilding these transmissions, you find that seals, bearings, and synchronizers have usually reached the end of their service life. Gears rarely fail unless abused, but they do need to be inspected for chipping, excessive wear, and any other potential issues. If your transmission is popping out of gear, grinding into gear, or has significant whining, it may be time for a rebuild. The M-22 transmission had special gears that used a helical cut for strength, but resulted in increased gear noise.

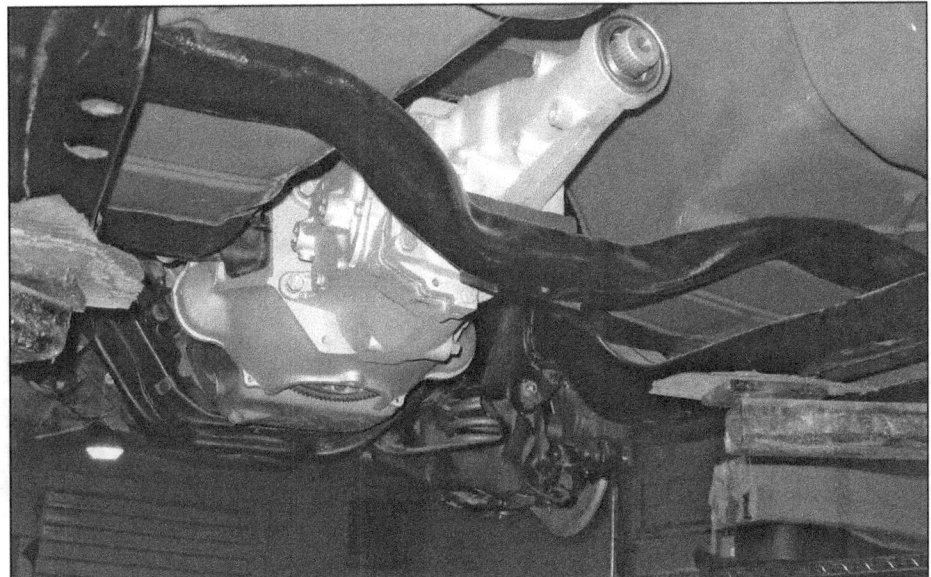

The Muncie M-21 was installed in the 1973 Trans Am. To identify the transmission, refer to the seven-digit serial number that is found on the passenger's side of the case. The serial number codes are provided online. Keep in mind that the casting numbers are Muncie part numbers, not GM part numbers. You find the date code on the side cover. A month designation of 1-12 is shown in one of the two half-inch circles while another circle has the day of manufacture.

CHAPTER 7

This is a Turbo 400 automatic transmission. Notice the rectangular plate located on the side just behind the chain. This plate has the transmission stamping on it to identify the application.

Removing the side cover of the transmission lets you view the condition of the gears. When inspecting the gears, look for any chipped or worn teeth. Generally, the worn teeth have very sharp edges. You also want to look for any color changes in the metal. Blue in the gears is a sign of the transmission having been overheated. Overheating generally results from leaks rendering the transmission low on fluid. Overheating also can indicate hard usage from abuse. If you see any blue, I recommend a complete rebuild and replacement of the affected parts.

So, if any part of the transmission needs repair or replacement, it is a good idea to rebuild the transmission while it is apart. It makes sense, as the labor is essentially the same whether or not you are rebuilding the transmission. If you endeavor to rebuild the transmission yourself, Paul Cangialosi goes into the entire process step-by-step in his book *Muncie 4-Speed Transmissions: How to Rebuild and Modify*.

The removal of either transmission is not difficult. It is best to have a lift available and use a transmission jack. Whether you are removing a manual or automatic transmission, they are both fairly heavy. I do not recommended removal to be performed with just muscle: use mechanical support.

Manual Transmission Removal

The process for removing a Turbo-Hydramatic 350, Turbo-Hydramatic 400, or Muncie 4-speed is similar. It is not all that difficult but is labor intensive. As with other restoration processes, you need to pay attention to how you remove the bolts, take notes, and take plenty of pictures to document the removal process. You will need these tools: a pry bar, 1/4- and 3/8-inch drive ratchet sets, open-end wrenches, and pliers. Following is a general overview of the removal process.

Use a socket and ratchet to remove the retaining nuts and straps on the driveshaft, and then you can remove it. A pry bar may be necessary to push the U-joint assembly out of the rear axle yoke. Slide the shaft out until the front yoke clears the output shaft.

Remove the transmission mount bolts with a socket and ratchet. Use an open-end wrench to disconnect the

TRANSMISSION REBUILDING

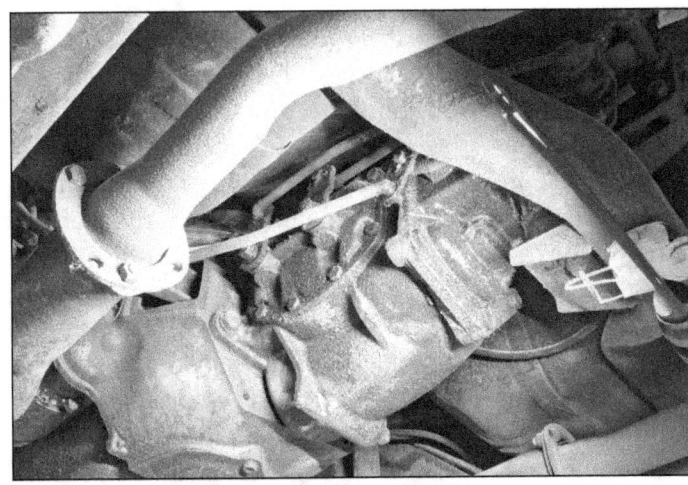
The 4-speed transmission has been installed.

The VIN on a BorgWarner Super T-10 is stamped in the side of the case. This particular Super T-10 was installed in a 1979 Macho Trans Am.

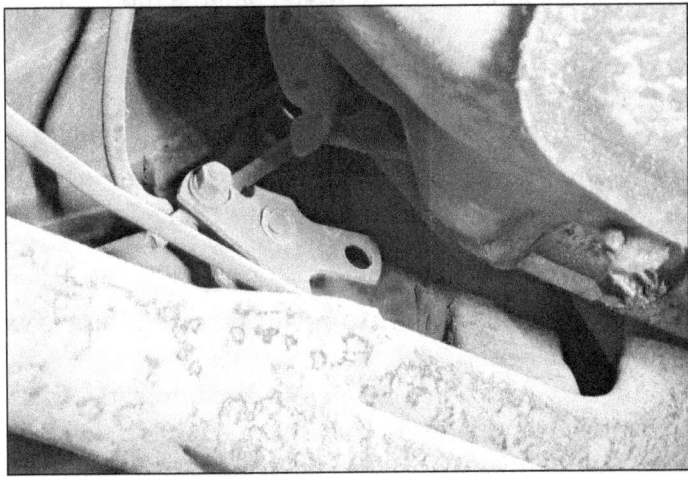
To remove the transmission from the vehicle, use a wrench to loosen the nut that retains the reverse lock-out rod. It's located at the base of the steering column.

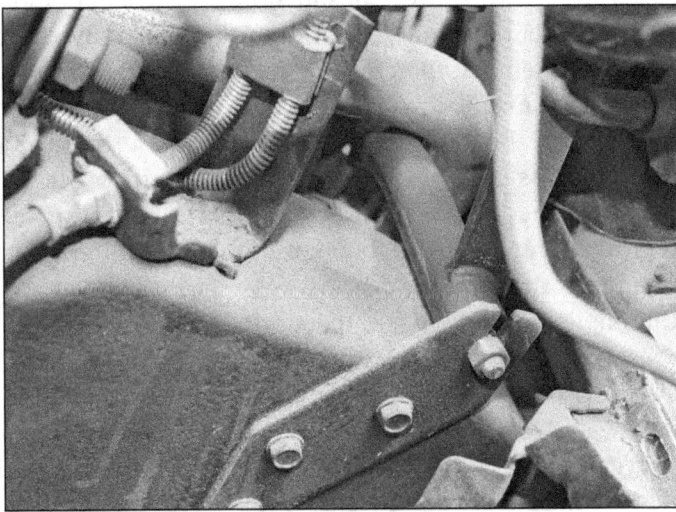
Use a socket and ratchet to disconnect the Z-bar clutch mechanism.

Remove the bolts that connect the transmission to the crossmember.

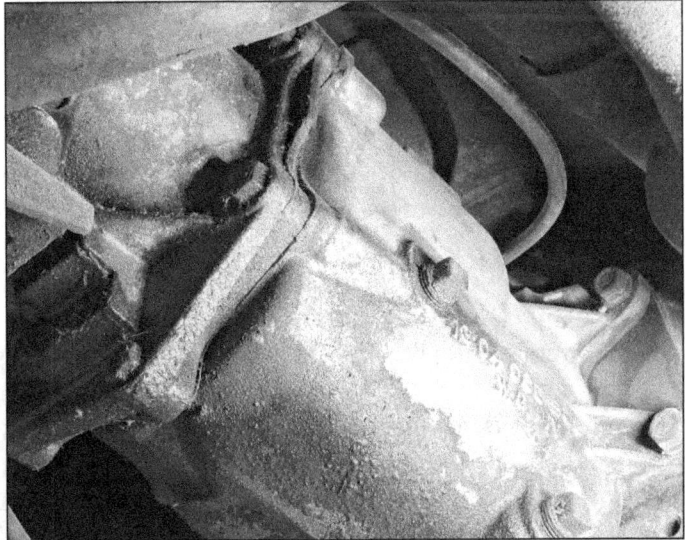
Remove the four bolts that hold the bellhousing to the transmission. Two are on each side on the housing ears.

TRANS AM & FIREBIRD RESTORATION 123

clutch pedal linkage at the clutch fork on the threaded part of the linkage.

Remove the shifter handle in the passenger compartment using a socket and ratchet. You need to push the shifter rubber boot down to access the bolts.

Use a socket and ratchet to remove the bolts that hold the bellhousing to the transmission. Make sure the transmission is properly supported. Place the transmission jack under the transmission and lift it slightly. Remove the transmission crossmember bolts that hold it to the frame and remove the crossmember. Slide the transmission back enough to clear the bellhousing and lower the transmission.

Once the transmission has been removed, remove the bellhousing bolts that attach the transmission to the engine. You need a ratchet and socket along with an extension and possibly a swivel to fully access the bolts.

After those bolts have been removed, pull the bellhousing away from the engine. The clutch assembly can then be removed with a socket and ratchet.

Once the clutch assembly is removed, you have access to the flywheel bolts. Those bolts thread into the back of the engine crankshaft. Remove them with a socket and ratchet. The throwout bearing also needs to slide off the clutch fork. Remove and replace the pilot bearing at this point. Use a flat-blade screwdriver to remove the bearing.

Manual Transmission Installation

Installation is not much different than the removal process. Following is a general procedure overview.

You need a clutch alignment tool to center the clutch properly to the flywheel. Most good-quality clutch kits come with this tool. The flywheel is attached to the engine. I recommend having the flywheel turned at a machine shop to provide a clean, flat surface for the new clutch to operate against. A flywheel is similar to a disc brake rotor. If the brake rotor is contaminated or warped, the brake pads do not operate smoothly or efficiently. The same theory applies to the clutch disc and the flywheel.

You should consider installing a billet flywheel because it weighs much less than the factory flywheel. The lighter flywheel enables the engine to turn faster as it has less weight on it. Make sure you count the ring gear teeth so you have the same number of teeth as on the flywheel you are replacing.

Once the flywheel is installed, install the clutch assembly. Use the enclosed clutch pilot tool to have everything line up properly. Once everything is in line, you can tighten the clutch assembly on the flywheel. It is important to align the clutch because it allows the transmission input shaft to slide in.

After the clutch is properly installed, place the throwout bearing and clutch fork into the bellhousing's side opening. Now you can install the bellhousing to the engine block using the removed bolts. After the bellhousing has been installed, the transmission can be "stabbed," or installed.

The transmission should fit flush against the bellhousing. If it does not go in fairly easy, recheck all your prior work. Do not try to force the transmission in by tightening the bolts against the bellhousing. The transmission ears may crack or, worse, break off.

Finishing Touches

Once the transmission is installed, reconnect the clutch linkage using an open-end wrench. Install the transmission mount to the crossmember using a socket and ratchet. Install the transmission crossmember to subframe bolts using a socket and ratchet on one side and an open-ended wrench.

Go back into the passenger compartment and connect the shifter handle using a socket and ratchet. Make sure you pull the rubber shifter boot back up over the bolts. Install the driveshaft by sliding the yoke onto the transmission output shaft. Place the opposite end into the rear axle yoke and install the retainer straps and bolts using a 1/4-inch ratchet and socket.

Automatic Transmissions

Rebuilding an automatic transmission requires a lot of skill and expensive specialized tools. The cost for an overhaul on a Turbo 350 or 400 with a new torque converter usually costs about $1,200. Given the complexity of removing and installing the transmission, it is a wise decision to have the transmission rebuilt by a professional. A reputable shop usually gives a warranty.

Automatic Transmission Removal

Following is a general procedure overview of the removal process.

First, remove the driveshaft. Then remove the rear U-joint retaining bolts and straps using a socket and ratchet. It may be necessary to use a pry bar to push the U-joint out of the rear axle yoke. Lower the rear of the driveshaft and pull the shaft back until the yoke clears the transmission output shaft.

TRANSMISSION REBUILDING

TH400 versus TH350

Only two automatic transmissions were installed on the second-generation Firebird: the GM Turbo-Hydramatic 400 and the GM Turbo-Hydramatic 350. The Turbo 400 was the more robust transmission and was fitted to a large-displacement engine. The kick down is controlled via an electric switch mounted on the inside of the firewall just above the accelerator pedal arm. The Turbo 350 can be identified by an additional cable attached to the throttle linkage. Both are 3-speed transmissions.

If you want to rebuild either of these transmissions, Cliff Ruggles covers them in detail in his two books *How to Rebuild & Modify GM Turbo 400 Transmissions* and *GM Turbo 350 Transmissions: How to Rebuild & Modify*. In both books, Ruggles, a veteran transmission service professional, provides photos and instructions for completing each crucial step of the transmission, disassembly, inspection, and assembly.

Use a socket and ratchet to remove the transmission mount bolts. Disconnect the shifter. The shifter cable is connected at the shifter arm, which is located on the driver's side of the transmission. Disconnect the reverse lockout rod also attached to the shifter lever by removing the arm retainer nut using an open-ended wrench. Slide the arm away.

If you have a Turbo 350, the kick-down cable needs to be removed at the throttle linkage. Simply compressing the spring clip at the mounting bracket and removing the cotter pin at the throttle arm releases the cable. Remove the transmission inspection plate located on the bottom of the transmission case and around the starter. Remove the torque converter bolts.

You need to rotate the flywheel manually with a large pry bar to gain access to all the torque converter bolts. Remove the bellhousing bolts that attach the transmission to the engine.

Place the transmission jack under the transmission and lift the transmission slightly. Remove the transmission crossmember outer bolts at the frame rails and slide the crossmember out of the way. Move the transmission back enough to disengage the input shaft of the transmission and to clear the flex plate.

Automatic Transmission Installation

Installation is pretty straightforward. If you take notes and take good pictures of the removal process, you will be able to re-install the transmission without much trouble.

You need to be aware of some specific techniques. On the Turbo 350 you want to make sure the kick-down cable is attached inside the transmission valve body area. The other end of the cable needs to be threaded behind the engine to the top of the intake manifold, so it is not in the way during the installation.

Make sure the cooling line nuts are clean and the threads are in good condition. The transmission dipstick tube also should be installed prior to re-installation. Once the transmission is flush against the engine block, slide the transmission crossmember under it to hold it in place.

Install the transmission bellhousing bolts to the engine using a socket and wrench. It may be necessary to use an extension and a swivel to obtain the proper seat on the bolt head. After the bellhousing bolts are about three quarters of the way in, install the torque converter bolts to the flex plate. You can turn the flex plate with a pry bar or a large flat-blade screwdriver. Tighten the bellhousing bolts after the torque converter bolts are tightened.

The transmission cooling lines should be installed at both ends using line wrenches.

Re-install the transmission mount to the transmission crossmember using a socket and ratchet. Attach the shifter cable and lockout rod. Install all electric connectors. Re-install the driveshaft.

Automatic Transmission Fluid

Fill the transmission using Dexron III automatic transmission fluid unless your rebuilder recommends something else.

On stock automatic transmission pans, the Turbo 350 holds 4 quarts of fluid plus the 4 quarts in a stock torque converter. The Turbo 400 holds 6 quarts plus the 4 quarts in a stock torque converter.

These quantities can be different, depending on the size of the transmission pan and torque converter.

CHAPTER 8

DRIVETRAIN

The Camaro and Firebird share many of the same drivetrain components, particularly the rear axle assembly.

As previously noted, transmission choices were minimal. The Firebirds were either equipped with an automatic or 4-speed manual transmission. The rear axle ratios varied depending on engine, transmission, and even sometimes because of options. The drivetrains were durable for the most part. There may be a difference of opinion on the 301 engines as far as their reliability and durability.

Differential

Over its model run, the second-generation Firebird was equipped with the 8.5-inch corporate 10-bolt and corporate 12-bolt differential.

Rebuilding your rear differential at home is suitable for many car owners because this is straight mechanical work. However, you need to pay close attention to details during the process. In addition, you need to rent or buy some specialized tools. If you choose to rebuild your own rear axle assembly at home, Jefferson Bryant's *Chevy Differentials: How to Rebuild the 10- and 12-Bolt* is an excellent guide with lots of detailed information and step-by-step instructions. If you choose to buy a new or reconditioned axle assembly, it comes with a new warranty.

Clutch

For your Firebird to stop without stalling the engine, it needs a way to disconnect from the engine. A clutch is needed because the wheels are not always turning when the engine is turning. The clutch allows a smooth engagement of the engine to the

The corporate 10-bolt rear axle was the mainstay of the second-generation Firebird. It was a robust axle assembly and the available axle ratios varied widely throughout its 11-year run.

DRIVETRAIN

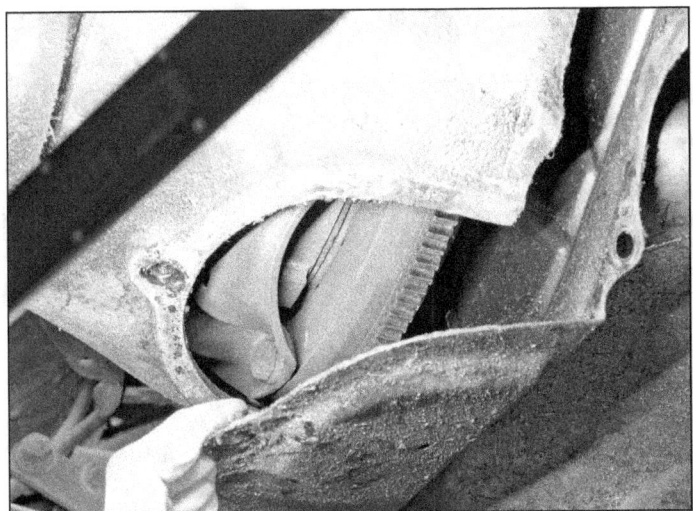

The clutch and pressure plate in a manual-transmission Firebird connects the engine and the transmission.

The bellhousing and clutch are installed along with ceramic-coated headers. The lockout rod is dangling on the left.

transmission by controlling the slippage between them. A clutch works based on friction between the clutch plate and the flywheel.

When the pedal is not depressed, the springs in the pressure plate apply force against the clutch disc, which then applies pressure on the flywheel. This mates the engine to the transmission, making them spin at the same speed. When the clutch pedal is depressed, the clutch linkage moves the clutch fork, which moves the throwout bearing against the diaphragm spring. As the spring is pushed inward, it causes the spring to pull the pressure plate away from the clutch disc. This disconnects the clutch from the engine.

If you hear a noise at idle and it goes away when the clutch pedal is depressed, the problem is most likely between the clutch fork and pivot ball.

Set the parking brake, put the car in neutral, and start the engine. With the Firebird running, listen for a low-pitched noise. If you hear a noise, the issue may be in the transmission.

Slowly push in the clutch pedal while listening for an irregular noise such as a higher-pitched rubbing noise. The noise may sound in rhythm with the engine. If so, you may have a throwout bearing issue.

If you depress the clutch pedal all the way to the floor and hear a squealing noise, you may have a defective pilot bearing or bushing.

If you do not hear noise while performing these techniques, your clutch is probably not the problem.

You could expect to get around 50,000 miles on a clutch. That, of course, depends on how you drive the car. Moreover, habitually driving with your left foot resting on the clutch pedal significantly reduces clutch life.

Checking and keeping the clutch in adjustment also is critical. Self-adjusting or hydraulic clutches are not available in second-generation Firebirds. The friction material on the disc wears out much like a disc brake pad wears and will require adjustment and then replacement when it wears out. Clutch slippage that is not correctable by adjustment is one of the most common signs that it's time to replace the clutch disk.

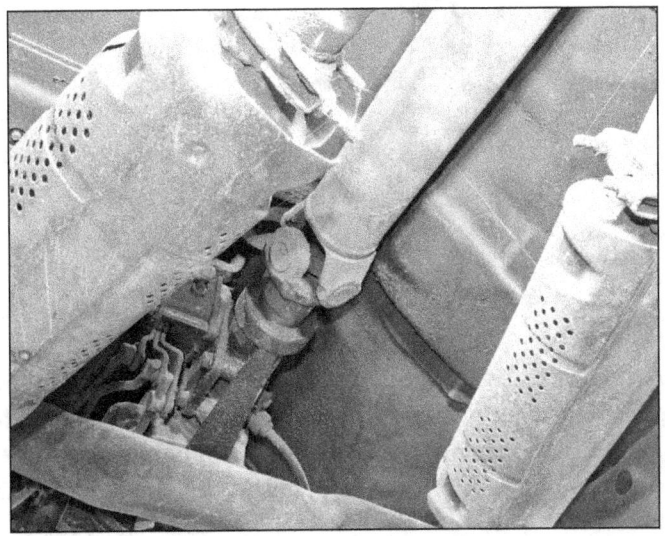

The driveshaft is one heavy piece of steel, so take the necessary safety precautions when removing it from the car.

TRANS AM & FIREBIRD RESTORATION

Driveshaft Recondition

Remove U-Joint at Rear Differential

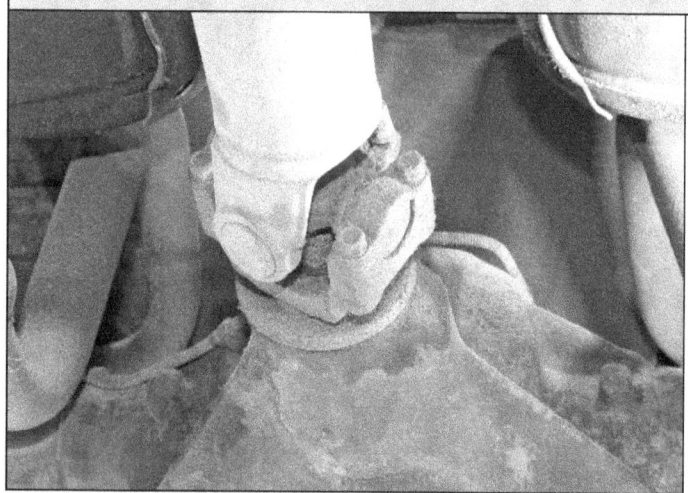

1 Two small bolts at the end of the shaft hold in each side of the U-joint at the rear axle yoke. These bolts have often been subjected to years of corrosion. If the differential seal has been loosened or cracked, the U-joint often has oil or grease in it. In addition, moisture and road debris can cover the U-joint, so these U-joint strap bolts are often frozen in place. First, soak them with WD-40 or PB Blaster; in extreme cases, you may need to use a propane torch.

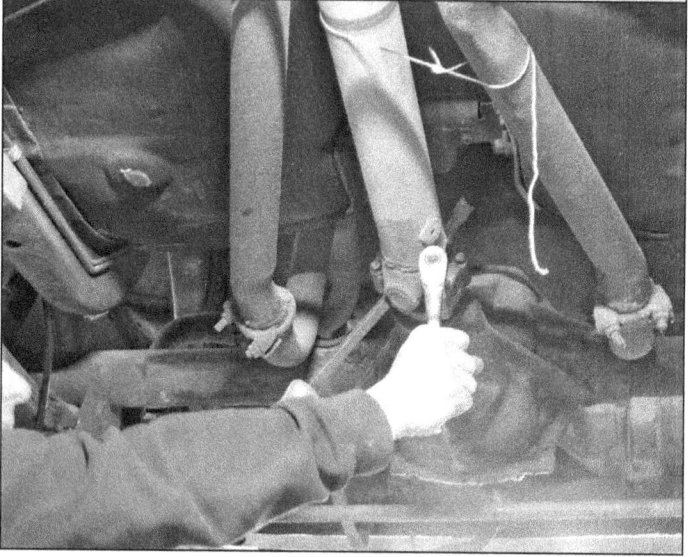

2 A ratchet and socket are typically used to remove the bolts and the small straps that hold the U-joint to the yoke. If the bolts are particularly stubborn, use a breaker bar or an impact wrench. Once the bolts have been removed, place a pry bar between the yoke and driveshaft. Gently push the driveshaft away from the yoke to break the U-joint free from the yoke.

Remove Driveshaft from Tailshaft of Transmission

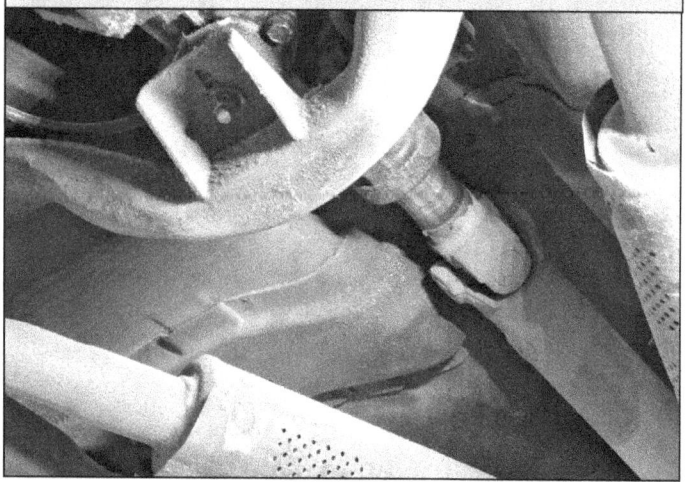

3 Once the driveshaft has been separated from the rear axle yoke, gently pull the driveshaft out of the yoke in the tail section of the transmission. The driveshaft is a heavy piece of steel, so be prepared to carry it to your workbench or storage area.

Inspect Driveshaft

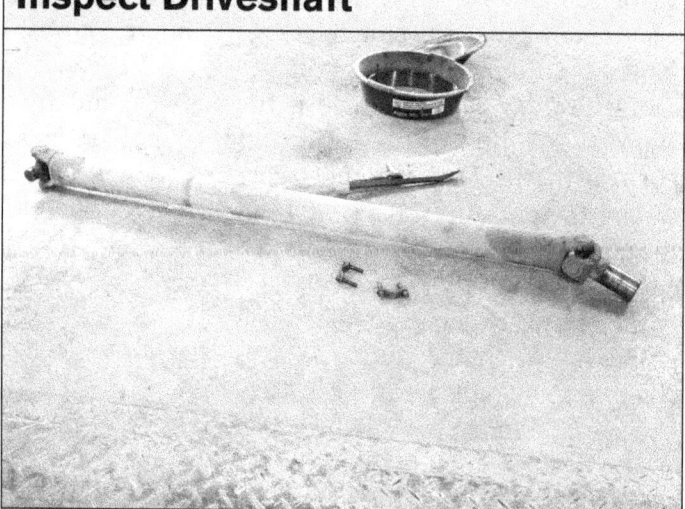

4 Lay the driveshaft on the floor and visually inspect it for any dents or irregularities. Check the welds at each end of the yoke on the shaft for any cracking. If you find any missing weights or damage to the driveshaft, I recommend sending it to a driveshaft shop to be repaired and balanced.

Remove C-Clips

5 *Place the driveshaft in a vise and remove the C-clip on the inner side of the yoke that holds the U-joint in place. Two C-clips reside at the rear of the driveshaft ears; four are at the front. The clips are held in by pressure and in a recessed area of the yoke.*

Inspect Loose U-Joint

6 *Once the C-clips have been removed, the U-joint is loose, and you need to prepare for the next step of pressing out the U-joint.*

Press U-Joint from Yoke

7 *Because many car owners do not have a hydraulic press in their home workshop, they take the driveshaft to a machine shop to have the U-joint pressed out of the fixed yoke. If you have a hydraulic press, place a pipe end large enough for the U-joint cap to slide through on the driveshaft. On the press end, align a socket or other round object that's about the same diameter as the U-joint.*

8 *As the press applies force to the U-joint, it pushes the U-joint cap through the yoke. Make sure everything is perfectly straight.*

Inspect Yoke Ears

9 *Once you have removed the U-joint, inspect the yoke ears for any distortion or cracks. Cracks can occur anywhere on the yoke ears. They can also occur at the welds where the yoke is attached to the driveshaft tube.*

Organize U-Joint Parts

10 *U-joints on a high-mileage car have often reached the end of their service life and replacing them is relatively inexpensive. Organize the U-joints and get them ready for installation. Remove the new U-joint from the box and tape the caps on to prevent them from falling off. Small needle bearings sit inside the cap, and it's critical that the needle bearings stay in place.*

Insert U-Joint in Fixed Yoke

11 Place the U-joint in the yoke on the shaft. Gently remove one of the caps that has not been taped.

Press U-Joint Cap into Fixed Yoke

12 Place the shaft and cap back into the hydraulic press. Place the cap that you removed onto the outer end of the shaft and then press it onto the U-joint so that the two caps are pressed into the shaft yoke.

Install Zerk Fitting in U-Joint

13 Remove the shaft from the press. Install the zerk fitting into the U-joint. This is best done with a small open-end wrench.

Install C-Clips

14 Install the C-clips onto the U-joint. These clips simply snap on and do not require tools. If you have difficulty, you can use small needle-nose pliers. The front yoke and U-joint are exactly the same as the rear. This process requires an extra step on a hydraulic press because all four sides must be pressed out.

Install Shift Yoke on Output Shaft

15 This is the tailshaft housing of the transmission and the splined output shaft. Slide the forward yoke over the transmission output shaft.

Install Driveshaft on Rear Differential Yoke

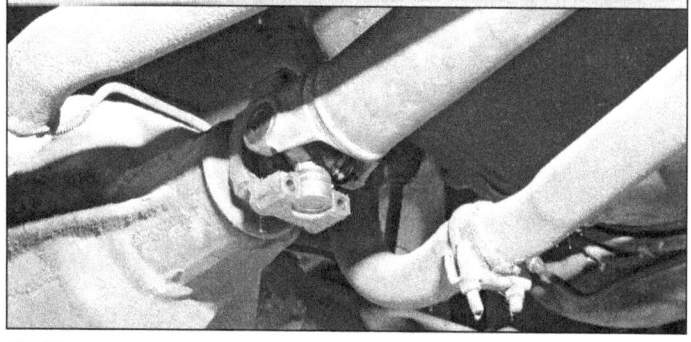

16 Place the other end of the driveshaft into the rear axle yoke. Slide the shaft forward enough to clear the axle yoke ears and then pull it back slightly to seat the U-joint into the seat of the rear yoke.

DRIVETRAIN

Install U-Joint Straps

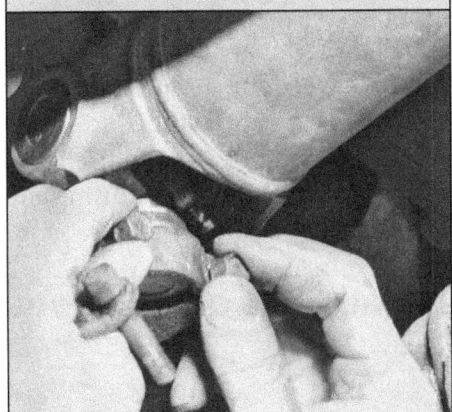

17 With the U-joint resting in place against the yoke, place the U-joint straps over the U-joint and thread in the bolts. Clean the U-joint straps and bolts before reassembly. This helps establish proper torque because no dirt is in the way. The bolts must have clean threads so they can be torqued to the proper rating.

Grease Zerk Fittings and Install Bolt

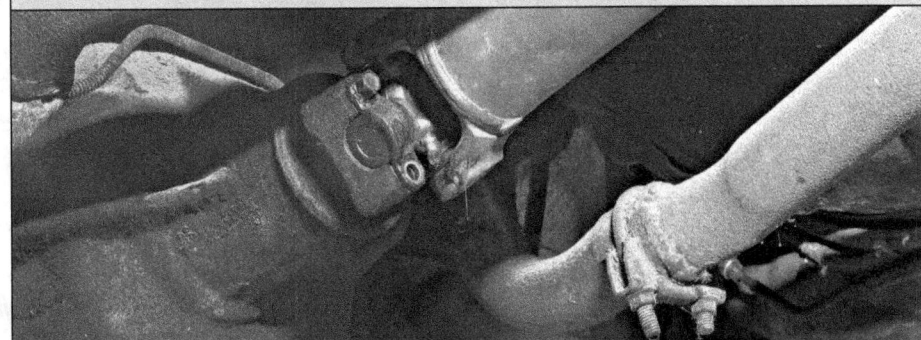

18 Once you have the straps installed, leave one bolt out for access to the zerk fitting. You do not want to grease the U-joint before it is installed because the grease pushes the caps off the U-joint. If you experience a vibration after installation and you did not feel one before, remove the driveshaft, turn it one-half turn, and reinstall it. Sometimes that cures the issue. If not, recheck your work. Otherwise, the shaft must be balanced at a driveshaft shop. Most manufacturers recommend NLGI Grade-2 grease with an EP additive (EP additives are meant for shock loads and frequent load/unload cycles such those of a universal joint). One such grease is Chevron Ultra-Duty EP2. Slowly add the grease until you see some ooze out. Make sure you do this slowly because too much grease is not a good thing.

Driveshaft

Inspection of the driveshaft requires you to visually look at every square inch of it for any dents or dings. Also watch for any evidence of missing weights.

If the Firebird was running and driving and there were not any vibration issues, then new U-joints are probably all that is required. If there are any visible issues or a vibration, then it is better to send the shaft to a driveshaft specialty company. A specialist can balance the tube or make a new one to fit and function as new, usually for less than $300. The stock driveshaft is more than robust and is able to handle much higher horsepower and torque than the factory ever offered.

Rear Axles

The 10- and 12-bolt rear axles that were installed in the Firebird are a similar design, and therefore, rebuilding the 10- and 12-bolt follows a similar procedure. Overhauling the rear axle is a long and methodical process, and it requires specialized tools and knowledge. Getting a rear axle to be free of noise on acceleration and coast takes skill in it setting up.

The 12-bolt axle was only used for the 1970 model year. A popular upgrade from the stock 10-bolt setup is to use a 12-bolt. Moser Engineering and Currie Enterprises both offer bolt-in 12-bolt rear axle packages with a variety of ratios available. These complete, ready-to-install rear axle assemblies can run about $3,200, depending on the options you choose.

Owners typically want to know the gear ratio of their differential. You can simply drop the rear cover and count the teeth on the pinion and on the ring. Then, divide the number of ring teeth by the number of gear teeth. That is the gear ratio.

Another, albeit slightly less accurate, way to tell which ratio your Firebird has involves little more than raising the rear tires off the ground. Block the front wheels and raise the rear wheels with a floor jack. Use tape or a grease pencil to mark the tire and the wheel well opening. Make a mark on the driveshaft with tape or a grease pencil. Turn the tire and count the number of times the driveshaft turns to one single revolution of the tire.

For example, if the shaft turns about 3.5 times to one revolution of the tire, the rear is about a 3.55 ratio. Given that the 3.55 ratio was not available in the Firebird, it most likely is a 3.42 ratio. The difference could be in the tire size or just a slight difference in turning ratio.

Rear Axle Rebuild Overview

If a rear is not set up perfectly, you will have problems. Even the setup for the ring and pinion-to-ring gear mesh is absolutely critical. At a minimum there is noise on the acceleration or coast side if not perfectly set up. An improperly set up rear that has been run can ruin the ring gear and pinion, which will require a complete replacement and you'll have to start over from scratch.

As I have said before, there are some things that are worth paying for to have done properly. Even if you are performing the rest of the restoration on your car yourself you can remove the rear axle housing and deliver it to the shop for the rebuild.

Gaining access to the differential and to change the oil is a relatively simple process even with the sway bar in place, but in this case, you remove the sway bar.

Remove Sway Bar Links and Mounts

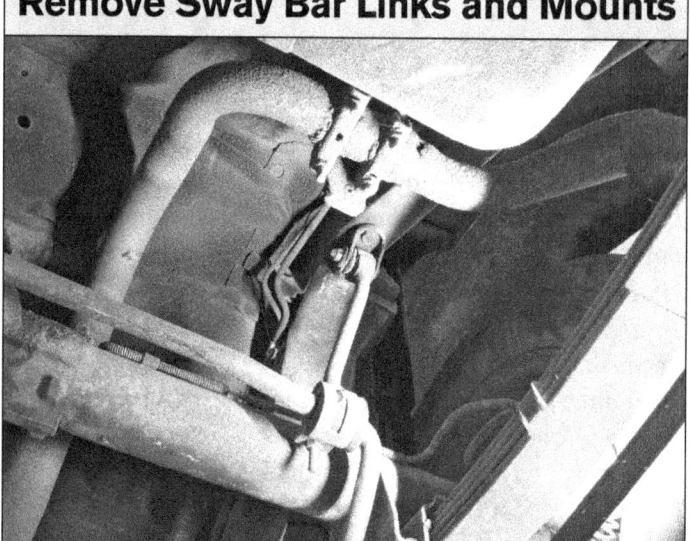

1 Remove the upper sway bar links at their uppermost mounts using a socket and ratchet with an extension for the upper links. A socket and ratchet work fine for the end mounts.

Move Sway Bar

2 Once the links have been disconnected, the sway bar can swivel out of the way.

Remove Cover Bolts

3 Most of the time the cover gasket has leaked. Although the bolts may be difficult to turn initially, these bolts should not be frozen. Using a socket and ratchet, remove the 10 or 12 bolts holding on the cover.

Drain Oil

4 Once all of the bolts have been removed from the center section cover, it often has to be pried off. If you have ever smelled used differential fluid, you know how bad it smells, and if you get it on your clothes, you probably won't get the smell out. Use a small pry bar or flat-head screwdriver to pry off the cover; be sure to break the seal all around the mounting surface of the cover. If the cover is particularly difficult, use a plastic mallet to tap the cover. Be sure to place a drain pan underneath to catch the oil. Let the oil drain before completely removing the cover. It is best to start prying at the bottom to allow the housing to drain before letting the entire cover come off. It can make a big mess if you just pop the cover off all at once.

Remove Cover

5 Once the oil has mostly drained, remove the cover. Then you can see the ring rear, side gears, and spider gears. If catastrophic failure has occurred, you should be able to see evidence of it. In this particular car, the gears and components appear to be in good condition.

CHAPTER 8

Remove Ring and Pinion

6 The ring and pinion is removed from the axle.

Place Carrier in Center Section

7 You can rebuild the axle assembly in the car or on the bench; the decision is up to you. However, if the rear axle has never been rebuilt and needs all new seals and bearings, it easier to rebuild on the bench. When you have completed the rebuild, the carrier is placed in the center section. You can tell that this is a limited-slip unit because of the clutch pack at the top.

Verify Gear Mesh

8 This is a newly assembled differential. The yellow grease on the gears is a way to see how the pinion and ring gear mesh together. The ring and pinion should mesh in the middle of the ring gear. The ring and pinion should not mesh too much on the coast or toe side; they should mesh in the middle of the ring gear.

Second-generation Firebirds used the corporate 10- and 12-bolt axle assemblies. This 10-bolt has been re-installed in this Firebird.

TRANS AM & FIREBIRD RESTORATION

CHAPTER 9

BRAKES

The stock front disc and rear drum brakes used on the second-generation Firebird were extremely robust and efficient. Depending on which road test you read, the disc/drum setup on the Firebird took about 160 feet to stop from 60 mph. The rear disc brake option was offered as part of the WS6 Special Performance Package starting in 1979, which helped the stopping power even more.

The new four-wheel disc brakes on the WS6 cars knocked some time from the stopping distance, bringing the Trans Am to 60 mph in only 146 feet.

When compared to braking systems other manufacturers offered at the time, nothing compared to the Firebird brakes.

Upgrades are available from various manufacturers, such as Brembo, Baer, SSBC, and Wilwood. These systems are also used with resto-modding, which is beyond the scope of this book.

Brake upgrades are available that fit behind the factory wheel, but I am not sure that the additional cost translates into braking power that is superior to a perfectly operating factory system.

Front Disc Brakes

Replacing the front disc brakes on your Firebird is not a difficult procedure. Using commonly available hand tools and following simple procedures, you can replace the brakes quickly and save some money too. Having a professional shop replace the brakes is something to consider, especially if you use one of the major chains that offer lifetime warranties.

You may need to replace your brakes for any number of reasons. You have to determine what needs to be replaced if you are only doing a repair. If the Firebird has been sitting for an extended period, it might be prudent to replace every component for safety reasons. Inspect the brake lines to make sure they are not rusted, leaking, or bent. The braking system of the second-generation Firebird is very good and is relatively inexpensive to replace.

This 1978 Formula W72 was a limited-performance model with a 400-ci engine, which produced 220 hp and 320 ft-lbs of torque. Here, the front brakes are shown.

CHAPTER 9

Brake Disassembly

Remove Front Wheel

1 Use a lug wrench or breaker bar and socket to remove the lug nuts from the front wheel that is receiving brake service. I advise breaking the torque on the lug nuts before jacking up the car. Use a breaker bar and socket. I do not recommend using an impact gun because the lug studs could snap or the studs could develop hidden cracks.

Locate Caliper Pins

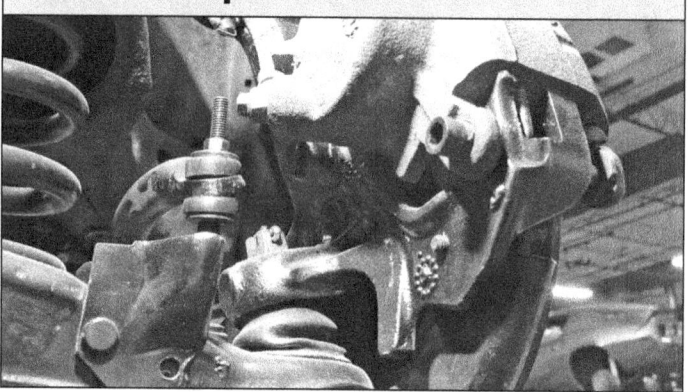

2 The first step is to remove the brake calipers. To do that, locate the caliper pins on the back side of the caliper. To gain easier access to the caliper pins, turn the steering so the rear is pointing outward.

Loosen Caliper Pins

3 Use a 3/8-inch Allen socket on a 3/8- or 1/2-inch ratchet to loosen the upper and lower caliper pins. Do not remove the pins yet because you need the caliper in place so you can loosen the rubber brake hose.

Remove Brake Line to Front Caliper

4 Pinch the rubber brake hose with locking pliers just tightly enough to keep fluid from draining. Using a 5/16-inch wrench to loosen the caliper bleeder to relieve pressure.

Remove the rubber brake hose at the caliper with a 7/16-inch wrench. It may be necessary to have a drain pan underneath or at least a shop rag to catch the residual fluid.

Lift Caliper off Brake Disc

5 The brake caliper should pivot and lift off the mounting bracket. If it's stubborn, wiggle the caliper off with a rocking motion.

TRANS AM & FIREBIRD RESTORATION

BRAKES

Remove the Rubber Brake Line

6 Use a 3/8-inch line wrench to remove the short section of rubber brake line from the steel brake line at the bracket.

Remove Spring Retainer Clip

7 A retainer ring is located at the back side of the brake line bracket. Use a flat-head screwdriver or pick to snag it and lift it out.

Remove Dust Cap

8 A dust cap is at the center of the brake rotor. Use a larger flat-blade screwdriver to get between the edge of the hub and the dust cap. Pop off the dust cap.

Remove Wheel Hub Cotter Pin

9 Use needle-nose pliers to straighten the cotter pin and yank it out. Once the cotter pin has been removed, you have access to the spindle nut.

Remove Spindle Nut

10 Use an adjustable wrench to turn the spindle nut counter-clockwise to loosen it. It is not necessary to use a socket and ratchet, as the nut does not have much torque on it. Remove the nut.

Slide Rotor off Wheel Hub

11 Slide the rotor out slightly to remove the keyed washer and outer bearing.

TRANS AM & FIREBIRD RESTORATION

CHAPTER 9

Brake Assembly

Remove Bearing and Grease Seal

1 You need to remove the bearing and grease seal from the rotor. To do this, reinstall the spindle nut and turn it clockwise a few threads.

2 Grab the rotor with your hands placed at the three and nine o'clock positions. Pull toward yourself quickly and forcefully to pop the rear bearing and grease seal from the back of the rotor. Inspect the bearing and seal. You need to replace them if you see any binding or excessive wear.

Remove Spindle Nut

3 Remove the spindle nut and bearing and clean the spindle. Apply fresh wheel bearing grease to the spindle.

Apply Grease to Wheel Bearing

4 Use your fingers to evenly spread a coat of wheel bearing grease over the entire surface area of the bearing. This is in preparation for inserting the wheel bearing inside the rotor. Grease needs to cover the entire space between bearing and the bore.

Install Bearing in Rotor Bore

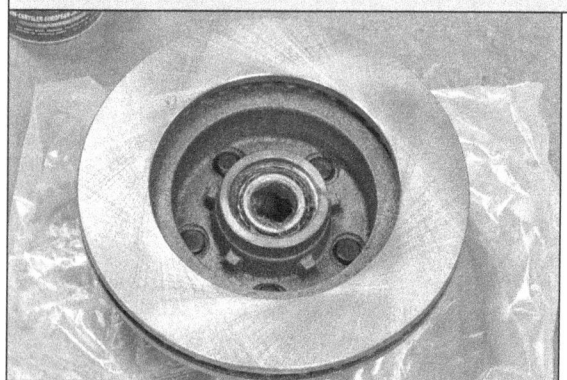

5 Bearings are inexpensive so I recommend installing new bearings when performing a brake job. Install a new wheel bearing after packing grease into the bearing orifices.

BRAKES

Install Grease Seal

6 Use a ball-peen or other suitable hammer to gently tap the new grease seal into position on the back side of the rotor.

Install Brake Rotor on Hub

7 Inspect the rotor and make sure the rotor is true and there is no damage or flaws. Slide it onto hub.

Install Bearing and Key Washer

8 Install the bearing and key washer by just sliding them over the spindle and into the rotor.

Install Spindle Nut

9 Use an adjustable wrench to tighten the spindle nut. Tighten the nut clockwise until snug.

Install Spindle Nut (CONTINUED)

10 Spin the rotor counter-clockwise and tighten the nut until you feel resistance against the rotor; the rotor still turns but not freely. Back the spindle nut off a quarter of a turn. Turn the spindle nut until an opening in the spindle is clear on both sides of the nut. Install a new cotter pin and bend the ends around the nut.

Install Dust Cap

11 Place the dust cap square on the spindle bore and use a hammer to lightly tap it around the circumference until the cap sits flush against the rotor.

Install Hose and Spring Clip

12 Install a brake caliper rubber hose line and retainer spring clip. Install the caliper. Line up the caliper with the bracket. Slide the pins through the caliper and use the Allen driver to torque the pins.

Lubricate Caliper Pins

13 Lubricate the caliper pins with wheel-bearing grease by simply wiping some on with your finger. Install the pins. Install the brake hose by placing one end at the caliper and installing a new copper washer, which should have been included with the new hose. Reuse the bolt you removed earlier.

Rear Disc Brakes (1979–1981)

The 1979 model year brought a major change to the Special Performance Package (RPO WS6). When you checked that option on the order form, you received four-wheel power disc brakes. Having rear disc brakes in 1979 was considered exotic and, in the GM family, they were usually only available on the Corvette. Rear disc brakes greatly simplified repairs and improved braking performance. The appearance of the rear rotors was also upgraded: They could be seen through 8-inch aluminum snowflake wheels that were also part of the option package.

Brake Kit Installation

A four-wheel-disc upgrade to a Trans Am or Firebird provides a significant safety and control upgrade. This bolt-on item was originally offered as optional equipment in 1979, and therefore, it does not negatively effect the collector value of a second-generation F-Body car. The brake upgrade was part of the WS6 Performance Package. It provides a serious performance upgrade compared to the standard hardware. The rear disc brake option (J65 RPO) could also be ordered to replace the rear drum brakes. In addition, a WS7 Performance Package was offered in 1979. The WS7 package was essentially the WS6 package without the rear disc brakes. In the following procedure, you see the installation of a Macho Trans Am kit.

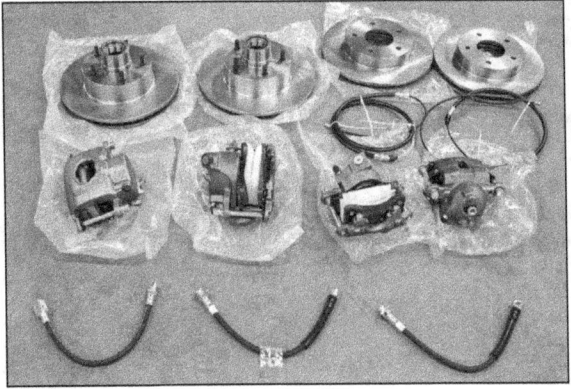

Here are the complete front and rear disc brake components to be replaced on the 1979 Macho Trans Am that is equipped with the WS6 Special Performance Package. This package included new-for-1979 four-wheel disc brakes.

Clamp Rear Brake Hose

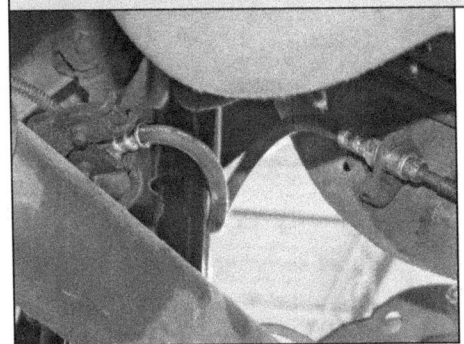

1 The rear hose that attaches the main front-to-rear brake line to the axle union should be clamped with small locking pliers toward the middle to prevent brake fluid from draining out completely while changing the calipers. Do not clamp at the end of the hose because it can permanently distort the hose.

Remove Rear Caliper Bolts

2 As with the front brakes, the rear brake calipers are held to the mounting bracket with Allen-head bolts. Like other parts subjected to corrosion, these may require a lubricant, such as PB Blaster, before they loosen. Use a 3/8-inch Allen socket to break the torque on the caliper retainer bolts.

Remove Steel Brake Line

3 Use a 7/16-inch open-end wrench to remove the steel brake line on each end of the axle where it attaches to the caliper flex hose. Disconnect the flex hose from the caliper.

Remove Caliper

4 Remove the caliper bolts and then remove the caliper by removing the bolts and lifting the caliper off the retaining brackets.

Remove Parking Brake Cable

5 Use locking pliers to grasp the end of the parking brake cable. Pull on the cable and get some slack from the cable itself so you can move the retainer ball out of the bracket. Bend and twist the retainer to the side with the opening. Remove the cable from its retainer.

Remove Caliper Spring

6 Compress the caliper spring by using hose-clamp pliers or other long-nosed pliers. Then remove the spring from the caliper pocket.

Remove Parking Brake Spring Clip

7 Use hose-clamp pliers to compress the tabs on the park brake spring clip. Slide the cable end out through the bracket.

Remove Accessory Parts

8 Many accessory parts are not included with the new caliper (bottom). In fact, the new caliper does not come with the park brake bracket, cable retainer, and the flex-hose adapter. Remove them from the old caliper (top) and transfer them to the new caliper. The brackets are keyed so they end up in the same location. The flex-hose adapter only goes on one way. The caliper brake bracket uses an 11/16-inch socket, the cable retainer bracket uses a 9/16-inch socket, and the flex-hose adapter uses a 7/16-inch socket.

Install Original Brackets and Flex-Hose Adapter

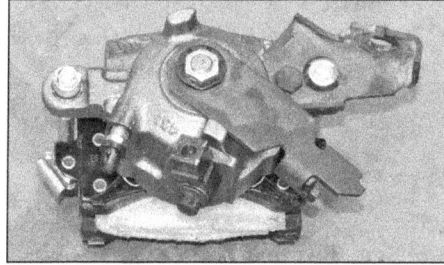

9 Here, the original brackets have been transferred to the new caliper, and the flex-hose adapter has been installed.

Remove Brake Rotor

10 Because brake parts are subjected to a lot of moisture and debris, they often rust together. If your Firebird has not had brake service, the rotor may be very difficult to remove. Use a ball-peen hammer to strike the rotor in several places to separate it from the hub. Do not use any type of heat source as the spindle could be irreversibly damaged.

Install New Rotor

11 Once the old rotor has been removed, you simply place the new rotor over the wheel studs.

BRAKES

Secure the Rotor onto the Hub

12 To keep the rotor secured to the hub, hand-tighten one lug nut until it seats against the rotor. This holds the rotor in place and keeps it straight.

Remove Parking Brake Bracket

13 Use a socket and ratchet to remove the 1/2-inch bolts that secure the parking brake bracket to the frame rail. These can be rusted so they may need a treatment of thread lube.

Remove Retainer Clip on Brake Cable

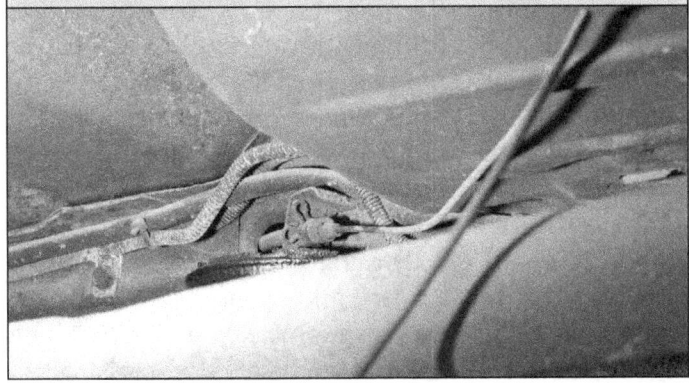

14 Remove the Mickey Mouse ear–style retainer clip located on the opposite side of the frame rail using needle-nosed pliers. If you have difficulty in getting the pliers into that tight space, you can try to pop off the clip with a flat-blade screwdriver.

Remove Parking Brake Cable

15 Attach locking pliers to the threaded rod on the main park brake cable to prevent it from spinning. Use a 1/2-inch wrench and socket to remove the cable from the retainer. Slide out the rear parking-brake cable.

Install Brake Calipers

16 Mount the calipers on the brake rotors and align them with the mounting bracket. Slide on the calipers at a 45-degree angle.

Install Cable and Calipers

17 Install the new cable and calipers in reverse order of the disassembly. The cable end snaps back into the bracket.

TRANS AM & FIREBIRD RESTORATION

CHAPTER 10

SUSPENSION

The chassis and suspension of the Firebird is GM's second-generation F-Body so it shares its architecture with the 1970–1981 Camaro. The Chevy and Pontiac teams in Trans-Am racing (as well as GM itself) developed the geometry of this suspension and it was a big step forward from the previous suspension in 1969. Similar to other GM chassis, the second-generation F-Body featured double-stamped A-arm front suspension, and the ball joints on a spindle join the upper and lower arms.

The suspension of your Firebird has an enormous impact on the driving experience. The suspension must be in good working order for the car to handle properly and drive as it did when new. The bushings and ball joints are wear items and are prone to failure from either use or age or both. After 33 years or more, the rubber bushings have most likely dry rotted and cracked, rendering them unable to perform their job properly.

Suspension rebuilding requires you to use the proper tools and follow the necessary safety procedures. Installed coil and leaf springs store a lot of energy, so you need to follow the correct disassembly and assembly procedures. You must use the proper spring compressors and spring removal techniques. If you do not, you risk serious injury or worse. Always make sure that the body is properly supported.

The tools you need to work on your suspension are a pickle fork, coil-spring compressor, hammer, sockets, and wrenches. A good floor jack also is needed and a hydraulic press is necessary for pressing the front suspension bushings and ball joints out and back in.

Inspection

Before you tear into the car and start disassembling the suspension, you should perform a thorough inspection to ascertain its current condition. The suspension should be in top condition not only for high-performance applications, but also for safety.

Sagging springs, broken ball joints, and failed bushings all can affect how your Firebird handles everyday driving. Even the smallest pothole or a dip in the road can cause a worn-out suspension to react improperly, resulting in an accident. You can closely inspect the alignment shims at the upper control arm

Up front, the 1970–1981 Firebirds were equipped with unequal-length upper and lower control arms. After 30-plus years, suspension components such as ball joints, tie-rod ends, shocks, and springs are often worn out and need replacement.

mounting points and count how many are installed on each side. If one side has many more shims than the other side, it can indicate an alignment problem or possibly some accident damage.

If the front end wasn't properly straightened after an accident, but rather had more shims added to attain the correct alignment, it's a problem. To verify if the front subframe has been bent, see if the alignment holes line up correctly. If the control arms are bent, it's difficult to see, but added shims may compensate for this.

If the Firebird has been in an accident and you have not noticed it until now, you need to enlist a shop with a proper frame machine to straighten the front end or the subframe may need to be replaced. If your frame is straight, it's a matter of replacing the worn bushings, ball joints, tie-rod ends, and other pieces so the car drives well and safely.

When contemplating which parts to replace on the suspension during your restoration project, I can say only one word: everything. Any part that is considered a wearable item should be replaced, and if you want to have a balanced and correctly operating suspension, you need to be sure that all parts are new and functioning like new. That's why you should not integrate old parts with new parts.

Look underneath the car to determine the condition of the four rubber bushings between the frame and floorpan. These compress, crack, and expand over time, so you may need to replace them.

Rear springs typically sag over time, but do not always require replacement. I rarely recommend replacing the front coil springs unless they have sagged. Why? When the factory specified the front coil springs, it was to a particular engine, transmission, and optional equipment. The 1970–1981 Firebirds have many different part numbers for springs. However, the aftermarket sources only list a few replacement springs. An incorrect coil spring can affect ride height (it may sit too high or too low), handling, ride softness or stiffness, and create other issues such as bottoming out when hitting everyday bumps.

Frame-Off Preparation

Before you start disassembling the suspension, you need a game plan. If you're planning to do a frame-off restoration, you can easily separate the front subframe and rear suspension from the body; the body can be mounted on a rotisserie. Once you have removed the front clip from the car, you can remove the front subframe, engine, transmission, and rear suspension; you're left with a body shell.

After the hood has been removed, you can pull the engine and transmission out through the top of the car. Then, you can remove the front subframe from the bottom. You can keep the wheels on the front spindles, and, with a floor jack supporting the front subframe, you can wheel it around on your garage floor very easily.

You need to remove all fuel lines, brakes lines, and the emergency brake cable. Six bolts hold the front subframe to the car, and once those are removed, you can simply roll the subframe out from underneath the car.

If you're doing a frame-off restoration, remove the two bolts at the bottom of the core support, the two bolts that go through the firewall in the mounting pad, and the two bolts that attach the subframe to the cage nuts.

Front Suspension

The front suspension is the most difficult part of overhauling your suspension. It is important to pay attention to where everything goes. Count the tie rod threads at the adjusters on both the inner and outer tie-rods. This gets your suspension close to the pre-disassembly settings. This allows the car to be movable and easier to steer before you take it to the alignment shop.

Shop Time and Cost

A properly equipped shop can replace your entire suspension in a couple of days with the right equipment and experience. If you want the shop to sandblast, prime, and paint the suspension components, expect at least two to three additional days for completion.

Costs for a shop to rebuild your front suspension, including degreasing, priming, and painting of all of the suspension components, can run about 20 to 30 hours times the shop's hourly rate. If you are performing a concours-type restoration, bodywork to the control arms may be needed to eliminate the rust pits that are commonly found on them. That kind of work drives costs up, but the arms look factory fresh and new. Overall costs also depend on the starting condition is of your suspension components.

CHAPTER 10

This is a complete front suspension deluxe kit with tie rods. Over time, bushings, ball joints, and chassis isolators absorb energy, crack, and wear out. Tie-rod ends and bolts are designed for only so much use. A kit such as this not only improves handling and comfort, but these fresh parts help the front suspension to function as designed and enhance safety. If your car has more than 70,000 miles or it's been 10 years or more since the front end components have been replaced, it's time to replace them.

This second-generation Firebird has experienced years of road grime that has accumulated on its upper control arm.

This upper control arm has had the steering knuckle removed. The upper nut holding the steering knuckle to the upper control arm was removed with a wrench until it was a few threads from the end. A pickle fork and a hammer were used to separate the control arm from the steering knuckle. The nut was then removed. The shaft seen here is part of the upper ball joint.

Contact alignment shops in your area and make sure they have the original specifications for your car. Some do and some do not want to be bothered with older cars. Do not have the front suspension aligned until the car is fully assembled because any weight differences change the settings and you'll have to revisit the alignment shop.

It is necessary to remove the cotter pin and nut to the upper ball joint. Support the lower control arm with a floor jack. Install a coil spring compressor onto the spring and tighten it so that the compressor holds the tension. Take the removed nut, turn it upside down, and re-install it onto the ball joint stem. Thread it several turns so that the nut is just covering the stem end. Hit the nut with a hammer to break the ball joint loose from the steering knuckle.

If that does not work or if you are not making much progress, you'll have to use a pickle fork. Hammer the pickle fork between the upper control arm and the upper part of the steering knuckle over the stem of the ball joint. Leave the castle nut installed so the nut prevents the upper arm from flying up when the tension is released. Once the tension is released, remove the nut slowly, and separate the upper arm and the knuckle.

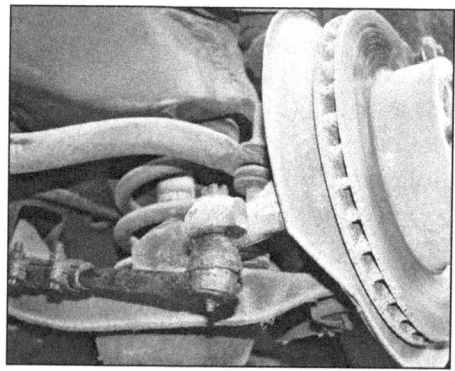

Here is the lower control arm and tie rod.

SUSPENSION

Remove the cotter pin and castle nut on the outer tie rod. Turn the nut upside down and thread it back onto the stem until flush. Hit the nut with a hammer until the tie rod pops loose. Remove the nut and pull the tie rod out of the steering knuckle end.

Remove the brake caliper, and using a wire, hang it from the frame. Do not allow the flex hose to hold the weight of the caliper.

Control Arm and Ball Joint Removal

Remove Control Arm Assembly

1 The nuts and bolts hold the lower control arm assembly to the subframe and can be removed using wrenches or a wrench and socket and ratchet. It may be necessary to soak the threads with PB Blaster if removal is difficult.

Inspect Upper Ball Joint

2 This shows the upper ball joint has been previously replaced (you can tell that because it is held in by nuts).

Inspect Upper Ball Joint (CONTINUED)

3 This is an original ball joint. It still retains the factory rivets.

Inspect Upper Control Arm

4 Two nuts hold the upper control arm that bolts to the arm shaft and subframe.

Remove Control Arm Nuts

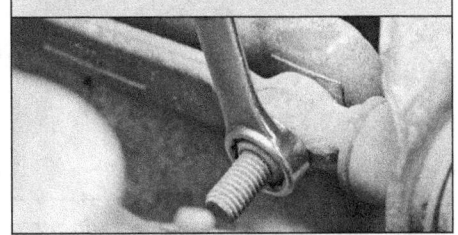

5 Use a 3/4-inch wrench to remove the nuts. If you find shims between the shaft and frame, remove them. You can reinstall them later.

Remove Ball Joint Pin and Nut

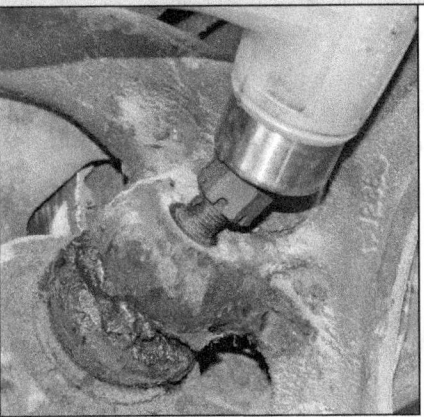

6 Remove the lower ball joint cotter pin and castle nut. Reinstall the nut upside down until flush with the stem. The steering knuckle sometimes requires a hammer to break it away from the arm.

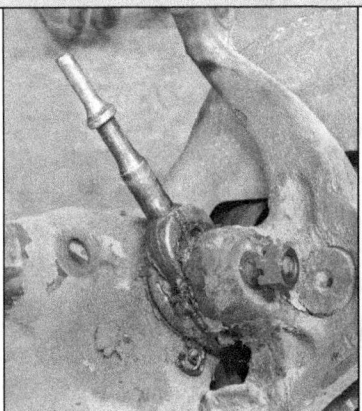

7 If using a hammer is not successful, try a pickle fork. It has tapered ends that allow the leading edge to get between the control arm and the steering knuckle. Hit the fork with a hammer; eventually the two components separate.

TRANS AM & FIREBIRD RESTORATION

CHAPTER 10

Inspect Suspension Components

8 Here are the components all apart.

Prep Seized Bushings

9 The old bushings generally do not remove easily. Drilling out the rubber parts helps release the bushing tension. This makes removal easier. When bushings are seized in the arm, removal is sometimes very difficult. It may be necessary to place the arm in a vise and then hammer and chisel the bushing out.

Remove Bushing Sleeve

10 The bushing sleeve requires a chisel and hammer to remove.

Remove Bushings

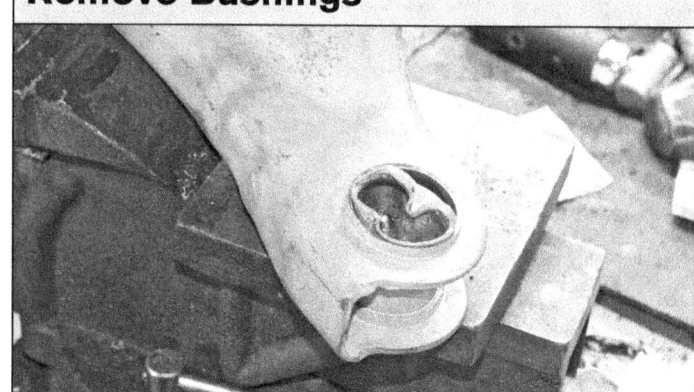

11 Now the bushing is ready to remove.

Press Out Old Ball Joint

12 Using a hydraulic press, press out the ball joint from the arm. Make sure there is room for the ball joint to pop out below. The press is basically a bottle jack with a handle and the process is not unlike jacking up your car to change a flat tire.

Inspect Removed Ball Joint

13 Now the ball joint has been removed from the arm.

SUSPENSION

Press in New Ball Joint

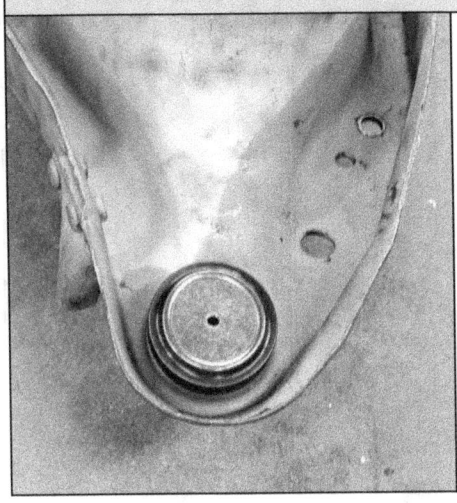

14 Press in the new ball joint using a hydraulic press and flat steel on one side. Make sure the opposite end is open enough to allow the ball joint to clear any obstructions.

Press in New Bushings

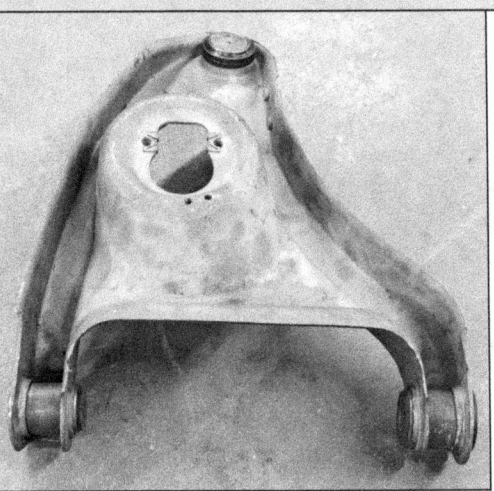

15 Press in the new bushings with a hydraulic press. Using a hydraulic press is not difficult, but it requires even pressure on the push side to force the bushing into the arm.

Press in the new bushings. If you are sandblasting, priming, and painting the suspension parts, I recommend that the sandblasting be performed once the bushings and ball joints are removed. Once you have finished sandblasting, press in the new bushings and ball joints. Tape and prime them followed by painting.

Installation of the ball joints and bushings usually damage the paint if done after painting. However, it is your decision as to the order of installation.

Control Arm Refinishing and Installation

Apply Epoxy Primer

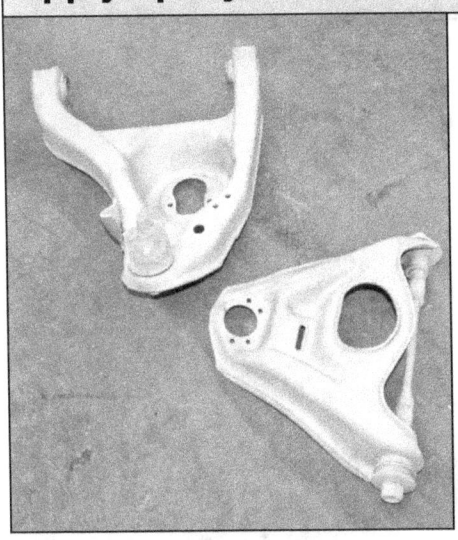

1 The control arms should have been sandblasted in a cabinet or scraped and cleaned with a degreaser before getting to this step. Make sure the metal is completely dirt- and grease-free by using Prep Sol.

Spray the control arms with DP-50 epoxy primer. The primer is sprayed straight without any reduction for thicker coverage and to provide additional durability.

Make sure the primer has completely dried and the primer finish is clean with no significant imperfections in the surface of the control arm. If the surface did pick up some contamination, sand the affected areas and respray with the epoxy primer.

Spray Paint Control Arms

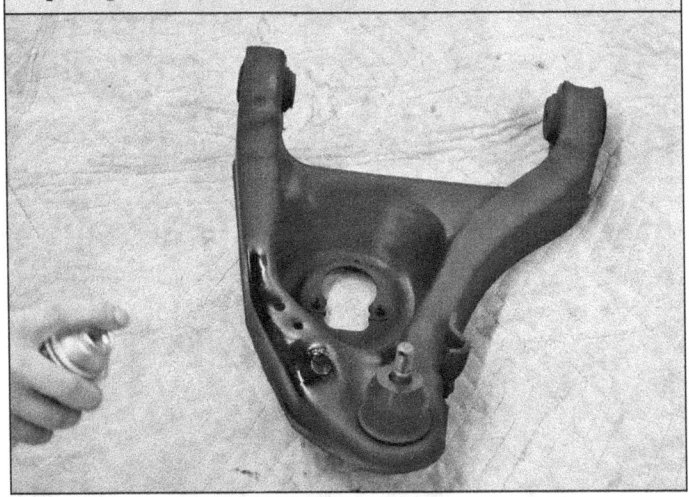

2 You can use a coat hanger or wire to hang suspension parts for painting. However, you can also paint suspension parts in a clean area of the workshop on the floor. Apply several light coats of paint. Spray one side and let it dry completely; then turn the control arm over and paint the other side. The color is a satin black or you can use a product called Hot Rod black. Eastwood also sells Chassis Black, which is close to the factory color. I do not recommend using any type of brush-on paint products.

CHAPTER 10

Remove Masking Tape

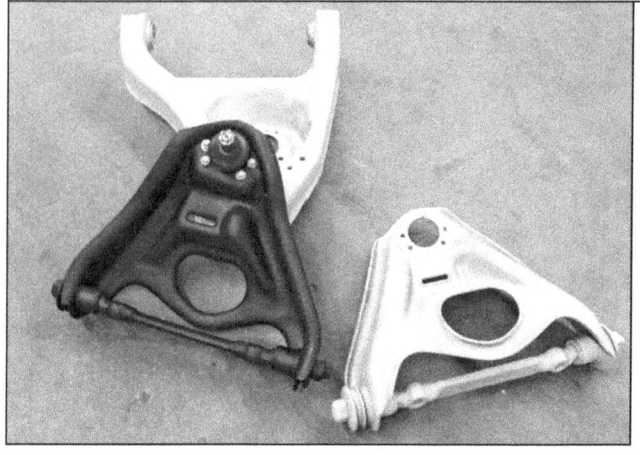

3 Simply peel the tape off that was used to mask the ball joint from paint overspray.

Tighten Ball Joint Nuts

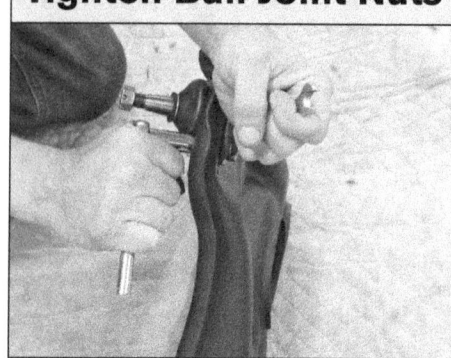

4 Tighten the nuts on the ball joints and confirm everything is ready for installation.

Install Suspension Components

5 At this stage, the complete suspension is ready to be installed. To install the upper and lower control arms, install the nuts and bolts into the subframe retainers. Install the coil spring into the subframe upper pocket and the lower control arm seat. Using a floor jack placed under the lower control arm, jack up the control arm until the lower ball joint stud pokes through the lower part of the steering knuckle. Install the nut on the ball joint stud and tighten. Place the upper control arm ball joint stub in the upper steering knuckle opening and attach the nut. Tighten the nuts. Make sure all the steering knuckle bolts are tightened prior to removing the coil spring compressor.

Install Control Arms, Spindles and Brake Rotors

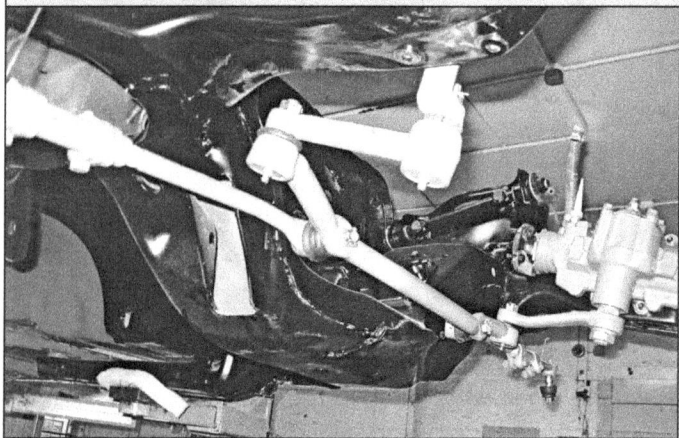

6 Steering cleaned, painted, and installed.

Completed installation.

150 TRANS AM & FIREBIRD RESTORATION

SUSPENSION

Rear Suspension

The second-generation Firebird rear suspension consists of leaf springs, rear sway bar, shocks, and a live solid rear axle. It is a tried-and-true setup. Installing urethane bushings in the leaf springs enhances performance of the rear suspension, axle pads, and sway bar.

The removal and assembly of these is quite simple. Three bolts hold the front spring pocket in, and one bolt and nut is held in at the back and through the lower shackle. The upper part of the shackle also has a single bolt and nut that slides through the rear part of the frame rail.

Two T-bolts on the inboard side and one U-bolt on each outboard side of the spring hold it and the rear axle in place.

Leaf Spring Removal and Replacement

Most parts deteriorate over time. The entire car rests on the suspension, and the rear springs have been placed under a load since the car was new. After years of being subjected to the weight of the car and/or aggressive driving, the springs lose their spring rate and need to be replaced. The bushings also deteriorate over time.

Well before a Firebird starts riding low in the back, you should have fresh leaf springs installed on your Trans Am or Firebird. This is not only for comfort, but also for safety.

If the springs are worn out and compressed, the suspension system of the car is out of balance, and handling can become dangerous.

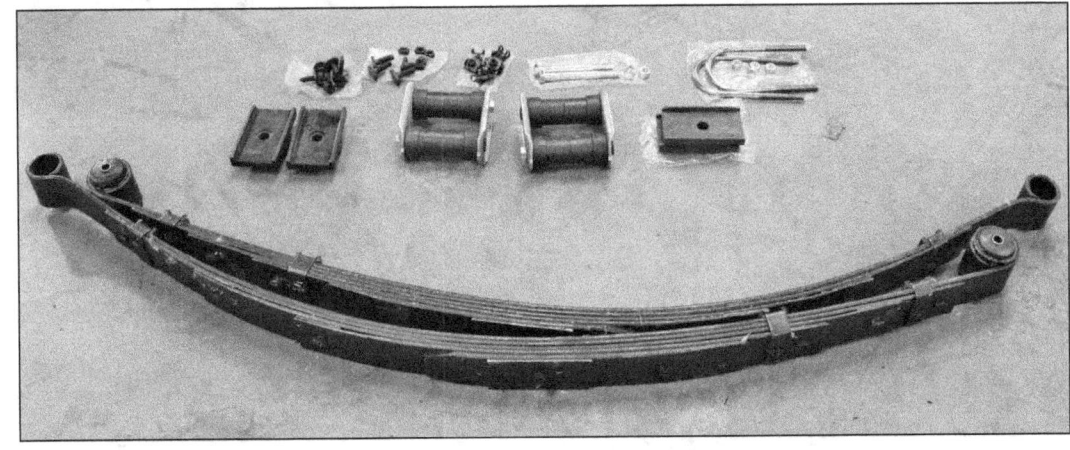

A typical rear-suspension restoration kit includes U-bolts, shackles, axle pads, and leaf springs.

Remove Rear Sway Bar

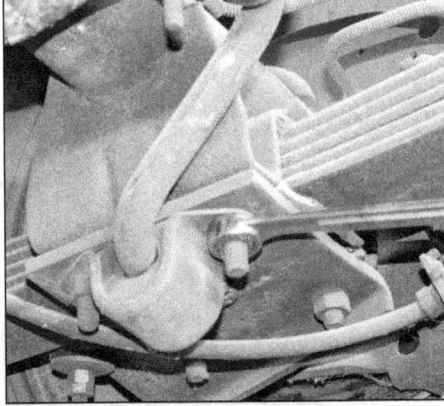

1 *Remove the lower sway bar nuts using a ratchet and socket. Allow the sway bar to swivel out of the way.*

Remove Rear Shackle Nut

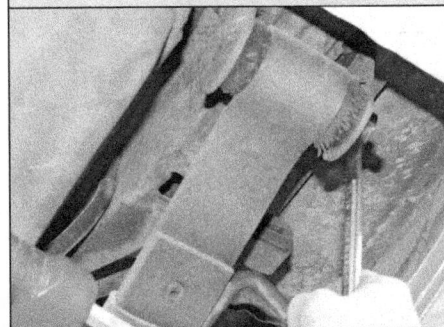

2 *The shackle nuts are often rusted together and may require an air ratchet to free them. You may need to soak the threads with PB Blaster for a few hours.*

Remove Mount Bolts

3 *Remove the three front mounting bolts with a socket and ratchet.*

TRANS AM & FIREBIRD RESTORATION

CHAPTER 10

Remove Sway Link Nut

4 Remove the upper sway bar link nut and put the sway bar to the side.

Install Shackle Bushing

5 Once the old hardware and parts have been freed, you can install the new shackle bushing. Slide the upper bolt through the frame rail.

Remove Leaf Spring Assemblies

6 Remove one leaf spring assembly side at a time. Support the rear axle to make installation easier.

Remove Front Mount

7 Remove the front mount from the old spring. This is the mount with the three bolts that you just removed in Step 3.

Install Mount

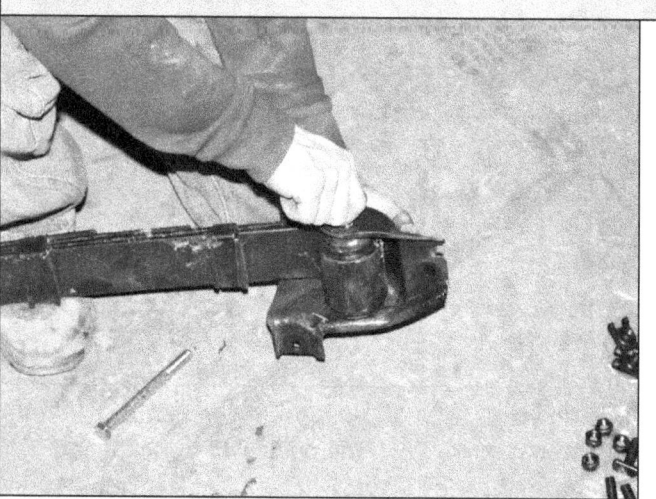

8 Install the mount onto the new spring by placing it over the bushing, as it was before you removed it. The single bolt and nut slides into the eye of the bushing through the bracket. Use a socket and ratchet with a wrench or two wrenches.

Replace Bolt Clips

9 Replace the bolt clips on the body by sliding them into place where the old one was just removed.

SUSPENSION

Install Mount and Spring

10 Install the mount with the spring attached onto the body. Use a ratchet and socket to install.

Install Leaf Spring

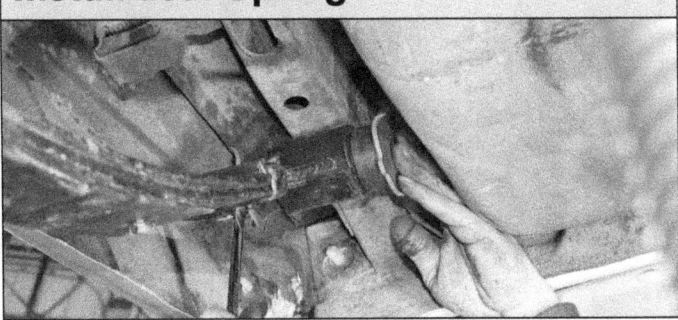

11 Install the rear part of the leaf spring onto the rear shackle. Place the rear part of the spring against the shackle and slide the bolt into the spring bushing center. Use two wrenches.

Install Upper Insulator Pad

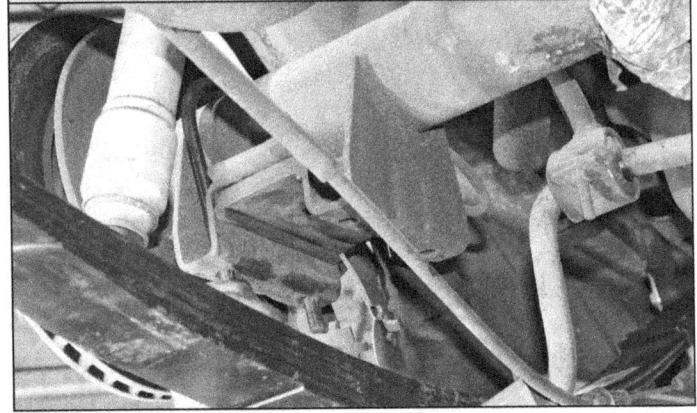

12 Place the upper insulator pad between the axle and spring. Make sure it sits flush.

Install Lower Insulator Pad

13 Install the new lower insulator pad below the spring. The center opening places it over the center spring stack bolt.

A rear-suspension restoration is essential for top performance and safety. The rear leaf springs have been installed. New hardware and bushings are also essential.

TRANS AM & FIREBIRD RESTORATION

CHAPTER 11

ELECTRICAL SYSTEM

The electrical system in your Firebird is the key to making the mechanical components operate at their best. Like the rest of your Firebird, the electrical system has aged over the course of three or more decades. Electrical wiring, terminals, gauges, interior lights, relays, and any number of the electrical components have been subjected to the ravages of time and, in some cases, the elements. You need to do a thorough visual inspection of the electrical connectors, wiring, connectors, and other components.

When the plastic casings and wires age, they become brittle so that the wiring can snap, fray, or become damaged. As wiring becomes older, it puts out more resistance and generates more heat; that is not a good thing.

Make sure you take the proper safety precautions before you start working on the electrical system. Generally, you should disconnect the negative battery terminal so the electrical system is not live to avoid electrical system damage and prevent an electrical shock. If you're doing mechanical work and fuel is around, you don't want an arcing electrical system to create a fire.

Keep in mind that you need to be careful when working around a lead-acid battery. You don't want to take any chances with battery acid. And always wear proper eye protection!

Electrical Harness

The wiring harness is the spine, or backbone, of the electrical system. As a rule, if you have an original wiring harness, it should be replaced. Electrical harnesses provide information to the gauges about the status of the engine and also provide creature comforts to the driver and passengers. The electrical harness needs to be in good condition for the

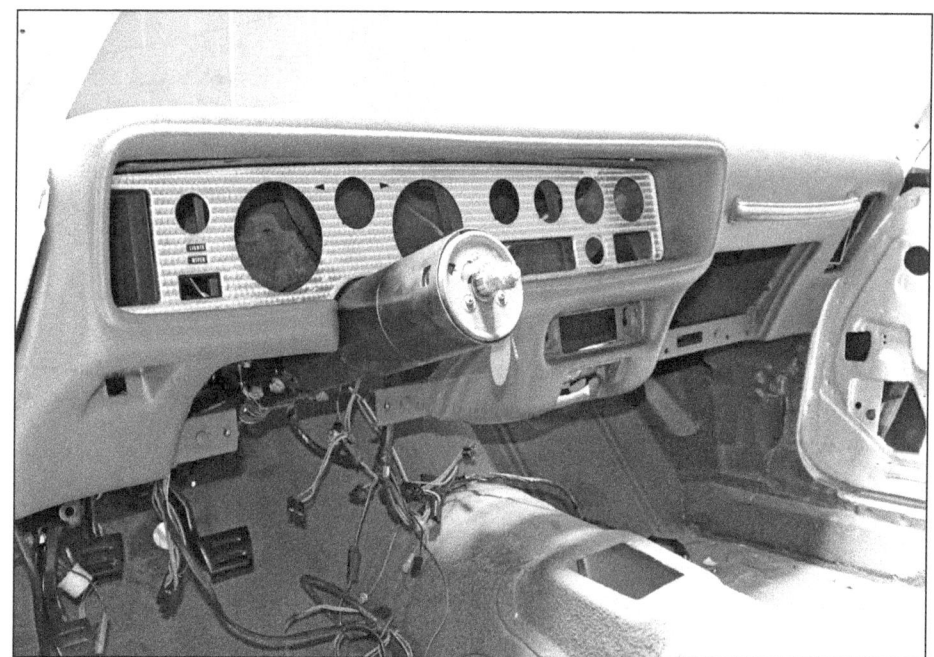

The dash harness is the main nerve center of the Firebird, so it's critical to install it correctly. A consistent electrical load and weather can severely impact the health and performance of the main wiring harness. After three decades, wires become brittle, worn, and sometimes stripped. Often the main wiring needs to be replaced.

electrical system to function as designed and operate at its best.

As your Firebird has aged so has the wiring harness. Depending on where your Firebird has spent the majority of its life, the condition of your harness can vary wildly. Southern climates tend to dry out the harnesses, causing them to become brittle. Northern climates tend to corrode the harnesses, especially at the connectors. Even if none of the climatic exposures have seriously compromised your harness, it still generally needs numerous repairs.

Stereo changes, backyard fixes, aluminum foil for fuses, and added electrical components greatly compromise the integrity of the electrical system. In most cases, these old harnesses need to be replaced, and keep in mind that if your harness fails and causes an unprotected electrical arc, it can lead to fire.

Deciding whether or not you can tackle the repairs on your electrical system greatly depends on your understanding of how electrical systems work. Unfortunately, diagnosing an electrical problem is not as simple as finding a blown fuse. If you do find a fuse is blown, simply replacing it usually does not solve the issue.

Fuses do not fail without a reason. Many things can cause a blown fuse: A gauge has gone bad, a ground issue, or a spike in the power system.

Electrical systems are time consuming and, in some cases, challenging to diagnose. If you are replacing the harnesses, you most likely do not require the services of a shop. Replacing the harnesses is basically a plug and play. All routing of the harnesses should be in the same layout as those you remove. Stock replacement harnesses are available from Ames Performance, American Autowire, and other distributors.

I do not recommend using any harness unless it is a direct reproduction. Painless and Ron Francis provide excellent harnesses. They do not correctly replicate the factory harnesses, but their harnesses can be used on modified cars that carry modern accessories and require more electrical current. When you order a replacement harness, you must specify the options on your car.

To perform basic checks, you need a test light and a multimeter. A multimeter comes with instructions on how to use it. Perform a continuity test to determine if a circuit is open or closed. If a circuit is open, then the circuit is off. If the circuit is closed, the circuit is on. An open circuit is not conducting electricity. A closed circuit has continuity.

Troubleshooting electrical problems for ignition switches, lights, and motors can be handled with some basic tips. The ignition switch in a car is just like any other low-voltage, multi-pole electrical switch, except that a car key turns it rather than a lever.

Ignition switches have four basic positions: START, RUN, ACCESSORY, and OFF. Most electrical systems remain live in the OFF position so it is a good idea to always disconnect the battery at the ground cable when working on the electrical system. When you turn the key to START, you have to keep it in place against a spring force, and as soon as you release the key, it returns to the RUN position. The main difference between START and RUN is that the START position powers the starter system.

Leaving the key in the RUN position powers all of the electrical systems in the car, except for the starter. The only circuit required to keep the engine running is the coil, which provides voltage to the spark plugs. If your battery goes dead or the engine starts misfiring, especially at night, it is probably because the alternator is not charging.

When the key is turned to RUN, the multimeter should indicate approximately 12.6 to 13.6 volts at the positive terminal of the coil. If there is not any indication of voltage, the system likely has an open circuit between the positive side of the battery and the positive side of the coil. That problem could be in the wiring, the ignition switch, or the coil.

If you have a starting issue, be sure that all of the accessories are operating properly with the switch in RUN. If the accessories such as the wipers, radio, fan motor, etc. work and you cannot get the Firebird to start, you most likely have a problem in the starter wiring. It is possible the car doesn't start due to failed points, coil, or solenoid.

Electrical Source Material

You need a solid foundation of the principles and concepts of electrical system operation. Although I provide specific instruction for electrical system repairs, Tony Candela's award-winning book, *Automotive Wiring and Electrical Systems*, provides excellent, easy-to-understand instructions for repairing electrical circuits and components.

CHAPTER 11

Troubleshooting Electrical Problems

Following is an overview of the general procedure for using a multimeter. It's invaluable for many situations when you are trying to solve an electrical mystery.

- Set the multimeter to the OHM setting. Note that although the probes are not touching anything, the multimeter indicates a reading of infinity. A reading of infinity means that the circuit is open. When you touch the two probes together, the reading changes to zero, which indicates that the circuit is closed or complete. A complete circuit is one that can conduct electricity; an open circuit cannot.
- Touch each probe to one of the terminals of the device or wire. If the reading changes to zero, the device or wire has continuity.
- To test a switch, place a probe on each pole of the switch. When you move the switch from the off to the on position, the meter reading should change from infinity to roughly zero, which shows that the switch is working.
- To test a component such as an engine, touch a probe to each pole. A reading of roughly zero indicates that engine has continuity and current can pass through it.
- A test light connects one end to ground while the other end has a sharp point that can penetrate the harness covering to check if there is power. If that particular wire has power, the test light illuminates.
- For example, if the dome light does not work but the test light illuminates, the dome lamp base may be defective due to corrosion or a bulb blown. If the test light does not light, the dome lamp harness could have a short or break.
- Before you go off on an extended electrical hunt, make sure the test light is working. Simply attach the ground to the negative post of a battery and the pointed end on the positive post. The lamp should illuminate. ■

Use a test light to find out if there is power to the dome lamp.

The other end of the test lamp is attached to a ground.

ELECTRICAL SYSTEM

Bear in mind that the electrical system also provides power to mechanical devices. It is important to check the mechanical component for proper operation before trying to diagnose a wiring harness problem. Using an alternative power source such as a battery jump box is one of the best ways to check the operation of these components. You could also run wires from the battery to check the function of the component.

The electrical system includes relays, fuses, and fusible links. The purpose of an electrical relay in a car is to switch a higher current. For example, the circuit that runs from the ignition switch to the relay actuates the relay, which connects the battery power to the device. The starter system typically has a relay in it. High draw-power options such as A/C and power windows usually have relays in place to control the power.

If your issue is not with the starter, maybe one or more accessories have stopped working. The first thing to check is the fuse. The fuse box is accessible under the dash to the left of the brake pedal. It is clearly labeled with the circuit that the fuse protects along with the proper amp fuse. Check the fuse by removing it and verifying that the wire in the glass is not broken.

The fuse, depending on the amperage, may either have a twisted thin wire or a broad flat-metal strip in it. Any breakage should be visible. Sometimes, if the failure was particularly violent, the glass is dark. You can be sure it is blown.

If the fuse is good, verify you have 12 volts on the terminal of the electrical motor. If the terminal has 12 volts, be sure that the device has ground. There may be a separate ground wire or it may be grounded to the body. If the component has power and ground and it still does not work, you must consider that the device has failed or the switch failed.

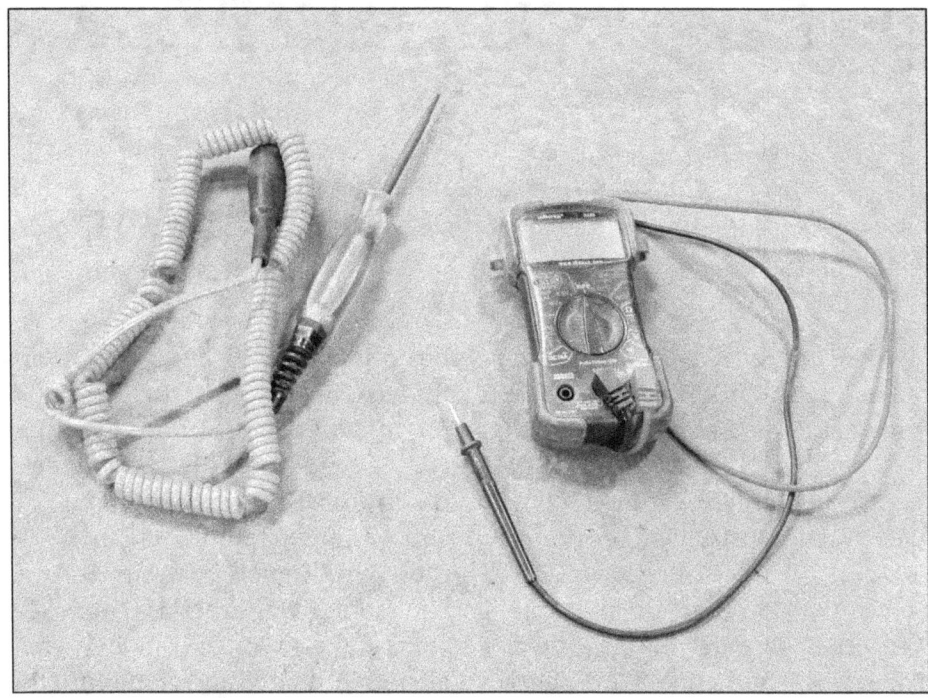

One of the tools you need to troubleshoot car-wiring problems is a simple multimeter. You can purchase a multifunction digital multimeter at a tool supply store.

Bolt-On Ignition Upgrades

Ignition technology has steadily improved since these Firebirds were new. The modern digital electronic distributors and ignition boxes provide a much stronger and more accurate spark for improved performance and fuel economy.

The 1970–1974 Firebirds were equipped with a breaker point ignition system, and this wearable system does not provide the reliability, or the spark energy, that you find in today's modern ignition systems.

The 1975–1981 Firebirds were fitted with High Energy Ignition (HEI), which was a huge step up in ignition performance. Adding an electronic or digital ignition system to your Firebird is a sensible and desirable upgrade. If you ever want to return the ignition to stock, you can remove the modern electronic ignition easily enough.

CHAPTER 12

INTERIOR

Beginning in 1970, Firebird was offered with an all-vinyl interior in standard and custom versions. It was well laid out and featured sensible controls, excellent ergonomics, and exceptional instrumentation. From 1971 to 1975, the interior continued to be offered in standard and custom versions. Although both interiors were highly functional and attractive, they were somewhat utilitarian.

From 1970 to 1976, Pontiac offered six different color interior codes, which changed from year to year. Black was a popular choice. Often interiors were adorned in various colors of vinyl, and many interiors were simply black vinyl.

In 1977, Pontiac introduced the cloth interior on the Firebird models. It was called a cloth contoured seat and was offered until 1981. In 1979, the 10th Anniversary Trans Am carried a special leather interior. The Trans Am and Firebird models were offered with vinyl and cloth until the second-generation came to a close in 1981.

The 1970 model year had low-back bucket seats with headrests. This was a one-year-only seat configuration.

The 1971–1981 Firebirds had high-back bucket seats. The foams and covers were changed through the years, dictated by whether the particular Firebird had a standard or deluxe interior. Other than that, the seats never changed.

The door panels were two-piece units with upper and lower trim panels from 1970 to 1977. In 1978 the door panel design was changed to a single panel with a single armrest attached to it. NOS parts are extremely difficult to locate; they tend not to have an extended shelf life as do steel parts.

The majority of interior parts are available today, but some significant parts are not. The lower door panels for the 1970–1977 are not reproduced. The 1970–1973 Firebirds have their shoulder belts mounted above the front seat sides of the roof and are held in with wire retainers. They also have a cloth bow-type headliner.

Restoring any of these interiors involves working with a variety of components and tools, and it involves many different procedures. Fortunately, the mechanically inclined owner can complete many of the interior restoration procedures at home. A rumor has persisted for a while now that Classic Industries is

Interior colors and fabrics varied widely from year to year, as did the availability of the standard or deluxe interior. This 1979 Trans Am SE is fitted with the optional deluxe cloth interior with hobnail inserts in black.

reproducing the dash; however, it is not currently offered.

PUI Interiors, OER, and Legendary Auto Interiors are all large manufacturers of Firebird reproduction interior parts.

Documentation and Damage Assessment

When performing disassembly of the interior, you should diligently document the process. Use a digital camera and a notebook to document how the parts were removed, including nuts, bolts, and screws. You will be able to reassemble the interior much easier and more quickly with this information, and it should reduce frustration. It does take patience and time, especially with the carpet and the dash.

The condition of the interior determines the amount of restoration work that needs to be done. If the car will be used mostly as a weekend driver, most owners can live with a faded and worn interior. If you want the interior to appear as new, it is often very difficult to be satisfied with a partial restoration. When an interior reaches a certain age and condition, it generally needs all of the major components restored or replaced. Almost any color starts suffering from sun fade, soiling, and general wear and tear over the years. Obviously, this wear occurs for every mile that you are sitting in the car. Black interiors tend to show most of the wear issues. However, black tends to show less sun fade and soiling so you might be able to get away with doing less.

Common failure areas include the headliner material drying out and falling down as well as abuse to the center console; it's leaned on continually and becomes broken over time.

Smoking was more in vogue when these cars were new, so cigarette burns are commonplace on consoles and seats.

Exposure to the elements from leaking weatherstrip and clogged door drains also contribute to the demise of the interior.

Seat padding starts breaking down and causes the seats to rely less on the cushions and more on the seat frames and springs. The durable seat covers become misshapen as a result. Seat belt webbing dries out from age.

The dash warps and cracks.

These are all common age-related issues with Firebirds. Usually, when an interior needs restoration work, it typically needs everything. When you add new seats, consoles, door panels, a headliner, or something else, the existing components look worn and dated by comparison. You may need to replace all of the interior pieces at once so you have a clean, consistent appearance to the interior.

Interior Carpet Installation

Remove Interior Carpet

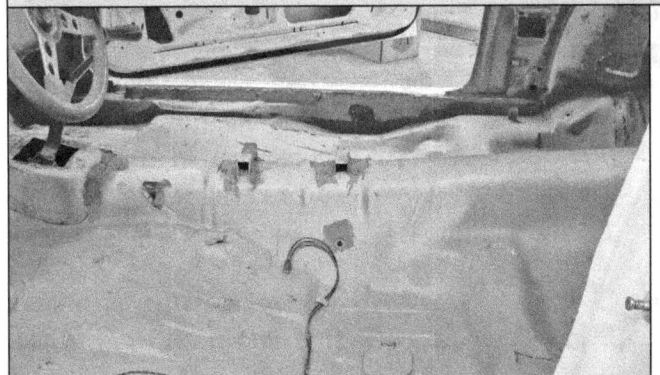

1. *This Firebird's old carpet has been stripped and is ready to be fitted. Prior to placing the carpet in the interior, make sure the floor is clean and all drains are seam sealed closed. You often have to strip the interior with a chemical to remove any residual adhesive and use a vacuum cleaner to pick up any debris or carpet fragments. Locate all the bolts you need for the seats and belts and have them ready.*

Route the seat belt wiring (if equipped) so you don't have to look for it when the new carpet is installed. Have a good-quality utility knife or carpeting knife for cutting the carpet. If the blade contacts sheet metal during the installation process, the blade dulls and may need replacement. Some cars had optional sound deadening. This insulation is available from distributors for less than $85. I do not recommend using any other type of aftermarket insulation as it can make the carpet installation much more difficult.

This carpet also appeared to be uneven. The carpets are molded and any change in the layout affects the fitment. I have used a spray-on product called Lizard Skin. It is a water-based product, weighs next to nothing, is sound-deadening, and fire-retardant. It sprays on thin enough to not affect the carpet fit. It also can be sprayed into areas that traditional mat sound deadening cannot reach, such as the inside of door shells, inner quarter panels, and hinge pillars, as well as the inside of the roof skin.

CHAPTER 12

Fit and Cut Out Carpet for Shifter

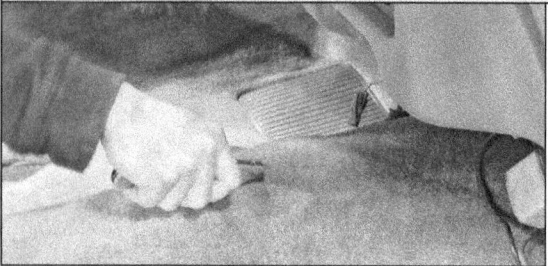

2 Classic Industries, among other companies, offers complete stock-type carpet sets for Firebirds, but they still need adjustment, cutting, and fitting for installation. A complete carpet set usually ranges from $130 to $200. It is a good idea to remove the carpet from the box and let it lay flat for a few days before installing. Placing it in the sun speeds up the process.

Place the carpet set on the floor with the heel pad on the driver's side for the pedals. Flatten all curves. Use a sharp utility knife to cut the carpet to allow the shifter base to stick through. Place an equal amount of carpet on each side of the shifter base. Also cut the carpet around the console mounting pads. This allows the carpet to flatten out better, and if you make a mistake, the center console will hide it.

Allow for Center Console Brackets

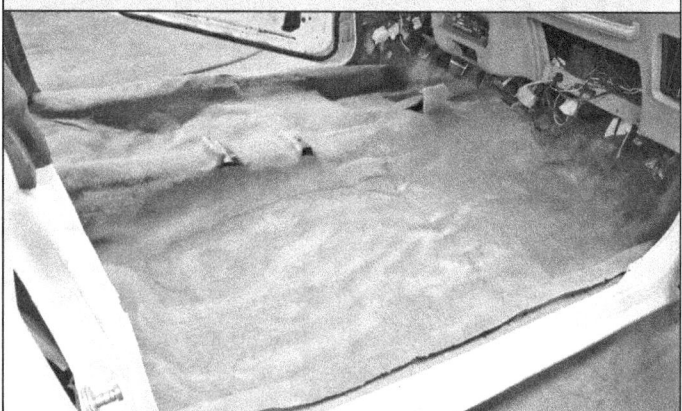

3 Trim the carpet so the center console brackets poke through (if equipped).

Interior Restoration Tasks

Interior restoration is far different than restoring other systems on the car because the interior contains many parts of various materials.

- Seats require replacing worn vinyl and leather seat covers, sacked-out or deformed foam buns, and backrests. Seats and headliners may require upholstery work.
- Cracked and worn steering wheels often require plastic and vinyl repair.
- Carpet requires fitting and cutting for the interior floorpan space, similar to home carpeting work.
- Steering columns involve mechanical work.
- Gauges, dome lights, and dash lights require electrical work.

Install Carpet Guard

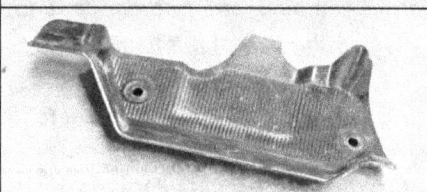

4 To anchor the carpet you need to install the carpet guard. This is the heavy-duty plastic panel that bolts to the floor in the driver's foot box. Verify that the carpet placement is correct. Use a socket and ratchet to install the carpet guard with two 10-mm bolts, or 3/8-inch bolts on earlier Firebirds. The bolts go through the carpet and anchor the carpet guard to the floor. It installs just under the steering column at the firewall.

Install Seat Belts

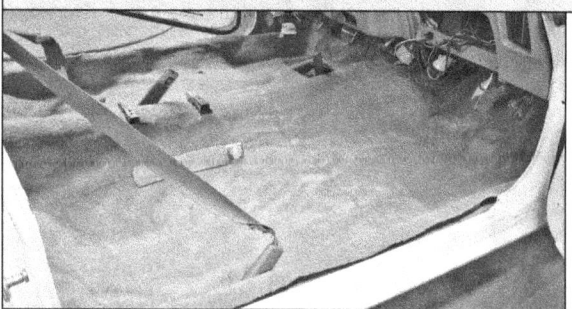

5 Locate the bolt holes for the seat belts and cut the carpet to accommodate them. Before cutting the carpet, locate the fitting and place a small "X" cut on top of it. This minimizes the amount of floor you see once the bolt is installed. Cut the hole for one anchor bolt at a time. Lift the carpet slightly and slide your hand underneath to the X cut. With your other hand, push the bolt through the carpet. Screw in the bolt to make sure it is not obstructed.

Cut Holes for Seat Track Bolts

6 *Four bolts hold the seat tracks to the floor and you need to accurately cut the mounting holes for the tracks before you actually mount them. Use a utility knife to cut small Xs over the correct locations. After you cut the seat track bolt openings, thread in the track bolts and snug them to the carpet to hold the carpet in place so it does not move when cutting other holes.*

Seat Track Holes

Cut the seat track holes first. Then, screw in the track bolts and snug them to the carpet. This holds the carpet in place so it does not move while cutting other holes.

Install Manual Transmission Shifter Boot

7 *For cars with a 4-speed, you need to install the shifter boot. The boot has a lower and upper lip at the base. Use your hands to work the carpet between the shifter boot lips, or channel.*

Install Manual Transmission Shifter Boot Retaining Ring

8 *Place the shifter-boot retaining ring over the boot and use a Phillips screwdriver to secure it to the floor. No cutting is required because the boot has pre-drilled holes, as does the floor. Firebirds equipped with automatic transmissions and floor-mounted shifters require a smaller cut for the shifter cable and the shifter assembly mounts.*

Install Wire Guards

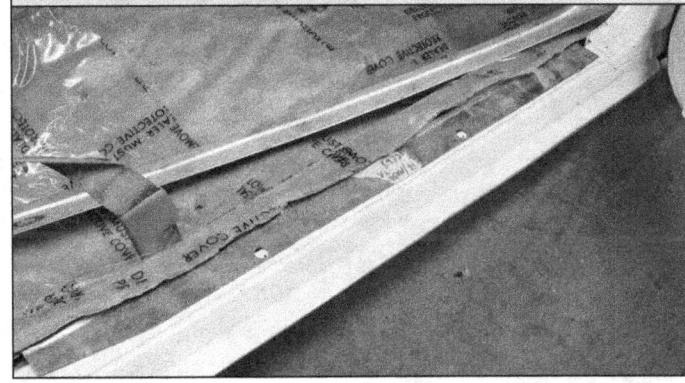

9 *Use a socket and ratchet to install four 7-mm bolts that hold the steel wire guards on the rocker panel.*

Install Sill Plates

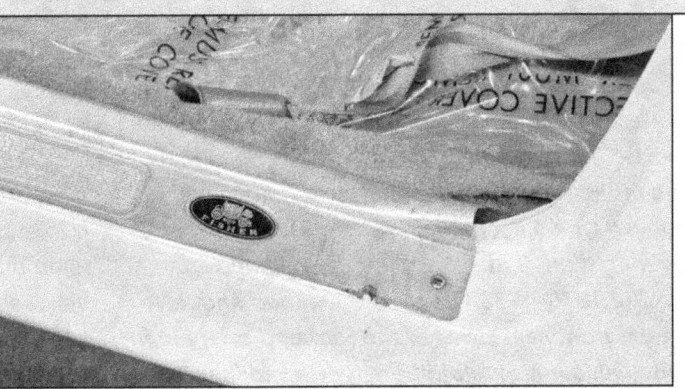

10 *Use a Phillips screwdriver to drive in the four screws that hold the sill plates to the rocker panels.*

CHAPTER 12

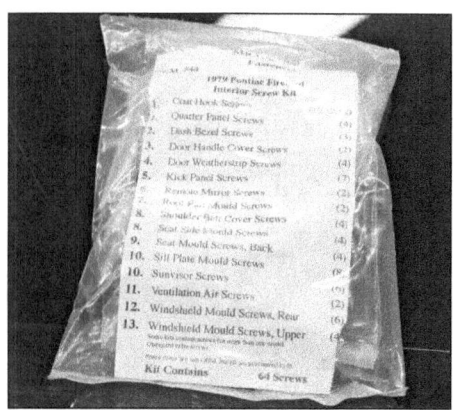

Purchase an interior screw kit from almost any distributor that sells reproduction parts; it will make assembly much easier and maintain a uniform look.

Install Rear Seatback Panel

11 This panel provides a partition between the backseat and the trunk. It helps deaden sound in the passenger compartment and provides a safety barrier from the contents in the trunk. Place the panel, with the insulation facing inward, against the rear deck support where the back upper seat will be installed.

Install Rear Seat Interior Panels

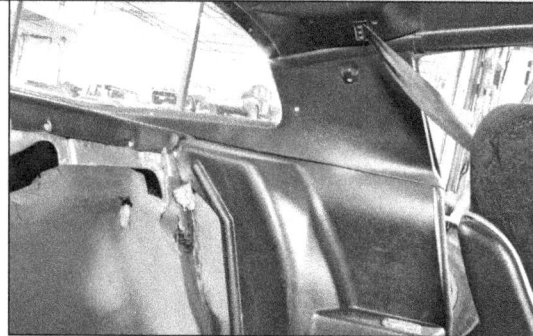

12 Install the rear seat side-trim panels first and then the sail panel inner trim. Each panel is held in with Phillips-head screws.

Install Headliner

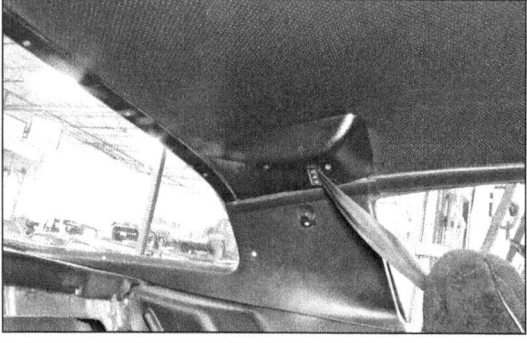

13 The 1974–1981 vinyl headliner is stretched over and glued to a cardboard panel. Phillips-head screws hold the perimeter of the trim panels and secure the headliner to the roof. Phillips-head screws also hold in the sun visor supports. The retractable shoulder belts have their mechanisms mounted in the roof above the rear seat held in with bolts that can be removed with a socket and ratchet. The retractors have a trim panel covering them that slides over the belt and attaches with screws. The 1970–1973 Firebirds have their shoulder belts mounted above the front seat sides of the roof and are held in with wire retainers. They also have a cloth bow-type headliner.

Install Kick Panels

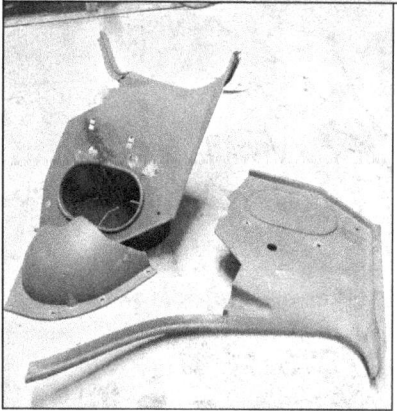

14 Plastic front kick panels are placed on either side of the front foot wells to protect the chassis and provide passenger comfort. The right side has a vent door built into it to allow fresh air to come in. A separate cover is on the right and attaches with Phillips-head screws. Reproduction kick panels are available but should be used only if originals cannot be located; the quality is not nearly as good.

INTERIOR

Install Upper Rear Seat

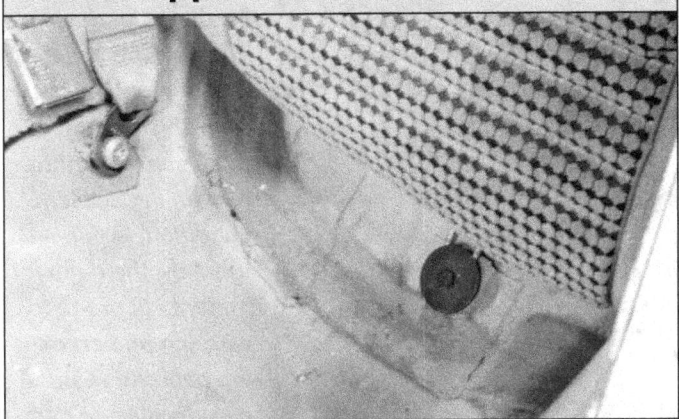

15 *Place the package shelf trim on top of the package shelf. Tuck the vinyl portion with the foam in the rear upper seat. Use tape to hold the vinyl in place and hold its shape. Install the rear upper seat. Three hooks on the rear support serve as upper retainers for the rear seat backrest. To install, simply lift and lower the upper seat frame portion onto the hooks (similar to hanging a picture). Center the seat by sliding it side to side until the lower wire retainers are centered on the bolt holes. Use a socket and ratchet to install a 7/16-inch bolt on each side and tighten. Make note of the lower seat floor retainers.*

Install Lower Rear Seat

16 *Place the vinyl tunnel trim piece over the tunnel and slide it under the upper rear seat. Place one of the lower seats just forward of the upper seat. As you look under the lower seat, slide the seat back. Stop when the seat frame wire is between the retainers. The technique is to push the lower seat from the front while pushing down to get the seat to pop into the retainer. Repeat for the other side.*

Plug-In Driver-Side Seat Wiring

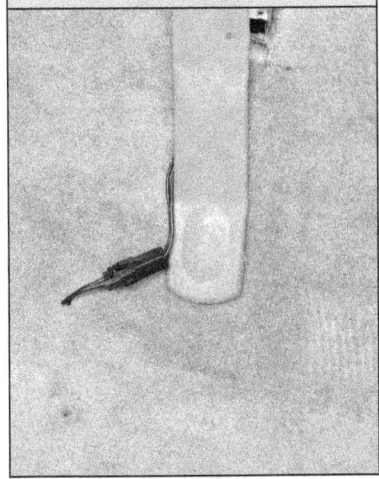

17 *Before you install the driver-side seat, locate the seat belt wiring harness under the carpet. Cut an access hole for it near the inner seat belt. The 1973 and later Firebirds have this wiring harness.*

Install Front Seat

18 *If you've mixed up the seats, you need to determine the location of a respective seat. The seatback release lever should be positioned on the outside edge of the seat (close to the door). Place the seat on the sliding tracks and slide the seat all the way forward to gain access to the rear track mounts. Thread in the 1/2-inch bolt on each side, but just snug at this time. Slide the seat fully back and repeat for the front track mounts. Once you have the bolts in the seat, test the movement of the seat. Make sure the seat slides freely back and forth on the track, and it is not jammed. Once you are sure the tracks are good, tighten the bolts securely.*

TRANS AM & FIREBIRD RESTORATION

CHAPTER 12

Dash

The second-generation Firebird dashboard remained similar throughout its production run. The radio opening changed during these years. The original dash featured a steel frame that had an ABS injection-molded backing with foam inserts and injection-molded vinyl in the correct grain material.

The dash is the nerve center of your Firebird. It houses the controls for the operation of the car and the instruments that show you what is going on. Removing the dash may seem intimidating, but it's really not that difficult. It is a tedious and exacting process that requires careful attention and patience, because there are many hidden fasteners and plastic clips.

Lift the center console compartment to reveal two 7-mm bolts. Remove them. Remove the two 7-mm bolts at the front of the console on either side of the front map pocket where the metal ears meet at the bottom of the dash.

When driving your Firebird, the dash is always within your line of vision so you want this conspicuous component to remain in excellent condition. Unfortunately, the dash material is prone to warping and cracking over the years. A deteriorated or damaged dash can make an otherwise sharp car look tired and old.

On automatic-transmission cars, use a screwdriver to pry the center shifter emblem off, remove the snap ring on the shifter handle, and remove the handle. Slide the shifter bezel off along with the indicator.

On manual-transmission cars, unscrew the shifter handle counter-clockwise. Remove the console and put it in a safe place. Place all of the removed components back into the console for safekeeping. Bag all screws and bolts and place them in the center compartment. Remove the 7-mm bolts for the glove box door.

Dash Removal

Remove Center Console Bezel

1 Remove the center console shifter bezel; it is the same for an automatic- or manual-transmission car. Four 5/32-inch Allen-head screws hold the automatic bezel and four screws hold the manual bezel. Simply use a short screwdriver to remove the bezel.

Remove Center Console Bolts

2 Use a socket and ratchet with an extension to remove the two 7-mm bolts at the bottom of the center console compartment.

INTERIOR

Remove Steering Column Cover

3 Two plastic twist screws secure the cover around the steering column itself. Use a flat-blade screwdriver to remove them.

Remove Instrument Cluster Bezel

4 Extricating this bezel is tricky and it bends easily, so be very careful. Two 8-mm bolts, located under the dash on either side of the steering column, secure the lower portion of the bezel to the steering column. They are very long and it is not unusual to find them missing. The bezel bends easily and, once bent, does not go back into shape without leaving behind some evidence of the prior damage.

Remove Steering Column Support Bolts

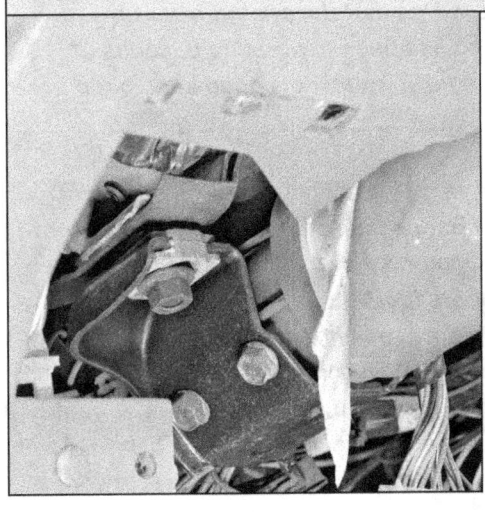

5 Remove the two 15-mm nuts from underneath the steering column that supports it and let it drop down.

Remove Headlight Switch Bezel

6 Pull out the headlight switch knob as if you are turning the headlamps on. Unscrew the black bezel by turning it counter-clockwise. This allows the dash bezel to clear the knob. Gently pull on the edges of the bezel to pop it loose from the dash. Using firm but gentle pressure rotate the top of the bezel and pull it toward you to remove the bezel.

Unplug Speedometer Cable

7 From the underside of the dash, reach up and unplug the speedometer cable by pushing the clip on the back of the gauge. The gauges are held in with 8-mm bolts.

Remove Speedometer Cluster Bolts

8 Use a socket and ratchet to remove four 8-mm speedometer-cluster bolts located at each corner. You need to be careful because these screws are sensitive and you don't want to break any of the gauge tabs or damage the plastic covers.

Remove Speedometer Cluster

9 Once the bolts have been removed and the gauge cluster has been freed from the dash, the electrical harness still needs to be removed. Pull the cluster straight out enough so you can put your hand behind the cluster. Reach behind and remove the main harness plug by depressing each end of the plug retaining tabs. If equipped with a tachometer, disconnect the pink-and-white harness.

10 The printed circuit board is located on the back side of the speedometer and tachometer cluster. (Your cluster board may look different; this example has already had the printed circuit board replaced and it is cosmetically different than the original.) Inspect your cluster printed circuit board to locate any cracks. If there were issues with the gauges not operating properly, the circuit board could be one of the culprits. Given that the printed circuit board is made of plastic and has been exposed to decades of extreme heat and cold, it would be a good idea to replace it.

Unplug Switches

11 Unplug the headlamp and wiper switches at connectors by pushing on the tab to release. Remove the two 8-mm bolts for the fuel/volt gauge cluster. Pull out the cluster and remove the two lightbulb retainers by tugging on them at the base. Remove the three 8-mm bolts for the A/C or heater control panel. Pull the A/C or heater control panel out slightly and disconnect the vacuum central port by gently prying it up and off with a flat-blade screwdriver.

Remove Blend Door Heater Cable

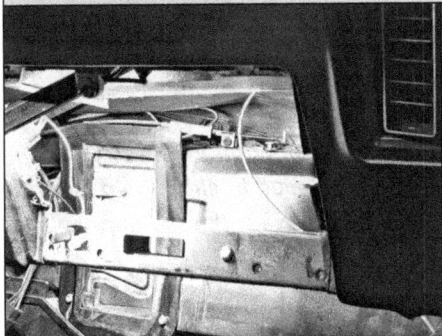

12 The blend door heater cable extends down to the top of the heater box located behind the glove box. Here the glove box has been removed and the blend door heater cable can be seen because of its distinctive yellow clip. It is held in with a single 8-mm bolt. Lift that clip off. Slide the control panel out slightly and disconnect the fan speed switch.

Store Control Panel

13 Once the control panel has been removed, place it somewhere clean so contaminants do not get into the vacuum ports.

Unplug and Remove Switches

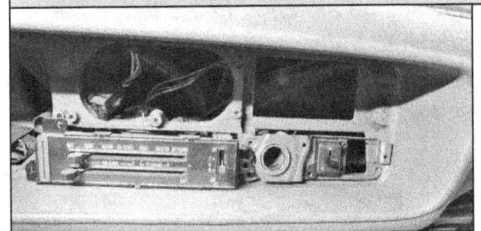

14 Reach behind the dash and unplug the lighter, defroster, and power door lock switches, along with the radio plugs. It may be necessary to wiggle the connector to remove it. Pull it by the connector, not the wire. The lighter panel may also house the power door lock switch (if equipped) on the earlier models or the rear defroster switch on the later models. The lightweight panel trim has plastic rivets that need to be gently pried off. Three Phillips-head screws are situated behind the trim panel. If equipped with A/C, remove the 8-mm bolts holding in the center vent.

Remove Dash Panel Fasteners

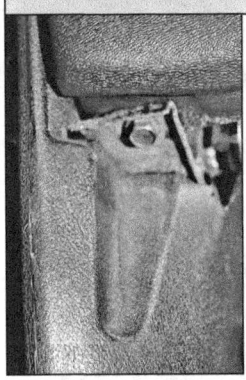

15 Locate the three 10-mm nuts and bolts that hold the top of the dash to the metal dash panel. Three nuts are located above the glove box opening and three bolts are located above the instrument cluster opening. Use a screwdriver or socket and ratchet with an extension to reach these fasteners. Once the nuts have been removed, locate the lower retainers that hold the bottom of the dash at each corner. They are at the notches at the forward edge of the kick panels. One 13-mm bolt is on each side.

Remove A-Pillar Trim Panel

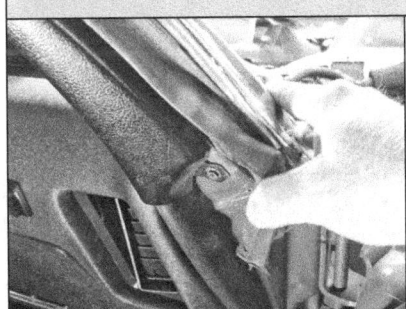

16 Use a Phillips screwdriver or socket and ratchet to remove the A-pillar inside trim panels. These are located on each side of the windshield. A hidden 7-mm bolt at the base under the weatherstrip on the hinge pillar holds them down. Just peel back the weatherstrip slightly to gain access and remove the bolt.

Remove Pillar Trim Molding

17 Remove the screws that secure the trim molding and gently pull back the Y-trim molding. Slide the A-pillar trim molding up and out. If your Firebird has a T-top, the molding looks slightly different than this, but it is still secured in the same manner.

Remove Dash Panel from Car

18 At this stage, all the fasteners that attach the dash to the car have been removed and now the dash can be lifted so the remainder of the removal work can be completed. Carefully and gently push the dash high enough so the studs clear the metal dash panel. You may need to slide the dash from side to side slightly to get the studs to clear the metal panel.

Disconnect Dash Wiring

19 Once the dash is clear of the metal panel, tilt it forward. Disconnect any wires that are attached and other wires that may be still connected. Disconnect the antenna lead from the back of the radio. Ground wires, courtesy lamps, A/C ducts, and other small relays may still be attached to the dash. The number of accessories attached to the back depends on the year and what options on your particular Firebird. When they are all disconnected, remove the dash.

Protect Dash

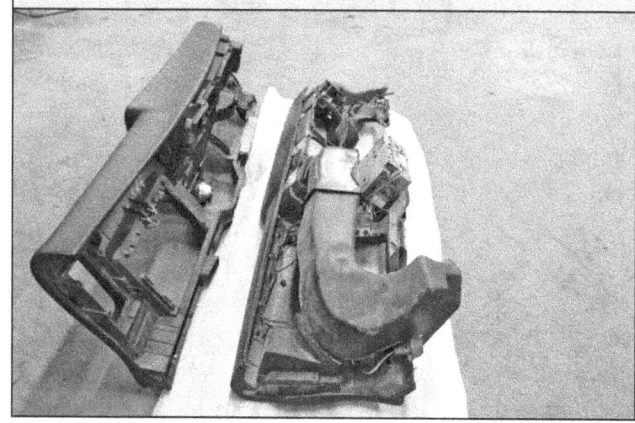

20 You need to work on your dash in a safe and clean spot in your shop. If you're working on the backside of the dash, be sure to protect the front of the dash by placing it on a carpet or other clean soft surface. This also makes removal of the components easier.

Protect Dash (CONTINUED)

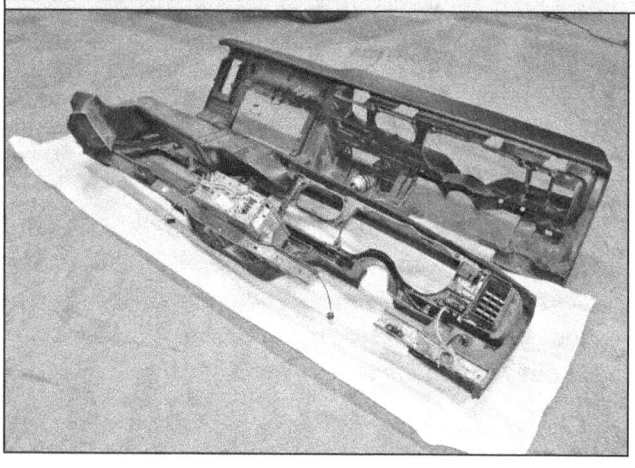

21 Once you have the dash removed, place it on a soft surface.

Remove Dash Components

22 Remove the radio knobs and retainer nuts that screw off the tuner and volume shafts in a counter-clockwise direction.

INTERIOR

Remove Dash Components (CONTINUED)

23 Slide the radio out from behind the dash. Remove the headlamp and wiper switches' 8-mm bolts, emergency brake handle, ashtray and slide panel, right and left dash vents, A/C and heater ducts, and glove box light switch and catch. If your car has the deluxe interior option, you also need to remove the grab handle that is above the glove box opening. Firebirds with standard interiors do not have this handle.

Completed dash installed. I chose to not install the radio because I sent it out for servicing and to have the 8-track rebuilt.

It's a good idea to purchase a used dash core and send it out to be restored before you begin to remove the components from the old dash. That way you can simply transfer the components instead of having to tag and store them until you have the new core.

Once you have the dash components installed but have not installed the glove box door, under-steering column, instrument cluster bezel, and center console, it is a good idea to start the engine to make sure everything is working and connected properly. Cycle through the A/C or heater modes to make sure the air is moving according to the control panel indicator. Check for vacuum leaks by listening for any hissing sounds in the dash area or when moving the control panel selector. Be sure the engine is not running rougher than it did before. If it does, you may have a vacuum leak.

Using a Shop

If you are sending your dash out to be restored, it is important to include these items with your dash: instrument bezel, right-side air deflector, glove box door, grab handle and escutcheons (if equipped), under-steering column panel, and radio bezel.

All of these items are necessary for the dash restoration so their fitment can be checked once the process is completed. I learned the hard way the first time I sent a dash. I sent only the dash and nothing else. When I began installation of the instrument bezel, I ripped the upper right corner because it was not flush in the radius.

I ended up removing the entire dash assembly again and sending it back but this time along with the bezel so the company could repair it. ∎

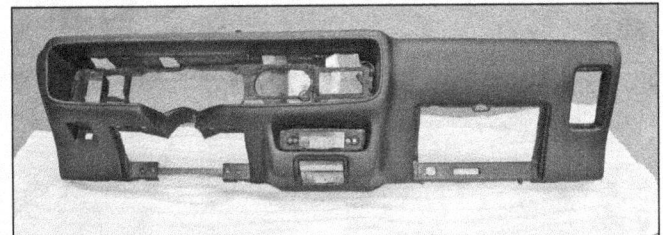

I have used Just Dashes for many years, and the company turns an old dash into one that looks factory new. If you are sending your dash out to be restored, you should take many photos and tag everything because the process to recondition the dash may take several months. It is also advisable to take notes as you disassemble the dash so you can reverse the order of assembly.

TRANS AM & FIREBIRD RESTORATION

CHAPTER 12

CHAPTER 13

OTHER SYSTEMS AND COMPONENTS

During the course of your restoration, you may have to replace and/or restore many other components on the car, including wheels and tires. When tackling cooling or fuel system restoration, take all precautions. Wear the proper clothing, use eye protection, and use nitrile gloves. These gloves prevent toxic chemicals from being absorbed into your skin, creating a health concern. Of course, when working around hazardous chemicals such as antifreeze or gasoline, properly store and dispose of them.

Cooling System

The cooling system on your Pontiac is simple, yet every component is required to perform correctly to maintain your engine at the proper operating temperature. The cooling system in your Firebird is vital to the operation and performance of it, and it is made up of many different components. Any one component not doing its job could lead to engine overheating.

Pontiac water pumps are notorious for failure and are one of the most common reasons for the engine overheating. The water pump shaft bearing often wears out and thereby reduces the pump's ability to properly function, and eventually it fails. A common warning sign of wear is if coolant drips from the weep hole in the water pump. This coolant drip will be on the floor below the front of the engine. Another way to check for proper pump operation is to grip the fan and move it side to side. If the shaft wiggles, pump failure is imminent.

Other factors can affect your Firebird's ability to maintain its cool. The radiator can be compromised either by leaking or clogging. Loose fan belts, a failed fan clutch, improper engine timing, a leaking head gasket, a clogged catalytic converter or, even worse, a cracked head or engine block are other reasons for overheating.

The decision to perform this task is really dependent on your abilities. Bear in mind that bolts can break, requiring drilling and tapping of the remnants. Sometimes these bolts are located in dissimilar metals, making the extraction even more difficult. A professional can replace the water pump in a fully assembled vehicle equipped with A/C in about four to

Pontiac offered different wheel options for Firebirds and Trans Ams over the second-generation production run. Although the 15 x 7–inch Snowflake wheel (shown) was optional for some models, it was standard on the Trans Am SE from 1977 to 1981.

five hours without any problems. It is not beyond the skill of a novice to perform the swap, but it is time consuming.

The tools required are a socket set, wrench set, scraper, sealant, possibly a bolt extractor, and heli-coil thread insert. It is highly recommended that the coolant be flushed and filled with fresh coolant.

Fuel System

The fuel system in your Firebird comprises a fuel tank, a sending unit for the fuel gauge, fuel lines (both steel and rubber), a fuel pump, and the carburetor. Fuel lines and hoses should be checked, not only because of age but also because of modern fuel formulations that corrode the fuel lines and cause failure. The gaskets in the fuel system also have a shorter lifespan because of today's fuel ingredients.

The build sheet provided instructions that the factory used to build the car as it went down the assembly line. It appears it was placed on the tank before the asphalt insulators were installed. The sheet is in remarkable condition given its location.

This 1974 Trans Am with the famed Super Duty 455-ci engine is undergoing restoration. The core support and radiator have been removed; many other components need to be taken out so the water pump can be accessed and removed.

The water pump is accessible on the 455 HO. As you can see, the alternator and power steering brackets bolt onto the water pump.

Fuel Tank Removal

Locate Fuel Tank Engine Straps

1 *The fuel system in your Firebird is basic. The fuel tank is located in the back under the trunk floor and held in place by two retaining straps.*

Remove Fuel Tank Engine Straps

2 *Two 9/16-inch bolts hold the straps that cradle the tank. One bolt is on each side behind the rear body panel.*

Remove Fuel Lines

3 *Fuel lines attach to hoses at the tank, and spring clamps hold these hoses. It is not unusual to find worm clamps also installed. These hoses need to be removed to facilitate removal of the fuel tank. As you lower the tank out of the body, disconnect the wiring plugs from the sending unit.*

Remove Fuel Tank

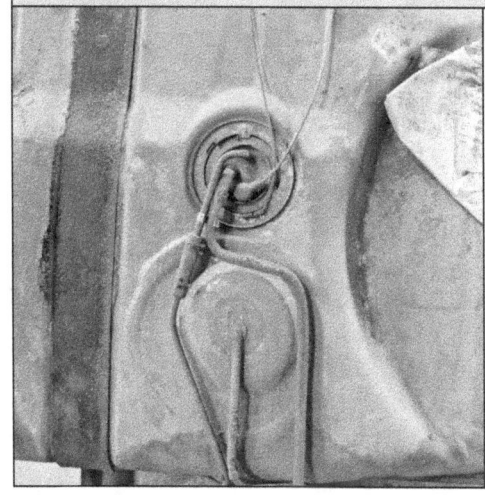

4 *Once the fuel tank is lowered, the fuel tank sending unit is on the top of the tank. The lock ring can be removed by using a brass punch to turn the ring counter-clockwise.*

When I removed the tank on this 1979 Macho Trans Am, I found a build sheet.

This particular Macho Trans Am had another build sheet that was found when the back seat was removed; this is a common area to find these sheets. A build sheet can be considered the birth certificate of your Firebird and absolutely confirms how your Firebird was originally built.

Wheels and Tires

The wheels and tires used on second-generation Firebirds evolved throughout the entire model run. With the introduction of radial tires in 1974, the suspension systems were tuned to allow the Firebird to handle them. The Rally II, honeycomb, snowflake, and Air Flow wheels were fitted to the Firebirds and Trans Ams at the factory.

You can find original and reproduction wheels in various sizes to fit your car. Originals are not cheap. Rally II wheels were offered in 14 x 7-, 15 x 6-, and 15 x 7-inch sizes. These five-spoke mag wheels feature a center cap and trim ring. These popular wheels were aluminum and gray-colored for a multi-tone appearance. The Rally II wheel stayed with the HM code and the trim ring was changed to a bright finish. The Rally

OTHER SYSTEMS AND COMPONENTS

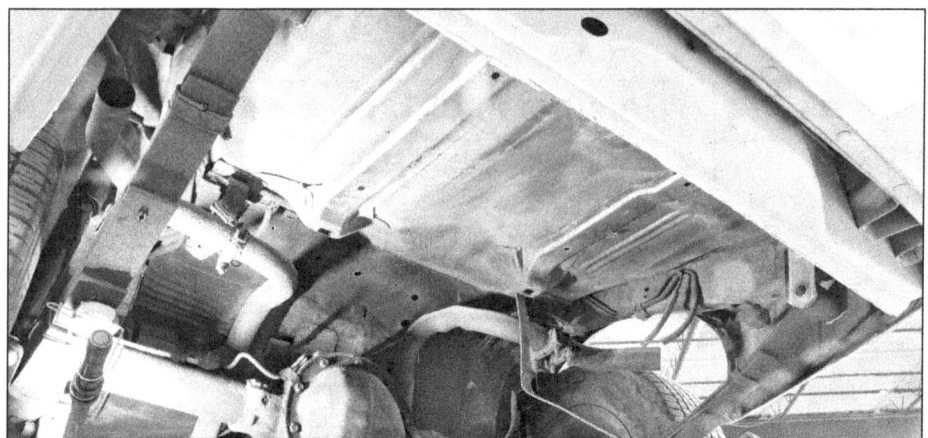

When the fuel tank has been removed, the underside of the trunk floor looks like this. If it has rust, you will be able to see it and repair it.

The rest of the fuel system is made up of fuel lines that run from the tank to the fuel pump.

The fuel pump has a steel line that runs up to the front of the Quadrajet carburetor. The fuel filter is located in the housing that the fuel line feeds into at the front of the carburetor.

II wheel stayed with the HM code, and the trim ring was changed to the brushed stainless finish for 1973 only. From 1974 to 1981, the trim ring was changed to a shiny finish.

Released in 1971 and discontinued after 1976, honeycomb wheels are readily identified with the Trans Am. This wheel came in two basic sizes, 14 x 7 and 15 x 7. These were offered in magnesium and gold-color finishes; they were also equipped with trim rings and center caps. The honeycombs retained the KP code. The radial tires were GR-70-15 sized.

In 1976, Pontiac offered a variety of wheels for Firebird and Trans Am models. Now the Rally II wheels could be ordered in matching body–colored centers. The honeycombs on the new-for-1976 Limited Editions were painted gold. The Formula received 15 x 7 Rally II wheels coded AE. The Trans Am Rally II wheels were coded HW whether they were body colored or not. The honeycomb wheels were coded HP.

Hitting the market in 1977, the snowflake design continued until the second-generation car production run ended in 1981. The snowflake wheel was available for Firebird and Trans Am models and came in 14 x 6-inch and a 15 x 7-inch sizes. The 15 x 7-inch wheel in white, gray, blue, gold, and red was offered on Firebirds. The snowflake wheel was available for the Firebird and Trans Am models and came in a 15 x 7–inch size. The 15 x 7–inch wheel in white, blue, and red was offered on Esprit Firebirds. Gray (argent) or gold Snowflake wheels were fitted to the Formula and Trans Am models. The body color determined color of the wheel.

The 1978 models received another change in optional wheel availability. A new 15 x 8 snowflake wheel featured a 1-inch step on the outer edge of the wheel. This wheel was not available as a standalone; it was available only with the WS6 Special Performance Package. This wheel design became the immediate favorite and is still the most sought-after wheel today.

In addition to the Skybird, a new Redbird became available on the Esprit and it featured 15 x 7 red snowflake wheels. The GR-70 tire stayed even for the wider 15 x 8 wheels.

The code for the Rally II was HW, the gray 7-inch snowflake was coded KJ, the gold 7-inch snowflake was KH, the blue 7-inch snowflake was JB, the gold 15 x 8 snowflake was JF, and the gray 15 x 8 snowflake was JJ. The gold SE and black SE wheels received paint on the lip of the wheels.

In 1979 the transition to metric sizing began. For GR70-15 tires, the new size was 225/70R15. Although they were dimensionally similar, the tire didn't change in any way; the system simply made tire sizing more exact.

CHAPTER 13

The Firebird used many different wheels during its 11-year model run. The standard wheel for the Trans Am throughout the entire run was the 15-inch Rally II. The 14 x 7-inch Rally II wheel was standard on the Formula. A number of other optional wheels were available. This 1978 W72 Formula has the optional gray 15 x 8–inch snowflake wheel.

In 1973 the Rally II wheel was redesigned to a full 15 x 7 inches wide. The center cap now had a brushed aluminum finish with a red dart (as Pontiac called it). Most people refer to it as an arrowhead. The trim rings were brushed stainless and the lug nuts had a stainless cap over a common lug nut, giving it a finished appearance. The 15 x 7 code was either AE or HM.

The coding for the Rally II was HW, the 7-inch silver snowflake was JR, the 7-inch gold snowflake was KH, the red 7-inch snowflake was JA, the silver 8-inch snowflake was JT, the gold 8-inch snowflake was JF, and the Air Flow wheel was HA. The 8-inch wheel no longer had the painted lip on the 1-inch step. The step was now polished.

Although earlier Firebirds had body color–matched wheels, the 1980–1981 Firebirds carried the unfinished aluminum wheels. Among the snowflake wheels were two different constructions. The 1979 and older models had thinner wheels, and although these didn't affect on-street durability, there was a quality difference.

The Formula received a standard 14 x 7 Rally II wheel coded XG with an optional 14 x 7 honeycomb wheel coded JX. The 14-inch tire was a F70-14.

The 1970 Rally II wheel was standard equipment without the trim ring. This was a unique wheel because it still retained the 14-inch center with a 15-inch outer. This wheel is identified by a 1-inch space between the center and the outer. This wheel can be identified by the code JW stamped on the outer face of the wheel near the valvestem. The 1971 wheel also was of the same design and coding but came standard with trim rings. The 1972 version used the same design but changed to a KR code. The center caps were chrome with a red center with black PMD letters. The lug nuts had an insert with black or red centers. The 15 x 7 honeycomb wheel on the Trans Am was a no-cost option starting in 1971. These wheels received a F70-15 tire.

OTHER SYSTEMS AND COMPONENTS

The Trans Am 15 x 7 honeycomb wheel was coded KP.

The wheel options for 1975 remained the same with the Rally II HM code. Honeycomb wheels without trim rings were coded HP. Honeycombs with trim rings were coded AE.

In 1977, Pontiac introduced more optional wheel offerings. The optional wheel was a cast-aluminum 15 x 7 that was commonly referred to as a snowflake wheel. The Rally II body-colored wheel remained available. The snowflake wheel was gray or gold, but the new Esprit Skybird option came with baby blue–colored snowflake wheels.

This bulletin clarified the correct gold coloring for the 1978 version of the 15 x 8 snowflake wheel. The face of the wheel was a solid color, not the bare aluminum.

The 1979 15 x 8 snowflake wheel was part of the WS6 and WS7 Performance Packages.

The 15 x 8 Air Flow wheel was introduced in 1979 as part of the 10th Anniversary Trans Am. These wheels were silver. The same wheel was used in many different forms in 1980 and 1981. They could be had in silver on regular Turbo non-SE Trans Ams and Formulas, gold colored on the SE Turbo Trans Am, and white colored (shown) on Pace Car–optioned Trans Ams. All of these wheels interchange among Firebird years and models. The most popular swaps are adding the honeycombs on pre-1977 models and 15 x 8 Snowflakes on 1977 and later years.

Pontiac introduced the radial tuned suspension (RTS) in 1974. The company began using radial tires and moving away from bias-ply tires. RTS also ushered in special spring settings, changed bushing durometers, and the rear sway bar was reduced to .812 inch on the Trans Am. On the Formula and other Firebirds, the rear bar was reduced to .56 inch.

An RTS badge was affixed to the top right of the glove box door from 1975 to 1981. It's placed above the steering column on the instrument bezel and between the speedometer and tachometer gauges.

SOURCE GUIDE

American Autowire
americanautowire.com

Ames Performance Engineering
amesperf.com

Automobile Restoration
premierrestony.com

Frank's Pontiac Parts
frankspontiacparts.com

Hemmings Motor News
hemmings.com

Innovative Products Technologies
innovativeprodtech.com

Just Dashes
justdashes.com

Meepzor Vehicle Services
vintageautoexperts.com

Old Air Products
oldairproducts.com

Original Parts Group, Inc.
originalpartsgroup.com

Phoenix Graphix
phoenixgraphix.com

Phoenix Transmission Products
phoenixtrans.com

Pontiac Historical Society
phs-online.com

Premier Restorations of NY
150 Rt. 17
Sloatsburg, NY 10974
845-712-5566
premierrestony.com

Python Restoration
pythonrestoration.com

Racekrafters Performance
racekrafters.com

Ram Air Restoration
ramairrestoration.com

Restore a Muscle Car
restoreamusclecar.com

Rock Auto Parts
rockauto.com

The Parts Place
thepartsplaceinc.com

The Premier Firebird Gallery
firebirdgallery.com

Year One
yearone.com

www.ingramcontent.com/pod-product-compliance
Lightning Source LLC
Chambersburg PA
CBHW081446070526
44586CB00019B/2252